WORSHIP THROUGH LATIN AMERICAN EYES

Worship and Witness

The Worship and Witness series seeks to foster a rich, interdisciplinary conversation on the theology and practice of public worship, a conversation that will be integrative and expansive. Integrative, in that scholars and practitioners from a wide range of disciplines and ecclesial contexts will contribute studies that engage church and academy. Expansive, in that the series will engage voices from the global church and foreground crucial areas of inquiry for the vitality of public worship in the twenty-first century.

The Worship and Witness series demonstrates and cultivates the interaction of topics in worship studies with a range of crucial questions, topics, and insights drawn from other fields. These include the traditional disciplines of theology, history, and pastoral ministry—as well as cultural studies, political theology, spirituality, and music and the arts. The series focus will thus bridge church worship practices and the vital witness these practices nourish.

We are pleased that you have chosen to join us in this conversation, and we look forward to sharing this learning journey with you.

SERIES EDITORS:

John D. Witvliet
Noel Snyder
María Eugenia Cornou

WORSHIP THROUGH LATIN AMERICAN EYES

Interdisciplinary Essays on Contextual Practices

EDITED BY
María Eugenia Cornou
AND
Noel A. Snyder

CASCADE *Books* • Eugene, Oregon

WORSHIP THROUGH LATIN AMERICAN EYES
Interdisciplinary Essays on Contextual Practices

Worship and Witness

Copyright © 2026 Wipf and Stock. All rights reserved. Except for brief quotations in critical publications or reviews, no part of this book may be reproduced in any manner without prior written permission from the publisher. Write: Permissions, Wipf and Stock Publishers, 199 W. 8th Ave., Suite 3, Eugene, OR 97401.

Cascade Books
An Imprint of Wipf and Stock Publishers
199 W. 8th Ave., Suite 3
Eugene, OR 97401

www.wipfandstock.com

PAPERBACK ISBN: 978-1-6667-0260-6
HARDCOVER ISBN: 978-1-6667-0261-3
EBOOK ISBN: 978-1-6667-0262-0

Cataloguing-in-Publication data:

Names: Cornou, María Eugenia, editor. | Snyder, Noel A., editor.

Title: Worship through Latin American eyes : interdisciplinary essays on contextual practices / edited by María Eugenia Cornou and Noel A. Snyder.

Description: Eugene, OR: Cascade Books, 2026 | Series: Worship and Witness | Includes bibliographical references.

Identifiers: ISBN 978-1-6667-0260-6 (paperback) | ISBN 978-1-6667-0261-3 (hardcover) | ISBN 978-1-6667-0262-0 (ebook)

Subjects: LCSH: Worship. | Social Science—Ethnic Studies—Latin American Studies. | Postcolonialism. | Liturgics.

Classification: BV178 W67 2026 (paperback) | BV178 (ebook)

VERSION NUMBER 01/16/26

INTRODUCTION

THE GATHERING

Every Sunday, millions of Christians worldwide gather for public worship. They may use different languages, sing distinct melodies, and perform rituals according to different traditions and in diverse styles. Still, there is a common element among all Christians: the practice of worship. The centrality of public worship in Christian life makes its study essential and relevant. The rapid growth of Christianity in Central and South America, Africa, and Asia in recent times and the vitality of the congregations in these regions make it important to widen the scope of worship studies to include more case studies and voices from outside Western Europe, the United States, and Canada.

Around two decades ago, the Calvin Institute of Christian Worship held two gatherings of scholars to focus on the study of "non-Western Christian worship." These meetings resulted in the publication of *Christian Worship Worldwide*, a book of essays edited by Charles E. Farhadian, focused on "expanding horizons" in the study of contextualized worship practices around the globe. The book you now have in your hands continues with that effort of "expanding horizons," but with a twist. In this case, the goal was to listen to and learn from a community of scholars from the global church whose voices are usually underrepresented in academic publications. Thus, in the summer of 2018, the Calvin Institute of Christian Worship invited a group of talented Latin American Christian scholars for one week to reflect on the contextual practice of worship using various disciplinary lenses and methodologies. In this seminar, each scholar presented a case study from a context with which they were familiar, on the theme "Strengthening Public Worship Practices: How Theological Disciplines Can Enrich and Deepen Congregational Life." After a collaborative group revision process, these essays resulted in this collection.

Each contributor to this book observes, describes, and interprets worship through Latin American eyes. Perspective is vital to this work. Its authors are women and men from different countries, are experts in varied academic fields, and represent a range of Protestant Christian traditions. They bring diverse religious backgrounds and worship experiences to this work. Nevertheless, they all belong to a collective that writes with Latin American eyes.

LATIN AMERICAN EYES?

Allow us to say a brief word about the term "Latin American." Using labels to designate groups of people may be helpful but also highly problematic. Every possible term we could use to name this book's authors collectively may be contested. "Hispanic" was rapidly disregarded because of its reference to the Spanish language; three of our writers are native Portuguese speakers.

We are also aware of the difficulties of using "Latin American." "Latin America" is a social and geopolitical construct whose existence may be credited to different impulses and interests, internal and external to the region, shaped by conflicting views on race, anti-colonial sentiments, and a complex imperialist/anti-imperialist dynamic.[1] Coined in the nineteenth century, this term has no evident historical origin, and its meaning has evolved and changed throughout the years. Yet, in different ways "Latin America" has been frequently used to signal otherness and to justify policies and practices of marginalization and exclusion.

However, acknowledging the limitations and challenges involved with using "Latin American eyes" and explicitly resisting any essentialization related to the term, the writers of this work bring a collective wisdom that emerges from a common ground.

Each of these authors experiences their Latin American identities differently. Yet despite all their differences, the scholars who contribute to this volume have been shaped by cultures resulting from some common elements: a Spanish or Portuguese colonial past, the experience of

---

1. See Gobat, "Invention of Latin America" and Brown, "'Latin' America Is Dead."

mestizaje (mixing of indigenous peoples, African and European descents, and cultural hybridity), the effects of migration, a pervasive Roman Catholic environment, the influence of the recent emergence of a Pentecostal/Charismatic spirituality, and societies dealing with poverty and inequality in a complex continental dynamic.

Our use of "Latin American" seeks to gather these common elements together to include a broader range of racial, national, linguistic, and class diversity. Despite the complexity of choosing a label, we hope that "Latin American eyes" conveys a sense of inclusivity while also resisting any homogenization and oversimplification of all the diversity our authors bring to this volume.

A MULTIPLICITY OF CONTEXTS, DISCIPLINES, AND PERSPECTIVES

Not all the authors are writing about Latin American or Latino-dominant contexts. It is their unique Latin American perspective that brings them together. A richness emerges when this common Latin American perspective combines in unique ways with the authors' multiplicity of scholarly fields, academic formations, and personal journeys. While each author reflects on a different worship practice or worshiping community, there are three major themes around which these essays converge.

The first set of essays addresses a key theme in Latin American culture: embodiment in worship. Leopoldo A. Sánchez M. opens this section by exploring Luther's theology of music through his own experience of playing the double bass, ultimately proposing a christological aesthetic as an embodied key for using instrumental music in worship. Nancy Bedford follows this with a close reading of the worship practices of a local community, identifying Pentecostality as a central theological motif embodied in these practices. Júlio Cézar Adam then reflects on an experimental seminar he designed in his Brazilian context to connect worship and daily life through theatrical performance and movement as a form of inculturation.

The second set of essays focuses on the intercultural encounters that happen when people, worship practices, and cultural artifacts cross borders. Marcell Steuernagel's essay highlights the complex questions raised by the changing dynamics of worship practices as music crosses borders in the Global South, applying an ethnomusicological analysis to case studies in Brazil, Mozambique, and India. Dinorah B. Méndez adds to this section by challenging the dominant narrative of the passive reception of a foreign musical tradition imported by missionaries through an analysis of cultural affinities in Mexican religiosity that have enabled contextualization by Mexican Protestant churches.

The third set of essays centers around faith formation in worship. Rooted in a multicultural church context in Spain, Israel Flores Olmos explores the role of testimony in public worship as a formative practice that builds community by weaving personal and communal narratives into the divine narrative. In the following essay, César Lopes notes the absence of lament as a regular practice in public worship and argues for reintroducing this practice as a countercultural formation that fosters empathy and solidarity. This section concludes with a case study by Elizabeth Tamez Méndez that describes a Latina congregation's efforts toward greater inclusion of youth in worship and presents a model for effective youth formation in the broader Latino Protestant context in the US.

LATIN AMERICAN SCHOLARS AS "WORSHIP DOCENTS"

Our colleague John Witvliet has introduced us to the concept of training worship "docents." When we teach alongside him in his undergraduate worship courses, our aim as instructors is to develop in our students a deep enough understanding of what is going on in worship that they can become like "docents" to others, describing more fully the historical, biblical, and contextual dimensions of public worship practices so that others can enter in with greater understanding. In commissioning and gathering these essays, we hope to cultivate a similar dynamic, allowing a group of Latin American scholars to guide our readers into a renewed understanding of public worship practices through learning from other cultural lenses.

As our world becomes increasingly interconnected on a global scale, there are abundant opportunities for cross-cultural exchange, but going beyond the superficial requires disciplined focus and attentive listening. We hope this book will provide an opportunity to listen to underrepresented voices and develop a more nuanced and multifaceted understanding of worship beyond familiar settings.

BIBLIOGRAPHY

Brown, Denise Fay. "'Latin' America Is Dead. Long Live Nuestra América!" *Canadian Journal of Latin American and Caribbean Studies / Revue Canadienne Des Études Latino-Américaines et Caraïbes* 38, no. 1 (January 2013) 1–16.

Gobat, Michel. "The Invention of Latin America. A Transnational History of Anti-Imperialism, Democracy, and Race." *The American Historical Review* 118, no. 5 (November 2013) 1345–75.

CONTENTS

Introduction | vii

—María Eugenia Cornou *and* Noel A. Snyder

List of Contributors | xiii

SECTION I: EMBODYING THEOLOGY

Theologian by Day, Double Bass Player by Night: Toward a Christological Aesthetic for the Use of Instrumental Music in Worship | 3

—Leopoldo A. Sánchez M.

Seeking Pentecostality: Worship Practices at Reba Place Church | 32

—Nancy Elizabeth Bedford

Liturgy, Daily Life, and Performance: An Experiential-Reflective Approach to Congregational Practice | 55

—Júlio Cézar Adam

SECTION II: CROSSING BORDERS

Songs from Other Heartlands: Church Music in the Global South | 81

—Marcell Silva Steuernagel

Contextualizing Evangelical Worship within Mexican Religiosity with Special Reference to Theology in Congregational Singing | 106

—Dinorah B. Méndez

SECTION III: FORMING WORSHIPERS

Narrated Lives and Testimonies as Part of Recapitulating the History of Salvation in Liturgy: Toward an Open, Multicultural Experience | 133

—Israel Flores Olmos

Learning Empathy: Removing Lament from the Null Curriculum in Public Worship | 150

—César Márques Lópes

Enriching and Deepening Congregational Worship Life by Developing Youth: Lessons from a Latino Congregation in Texas | 175

—Elizabeth Tamez Méndez

CONTRIBUTORS

Júlio Cézar Adam, Associate Professor of Practical Theology at Faculdades EST, São Leopoldo/RS, Brazil.

Nancy Elizabeth Bedford, Georgia Harkness Professor of Theology at Garrett-Evangelical Theological Seminary, Evanston, IL.

María Eugenia Cornou, Associate Director and Program Manager at Calvin Institute of Christian Worship, Grand Rapids, MI.

César Marques Lopes, President of the Comunidad de Estudios Teológicos Interdisciplinarios (CETI), San José, Costa Rica.

Dinorah B. Méndez, Resident Fellow, B. H. Carroll Theological Seminary, East Texas Baptist University.

Elizabeth Tamez Méndez, Director of Programs and Grants, Leadership Education at Duke Divinity School; Founder and Executive Director, New Generation3, Durham, NC.

Noel A. Snyder, Program Manager at Calvin Institute of Christian Worship, Grand Rapids, MI.

Israel Flores Olmos, Dean and Professor of Theology, Worship, and Missiology at Facultad de Teología SEUT, Madrid, Spain.

Leopoldo A. Sánchez M., Werner R. H. Krause and Elizabeth Ringger Krause Professor of Hispanic Ministries and Systematic Theology at Concordia Seminary, St. Louis, MO.

Marcell Silva Steuernagel, Assistant Professor of Church Music, Director of the Master of Sacred Music and Doctor of Pastoral Music Programs, Perkins School of Theology/Meadows School of the Arts, Southern Methodist University, Dallas, TX.

SECTION I

Embodying Theology

THEOLOGIAN BY DAY, DOUBLE BASS PLAYER BY NIGHT

Toward a Christological Aesthetic for the Use of Instrumental Music in Worship

Leopoldo A. Sánchez M.

The leader of a group I perform with regularly introduces me to audiences as "a theologian by day and a double bass player by night." Theology is my main calling, my professional vocation. Music has been for me a serious yet joyful pursuit, a form of disciplined play somewhere in that creative space between labor and rest. For years I kept my professional and musical lives separate, mostly so that music would not start to feel like my regular job as a professor of theology but more like a sabbatical time away from the daily rhythms of life at Concordia Seminary. But in the past few years I have tried to integrate these two dimensions of my creative life, acknowledging that both theology and music are gifts of God to be used for God's glory, in service to the gospel, and for the well-being of neighbors.[1]

---

1. I wish to acknowledge the Wabash Center for Teaching and Learning in Theology and Religion, where I first began to think about the need for such integration through participation in its 2014–15 Teaching and Learning Colloquy for Mid-Career Theological School Faculty on the theme of "Theology and the Arts."

Along this journey, Martin Luther's high view of music (including instrumental music) as a gift from above for gospel communication has been a source of inspiration. In this essay, I argue that Luther's theological interpretation of the function of instrumental music suggests a christological musical aesthetic that bears affinity with US Hispanic proposals for linking aesthetics to socially conscious discipleship in the world. I conclude with ideas about what a christological musical aesthetic might mean for instrumental musicians in worship.

Often the double bass is used in worship only for accompaniment of congregational singing, either doubling the main voice or providing *basso continuo* (that is, an improvised bass line based on a given chord structure). Integrating the double bass in other ways has been an interesting challenge. Two experiences come to mind.

First, for a midweek Lenten service's offertory, I played in both high and low registers the melody (with piano accompaniment) of the late-nineteenth-century French song "Après un Rêve" ("After a Dream"), by Gabriel Fauré (1845–1924). Although the original poem and Fauré's later musical interpretation were "secular," I played the melody in a way that would communicate a somber and meditative Lenten mood—an achievable musical effect given the low sonorities of the double bass and its warm, solemn, and broad timbre.

A church member came to me afterwards wondering what the title "After a Dream" referred to. The original poem portrays a man who dreams of flying away with his beloved and after waking longs to return to the dream. Could the lesser-known poem's picture of romantic love be appropriated evangelically to denote Christ's love for his bride, the church, in the style of Song of Songs? Perhaps, but I chose to use Fauré's melody without reference to its poetic inspiration. And in a sense, the melody was secondary. My main purpose was to use the instrument to speak a certain color or timbre to match the Lenten "blues," to communicate and embody a cruciform mood in the liturgical context.

On another occasion, I composed a musical interpretation of an artistic digital composite of clouds representing God's ongoing presence amid his people.[2] I explored various sonorities of the instrument to tell the exodus story, to describe God's leading Israel out of Egypt by a pillar

---

2. For a reflection on and link to the musical piece, see Sánchez M., "Telling the Exodus Story." The digital composite *By Night and by Day* is the work of artist Sarah Bernhardt and is part of her *Cloud Song* collection (https://www.sarahbernhardtart.com).

of cloud by day and of fire by night. In the tradition of word painting, a popular device used in sixteenth-century music to match an idea in a text with a corresponding musical effect, such as using low notes to express descent or high ones to communicate ascent, I used a melody from the Latin American song "El Señor es mi luz" ("The Lord Is My Light," based on Psalm 27) to guide my portrayal of God's presence with his people.[3] The psalm speaks of the Israelites' trust in the Lord's guidance and protection from adversaries during their wilderness pilgrimage, as well as their eschatological hope to dwell in the house of the Lord forever and see his beauty in his temple.

A variation on the melody used high-pitched harmonics, achieved by touching the strings without pressing them, to communicate a sense of Israel's calm in God's presence before crossing the Red Sea. The soothing harmonics were followed by energetic tremolos, made by rapidly moving the bow back and forth on each note of the melody, to represent the tumultuous movement of God's people away from their enemies as the pillars of fire and cloud went ahead of them through the great waters. To express Israel's proximity to the waters of salvation, the psalm melody is played by hitting the strings with the wooden part of the bow (a technique called *col legno*), evoking drops of water sprinkling faces and bodies as people prepare to cross the sea. Then a calm, flowing, lyrically bowed version of the theme depicted Israel's safe arrival to the promised land, anticipating the beatific vision of God's people in the presence of Christ. Next, a plucking Cuban *guaracha* (salsa) rhythm based on the song's chord progression expressed a mood of eschatological *fiesta* after the people's safe passage through turbulent waters into the promised land. Finally, the hymn's chorus was sung in Spanish with the double bass's wooden shoulders used for percussive accompaniment with a Panamanian *tamborito* rhythmic pattern. The main function of the instrument in this musical rendition was to paint an artistic picture of the biblical theme and to set up the same theme for a brief vocal rendition at the very end.

Experimenting with instrumental music in congregational worship and devotional settings has been deliberate, though at times more intuitive than premeditated. This essay is a more reflective, constructive attempt to explore some questions about the interaction between theology and instrumental music. How should we understand the relationship

---

3. "El Señor es mi luz" was originally written in Portuguese; I used the version in the Spanish hymnbook ¡*Cantad al Señor!*, 68.

between God's Word or the gospel voice and instrumental music? What are the uses of instrumental music in its own right? How should instrumentalists think about and approach their task and craft as accompanists or soloists in worship? In what ways and for what purposes should instrumentalists embody musical and theological intention in ritual performance? As a Lutheran Latino theologian and musician, I am especially interested in what the Lutheran tradition and US Hispanic scholarship might contribute to answering these questions.

MUSIC DIVINE: MARTIN LUTHER'S FORMATIVE APPROACH TO MUSIC

In a letter to Louis Senfl (ca. 1486–1543), a master polyphonic composer of the Renaissance, Martin Luther (1483–1546) wrote, "Except for theology there is no art that could be put on the same level with music, since except for theology [music] alone produces what otherwise only theology can do, namely, a calm and joyful disposition."[4] Luther observes that "the prophets did not make use of any art except music" to communicate the Word, "so that they held theology and music most tightly connected, and proclaimed truth through Psalms and songs."[5] In his commentary on Psalms, Luther likened the singing of psalms to the preaching of "sermons of the sweet Gospel which proclaim God's grace, honor, and praise," and compared the "accompaniment of string music" to the "deeds and miraculous signs" that accompany the gospel.[6] In these statements, the Reformer praised the value of both vocal and instrumental music as a divine gift and a means to gospel proclamation for the spiritual care of hearers, with the instrument primarily supporting the voice.

Although Luther prioritizes the gospel voice over its instrumental embellishment, both psalms and instrumental music serve to praise God.[7] Indeed, because of its association with Scripture, the psalm is

---

4. Luther, *Luther's Works*, 49:428.

5. Luther, *Luther's Works*, 49:428; similarly, "the priests and the Levites were ordained to sing and to accompany on stringed instruments such songs of thanks written by David" (Luther, 12:98). Lutheran composer and author Carl Schalk refers to Martin Agricola's *Musica instrumentalis deudsch* (written in 1529 and revised in 1545) as a notable example of Lutheran theological support for the use of instrumental music in church (Schalk, *Music in Early Lutheranism*, 54–55).

6. Luther, *Luther's Works*, 13:5

7. "God is to be praised by Christians, and He is praised today with both [voice] and with many other musical instruments" (Luther, *Luther's Works*, 10:152); "Still he

called a "new song" and "the harp is holy and the psaltery is holy."[8] The Word of God makes music holy and through it fosters holiness. Echoing a Pauline Spirit/flesh anthropology, Luther teaches that the Holy Spirit alone sanctifies music through the Word, making it an instrument of God's new creation and its accompanying virtues.[9] Conversely, music can be an instrument of the old sinful flesh and its vices. Although songs in and of themselves can be seen as "neutral in character," whether they are used "in congregations or in figural music" (the term "figural music" refers to polyphony in contrast to monophony), they can serve either "good" or "evil" ends.[10]

For Luther, what makes a song "new" or "old" is not the time of its composition, but whether it is a means of the Holy Spirit or of the sinful flesh. By this definition, Luther reasons that an old song can be quite "new" (like the spiritual songs Adam, the first man, would have presumably sung in paradise), or a new song "old." The question is whether the song is "spiritual" or not—that is to say, whether it fosters the fruit of the Spirit or the works of the flesh. Luther says:

> Old songs are all shameful, scurrilous, carnal and worldly songs, even if they should first be sung or composed today. New songs, however, are all psalms, honorable, holy, godly, and spiritual songs, even if they dated back to the time of the first man; indeed, these are the newest songs.[11]

Similarly, Luther's observation about the neutrality of songs suggests that the musical form itself, whether monophonic (single part or voice) or polyphonic (two or more parts or voices), does not make a song new or old. What matters is the theological content, use, and effect of the musical form on the hearer. In other words, the question is whether the musical

---

[David] established many divine services and prepared psalms and instrumental music for the praise of God" (Luther, *Luther's Works*, 13:167).

8. Luther, *Luther's Works*, 10:154.

9. "The Holy Ghost himself honors her as an instrument for his proper work when in his Holy Scriptures he asserts that through her his gifts were instilled in the prophets, namely, the inclination to all virtues, as can be seen in Elisha [2 Kgs 3:15]" (Luther, *Luther's Works*, 53:323).

10. Luther, *Luther's Works*, 53:323. Monophony is music in which a single part or melody is sung or played by either one or several people. The most important Western example of monophonic music is Gregorian chant. Polyphony is the singing or playing of two or more relatively parallel and independent parts. When polyphony is used to accompany a tenor or main melody, it may be called homophony.

11. Luther, *Luther's Works*, 10:154.

form serves a shameful or honorable end, whether music as a cultural sign can communicate, embody, or express the gospel sign to the glory of God and the benefit of the hearer.[12] Luther's comments on the spiritual function or use of music apply to both vocal and instrumental music, which in the Renaissance were approached interchangeably with instruments mostly doubling the voice.[13]

Luther's positive reception of church music included medieval monophonic chant as well as the polyphonic music of his day. He spoke highly of Josquin des Prez (d. 1521), a famous Renaissance composer of polyphonic works, judging that "God has preached the gospel through music" like that of Josquin, "whose compositions flow freely, gently, and cheerfully, are not forced or cramped by rules, and are like the song of the finch."[14] Prior to the arrival of chordal harmony in the Baroque period (1600–1750), making two or more equal and independent musical lines sound good together required great skill. Before the High Renaissance, polyphony—to use Luther's words—did not always "flow freely, gently, cheerfully." Before Luther's day, the use of polyphony in the church was at times suspect. To medieval church ears used to monophony or plainchant, some early forms of polyphony were felt to get in the way of "devotion, the true aim of all worship," even if they were not always completely banned.[15]

---

12. In Lutheran theology a gospel sign is a created means that by God's command delivers God's grace or forgiveness (gospel) to people (e.g., sacraments, such as baptism and the Lord's Supper). These sure and certain signs of grace are distinguished from other created signs that do not promise grace but can still be useful pedagogically to teach and admonish God's people with God's Word (e.g., a crucifix). For a Lutheran reflection on how music can function as a sign in both categories, see Sánchez M., "Theology in Context."

13. In contrast to the Baroque period (1600–1750), which increasingly featured "independent instrumental parts complementing rather than doubling vocal lines," Renaissance composers tended to assume that "vocal and instrumental idioms are essentially interchangeable" (Bonds, *Antiquity*, 207).

14. Luther, *Luther's Works*, 54:129–30; Schalk notes that Luther had grown up with and had an ear for the music of the Flemish School, whose "style was characterized by a clear texture, smooth-sounding polyphony and homophony, controlled expressiveness, and well-organized principles of compositions, including a controlled use of dissonance and consonance" (Schalk, *Music in Early Lutheranism*, 20).

15. For example, Pope John XXII declared in his bull *Docta sanctorum patrum* (1324–25) that while polyphonic forms should not be ordinarily used in the Mass in place of plainsong because "they hinder the melody" so that "devotion ... is neglected, and wantonness ... increases," he also states that "it is not our wish to forbid the occasional use—especially on feast days or in solemn celebration of the Mass and the Divine Office—of some consonances, for example, the octave, fifth, and the fourth,

By the sixteenth century, masters like Josquin had developed polyphony in ways that could make a tune flow and sound pleasant—or as Luther put it, "like the song of the finch." Luther seems most attracted to these polyphonic composers' masterful use of accompanying voices as an adornment to the main tenor melody or *cantus firmus* (fixed melody) of a hymn—a type of polyphony called homophony.[16] He welcomed the elaborate accompaniment of chorale melodies:

> Here it is most remarkable that one single voice continues to sing the tenor, while at the same time many other voices play around it, exulting and adorning it in exuberant strains and, as it were, leading it forth in a divine roundelay, so that those who are the least bit moved know nothing more amazing in this world.[17]

Luther's appreciation of music—both melody and embellishment—as a divine gift follows not only from God's ability to use the form to communicate or embody God's gospel truth in a culturally appropriate language, but also from God's ability to do something to the hearer through it. Music has a formative character. It is intended to create a certain kind of person, one devoted to God and his fellow human beings.[18] The psalmist's compositions are meant "both to praise and to thank God . . . and to serve his fellowmen by stimulating and teaching them."[19] What makes psalms "sweet" is not only their "beautiful text and beautiful tune, but . . . the theology they contain . . . the spiritual meaning."[20] Such theology and spiritual meaning are meant to serve a pastoral function—namely, to comfort consciences with the gospel:

> That renders the Psalms lovely and sweet, for they are a solace to all saddened and wretched consciences, ensnared in the fear of sin, in the torture and terror of death, and in all sorts of adversity

---

which heighten the beauty of the melody" (Bonds, *Antiquity*, 76).

16. In his request to Senfl for the arrangement of a favorite tune ("In peace [I will both lie down and sleep]"), Luther shows his appreciation for the basic characteristics of the homophonic style of polyphony: "For this tenor melody has delighted me from youth on, and does so even more now that I understand the words. I have never seen this antiphon arranged for more voices" (Luther, *Luther's Works*, 49:428).

17. Luther, *Luther's Works*, 53:324.

18. "The psalms and music have been designed to arouse devotion. But if they are handled with excessive noise, they quench the spirit rather than restore it" (Luther, *Luther's Works*, 10:42).

19. Luther, *Luther's Works*, 15:273.

20. Luther, *Luther's Works*, 15:273.

and misery. To such hearts the Book of Psalms is a sweet and delightful song because it sings of and proclaims the Messiah."[21]

Minds can be "moved by music," and music "alone produces what otherwise only theology can do, namely, a calm and joyful disposition."[22] Luther argues that "it is the function of music to arouse the sad, sluggish, and dull spirit."[23] His view of the power of music follows in part from his reading of 1 Samuel 16:23, where David's playing of the lyre made a harmful spirit depart from Saul.[24] In Luther's cosmological view, in which God fights against the evil one for the souls of humankind, God can use music to "cast out Satan, the instigator of all sins, as is shown in Saul, the king of Israel."[25] Like theology, "music, too, is odious and unbearable to the demons. . . . Manifest proof [of this is] that the devil, the creator of saddening cares and disquieting worries, takes flight at the sound of music almost as he takes flight at the word of theology."[26] It should be noted that Luther's assessment of music's "capacity to exorcise the devil himself" does not arise from an esoteric or magical view of music, but rather from his understanding of music not "as an end in itself, but as a function of theology."[27] For instance, as an instrument of the Holy Spirit, music can inspire good virtues as in the case of Elisha, who prophesied after hearing a musician play (2 Kgs 3:15).[28] Under the Spirit's baton,

---

21. Luther, *Luther's Works*, 15:273–74.
22. Luther, *Luther's Works*, 49:427–28.
23. Luther, *Luther's Works*, 10:43.
24. In *A Preface to All Good Hymnals* (1538), Luther writes:
"But God in me more pleasure finds
Than in all joys of earthly minds.
Through my bright power the devil shirks
His sinful, murderous, evil works.
Of this King David's deeds do tell
Who pacified King Saul so Well
By sweetly playing on the lyre
And thus escaped his murderous ire" (Luther, *Luther's Works*, 53:320).
25. Luther, *Luther's Works*, 53:323.
26. Luther, *Luther's Works*, 49:428.
27. "Él no concebía a la música como un fin en sí mismo, sino como *ancilla theologiae*; es decir, al servicio de la teología. Por esta razón, la música es un don dado por Dios y no por el hombre. No entra en juego la capacidad musical del intérprete ni tampoco la música como un fin en sí mismo, sino en función de la teología. Lutero considera a la música casi como si tuviera la capacidad de exorcizar al mismo diablo" (Granados, "Martín Lutero y la música," 136).
28. Luther, *Luther's Works*, 53:323. In *A Preface to All Good Hymnals*, Luther writes: "For truth divine and God's own rede

music can thus perform a formative function, channeling emotions or affections in virtuous ways or for divine purposes.

> She is a mistress and governess of those human emotions . . . which as masters govern men or more often overwhelm them. . . . For whether you wish to comfort the sad, to terrify the happy, to encourage the despairing, to humble the proud, to calm the passionate, or to appease those full of hate—and who could number all these masters of the human heart, namely, the emotions, inclinations, and affections that impel men to evil or good?—what more effective means than music could you find?[29]

Luther's thoughts on music as a master of our affections anticipates the burgeoning Baroque interest in "representing" a "predominant emotion" or "affect" through a musical idea with the intent of "creating in the mind and spirit of listeners a corresponding emotional state."[30] But how does Luther justify theologically the use of instruments as a means to move the emotions, and what affections should those instruments attempt to represent musically and then produce in the heart? More broadly, how does Luther's christological reading of Scripture shape the use and effect of instruments in worship or devotion?

MUSIC THAT PREACHES: THE CRUCIFORMITY OF LUTHER'S FORMATIVE USE OF INSTRUMENTAL MUSIC

We have seen that, for Luther, both the tenor melody and its polyphonic instrumental adornments, though neutral in themselves, can fulfill a formative function in hearers by moving and channeling their affections in ways that serve divine purposes. Under the operation of the Holy Spirit, music can function as an instrument or vehicle that fosters true devotion to God and service to neighbor. It does so through the proclamation of Christ and his gospel for the comfort of consciences and for growth in spiritual virtues. Delivering the holy Word in a compelling

---

The heart of humble faith shall lead;
Such did Elisha once propound
When harping he the Spirit found" (Luther, *Luther's Works*, 53:320).

29. Luther, *Luther's Works*, 53:323.

30. Bonds, *Antiquity*, 193; James Crockford observes that Luther's overall positive view of music as an instrument of the Spirit to instill virtues and drive out the devil does not allow him to consider the ways in which the devil can use music to move the affections in a negative way. See Crockford, "Get Happy."

way that touches the heart and kindles the senses, music can be used by the Holy Spirit in its work of driving the evil one away by convicting the proud and encouraging the desperate, by killing the old flesh ("the carnal and outer man") and making alive the new creature ("the new man, . . . a man of grace, a spiritual and inner man before God").[31] Incorporating hearers into Christ's death and resurrection, music takes on a cruciform character, raising the spiritually dead to life and thus bringing about a new creation out of suffering and death.

Further exploration of the cruciform character of instrumental music comes to us in Luther's reflection on the spiritual or mystical meaning of musical instruments in the psalms. In a meditation on Psalm 33:2 ("Praise the LORD with harp: Sing unto him with the psaltery and an instrument of ten strings" [KJV]), Luther draws upon a practice going back to the fourteenth century of contrasting "low" (*bas*) and "high" (*alta*) instruments based not on their range or register but on their volume or dynamic level.[32] Accordingly, each instrument's sonority signifies a truth concerning Christ's human and divine identity.

> In the first place, the harp is Christ Himself according to the human nature, who was stretched on the cross for us like a string on the harp. Thus to confess with the harp means to think about the acts and sufferings of Christ according to the flesh, for such meditation has its resonance from below, from humanity to divinity. . . . The psaltery is the very same Christ according to divinity, as He dwells among the ten choirs of angels. And thus to confess with the psaltery means to think about divine and heavenly things and about the angels. And this meditation sounds down from above.[33]

Musical instruments can teach both a Christology from below, which takes as its starting point the humiliation of the incarnate Christ, or one from above, which begins with his divinity. The spiritual or mystical meaning of the psalm's low and high instruments becomes, broadly speaking, none other than the christological sense of the psalm, and moreover it suggests concrete ways in which instrumental music can

---

31. Commenting on Psalm 33:3, Luther writes: "Only a new man can sing *a new song*. But the new man is a man of grace, a spiritual and inner man before God. The old man, however, is the man of sin, the carnal and outer man before the world. The newness is grace, the oldness, sin" (Luther, *Luther's Works*, 10:154).

32. For examples of high and low instruments before and during the Renaissance, see Bonds, *Antiquity*, 90, 149.

33. Luther, *Luther's Works*, 10:153.

actually invite hearers (and performers) of the psalm to meditate (or foster meditation) on the sufferings and glory of Christ.

As part of the christological meaning, each instrument's sonority can signify a tropological or moral truth concerning the believer's identity in Christ. Luther gives examples of such readings from Cassiodorus (ca. 490–583) and Augustine (354–430), early commentators on Psalm 33, who correlate Christ's earthly life and self-giving suffering for others with believers' participation in such a Christlike life through their devotion to God embodied in their good works, their experience of and response to adversity, and their sacrificial life in service to neighbors.

> In a mystical sense, according to the same author [i.e., Cassiodorus], the harp denotes the works of earthly prosperity or adversity, by means of which God is praised as it were from the lower parts, whereas the psaltery denotes the commandments of the decalog, which we receive as coming from above and which we then observe. Augustine's view is the same. However, he adds this besides, that the harp denotes the mortified flesh, by offering our bodies as a living sacrifice, holy, etc. (Rom 12:1).[34]

Luther draws a contrast between the Word and music. The former is intelligible in the sense that its meaning is "articulated by syllables that are intellectually significative," while the latter offers "only a sound that is perceived by the senses."[35] Instrumental music like that of the psaltery is more akin to the parable, Luther says, which works "like a sound that is neither articulated nor distinct" and has a hidden meaning that needs to be uncovered.[36] A christological principle is at work in Luther's mystical interpretation of musical references in the psalms, namely, that in the incarnation Christ is capable of revealing his divinity (and thus his divine teachings) through his humanity.[37] God can use sound, and thus vocal and instrumental music, to invite us to learn from Christ and live

---

34. Luther, *Luther's Works*, 10:153–54.
35. Luther, *Luther's Works*, 10:228–29.
36. Luther, *Luther's Works*, 10:229.

37. "For as through the incarnation of Christ the Word of God was added to the flesh, so the Spirit was revealed through the same. The Spirit is like the word of the voice and like the Godhead of the flesh. And so the prophet wants to say that Christ will open the word, the Spirit and hidden Godhead, on the psaltery, that is, He will reveal them in the parabolic voice and sound" (Luther, *Luther's Works*, 10:229). In these texts, the word "Spirit" appears to be used not in a hypostatic sense to refer to the person of the Holy Spirit, but in a substantial sense as a reference to the "Godhead," or divinity, of Christ.

in Christ. But the parabolic nature of instrumental music in particular requires a theological interpretation and use.

Another example of Luther's threefold mystical interpretation of Scripture (which assumes a distinction between literal and other senses) comes from his reading of Numbers 10:1–10, where God commands Moses to employ two silver trumpets for various purposes. The trumpet's sound calls the Israelites to different actions: "when they should go to war, when they should celebrate feasts, when the people should gather."[38] The text invites God's people—that is, the church of all times—to prepare spiritually for "war against vices and demons" (tropological), to feast in "instruction and refreshment in spiritual things" (allegorical), and simply to gather together (literal).[39] This is a christological interpretation of the text in the sense that the church of Christ is here called to gather in his name, to be refreshed in his instruction, and to share in his victory against the evil one. The sounds of trumpets embody a message that links Christ's life to ours.

As we noted before, in the Psalms the church is also called to share in Christ's sufferings and glory. We see Luther move toward this cruciform interpretation of the trumpet's sound in his teaching on Psalm 81 and its reference to the Feast of Trumpets as a preamble to the Day of Atonement (Lev 23:23–32). According to Luther, the psalm as a whole invites the church to a life of repentance and faith. The psalmist preaches both "penitence and affliction and the cross" so that "everyone's soul should be afflicted" and so that "the new life which comes into being through... Christ, by whom the soul is illuminated through faith" might shine forth.[40] Already in the Feast of Trumpets, "the cross of Christ and penitence began to be proclaimed by means of the apostolic trumpet."[41] To blow the trumpet "at the new moon" signifies "the day of beginning grace," that is, the New Testament church's apostolic work to "openly proclaim Christ crucified."[42] The proclamation of "the Word of the Gospel concerning Christ, the God, who was slain according to the flesh" involves "not only the cross that He Himself carried, but also the one we should carry."[43] Note how the sounds of trumpets are like a musical

---

38. Luther, *Luther's Works*, 10:229.
39. Luther, *Luther's Works*, 10:229.
40. Luther, *Luther's Works*, 11:101.
41. Luther, *Luther's Works*, 11:101.
42. Luther, *Luther's Works*, 11:105.
43. Luther, *Luther's Works*, 11:101–2.

parable with a hidden spiritual meaning that is only unveiled, received, and acted upon in the light of God's revelation in Christ and the apostolic announcement of this mystery of salvation.

In his interpretation of Psalm 81, Luther once again uses the popular distinction of his day between "high" and "low" instruments to unveil the psalm's meaning. The high sonority of the psalm tune and the lyre, signifying glory and majesty, stands in contrast to the low sonority of the harp and the timbrel, signifying patience, suffering, and afflictions. Referring to the christological hymn in Philippians 2, one of Luther's tropological interpretations of the psalm exhorts believers to take from Christ not the form of God but the form of a servant in their dealings with others:

> Many take Christ as a miracle worker and want to follow Him in the glory and majesty of works but are unwilling to do so in sufferings. These take the sweet lyre, but not with the harp, and they raise a psalm but do not sound the timbrel. They want to reign with Christ, be elevated with His honor in the church's offices, have the administration from above with relation to others, and let hierarchical acts flow downward. That is, they want to sound downward and be heard and received with reverence, obedience, and politeness. But they, in turn, do not want to sound upward through obedience and reverence to God and His representatives. They all want to imitate the form of God in Christ and not the form of a servant (Phil 2:6–7). The form of God is the lyre, producing great works by teaching, guiding, and commanding. But the harp is the form of a servant, obedient, patient, bearing affliction. Thus they do not sound the timbrel but raise a psalm. As for you, take note that the sweet lyre is with the harp.[44]

Later in the same section, Luther suggests that the technique a musician employs to handle or perform his instrument can convey in the "literal music" the attitude people in authority should have toward those under them, which is "figuratively" expressed in the christological hymn.[45] For instance, the musician who sings while strumming the lyre expresses the spiritual virtue of a leader whose words (mouth) are in sync with his works (strumming), thus serving "as an example for others" of someone whose life reflects "the spirit to be ruler over the flesh."[46] Here Luther suggests that musicians can interpret the Christian story in a musical

---

44. Luther, *Luther's Works*, 11:103–4.
45. Luther, *Luther's Works*, 11:104.
46. Luther, *Luther's Works*, 11:104–5.

way appropriate to the instrument itself (i.e., singing while strumming) and embody such story in their own musical attitude and delivery (for instance, to signify that a person does what he says). The instrument becomes an extension of the musician's interpretative intention as a theologian and artist. The musician not only transmits a theological message about Christ or the Christian life, but interprets such message musically through the instrument and embodies it ritually for others.

Consonant with Luther's focus on the pastoral function of theology, instruments serve a preaching function. Returning to the Spirit/flesh Pauline paradigm, instruments are an aid in bringing the old flesh to die and in raising a new creature with Christ. Reflecting on Psalm 98:6 ("With trumpets and the sound of the horn make a joyful noise before the King, the LORD!" [ESV]), Luther distinguishes between the high trumpets played on "festive and joyous occasions" and the low horns played "in times of sorrow and affliction."[47] Just as there are two kinds of brass instruments in the psalm, "there are two kinds of preaching in the church: to rejoice with the rejoicing, to weep with the weeping; to be exhorted to joy in the Lord and to be exhorted to grief and penitence in oneself.... Thus to teach the spirit to rejoice and the flesh to be sad."[48] In Luther's anthropology, the spirit refers to the whole person in whom the Spirit lives, and the flesh describes the whole person in sinful opposition to God.[49] Accordingly, the two kinds of preaching correspond to the sound of the trumpet that proclaims the "righteousness which is for us from God" or "the salvation of the spirit and the new man," and the sound of the horn that announces "judgment" or "the humiliation of the flesh and of the old man."[50] According to the moral or tropological sense of the psalm, the twofold preaching of judgment and righteousness, which invites us to share in the sufferings and the glory of Christ

---

47. Luther, *Luther's Works*, 11:273.

48. Luther, *Luther's Works*, 11:273.

49. On Luther's use of "the antithesis *caro-spiritus*" (i.e., flesh-spirit), Regin Prenter has shown that it corresponds to the old creature (Lat. *homo vetus*) and the new creature (Lat. *homo novus*). He argues that "the contrast *caro-spiritus* is not anthropological, so that *spiritus* means the most noble part of man, the source of his idealistic striving for God and the spiritual realities, and *caro* the sensual nature, by which man attaches himself to all the base, the outward and corruptible. No, this contrast is a theological one: *spiritus* is the whole of man, if it is dominated by the Spirit of God; and *caro* is the whole of man, if it lacks the Spirit of God" (Prenter, *Spiritus Creator*, 5).

50. Prenter, *Spiritus Creator*, 5.

(cf. Rom 6), is also meant to root out "sin and the vices" of the flesh and inculcate the "virtues" of the Spirit in the hearer.[51]

Luther's thoughts on instruments reveal an appreciation for their role in spiritual formation. Such a role assumes the status of music as a gift of God under the Holy Spirit's formative work of proclaiming Christ and shaping people after the likeness of Christ. Music that preaches strives for the devotional and congregational use of instruments to convey or embody in their sonorities, colors, rhythms, and other musical patterns those gospel truths that invite hearers and singers of the Word to become receivers of God's redemptive gifts in Christ and participants in Christ's life of struggle against the evil one and sacrificial self-giving to others. Using their instruments as an extension of their theological and artistic message, musicians themselves serve as instruments of the Spirit's formation of people in faith and love. Although such a formative role is seen mostly in terms of instruments supporting a text or voice, Luther suggests that this is not exclusively the case because instruments in their own way can also communicate a theological message, even if it is parabolic and thus requires interpretation for its proper embodiment and reception.

LOVING THE UNLOVABLE: ENGAGING US HISPANIC CONTRIBUTIONS TOWARD A CHRISTOLOGICAL AESTHETICS

We have heard from Luther on the relationship between theology and instrumental musical forms, paying attention to his mystical readings of the christological function of instruments in the psalms and the particular affects and effects they strive to create in people. One of Luther's important contributions to musical aesthetics lies in his integration of the christological and tropological (ecclesial, moral) understandings of the function of musical instruments, conveying the indissoluble bond between soteriology and ethics, justification and sanctification, faith and life. In this section, we begin a dialogue with US Hispanic contributions in the field of aesthetics, which exhibit a strong commitment to drawing out the organic connection between the mystery of Christ's beauty on the cross and the suffering of his crucified people. Although the following

51. Prenter, *Spiritus Creator*, 5; "Therefore to make music with hammered trumpets is to preach the mystery of the kingdom of heaven and to exhort to spiritual good things," and "to make music with the voice of the bronze horn is to preach and to reprove our sins and evils" (Luther, *Luther's Works*, 11:275).

studies do not deal specifically with musical aesthetics, they do give us some insight into the formative role of aesthetics in US Hispanic theology and thus a point of contact with Luther's own interest in the formation of persons through the use of music in worship and devotion.

In *The Community of the Beautiful*, Roman Catholic theologian Alejandro García-Rivera argues that the fundamental question of aesthetics is "What moves the human heart?"[52] It is a question with a religious dimension, the question echoed by St. Augustine's well-known words in his *Confessions*: "Thou hast made us for Thee and our heart is unquiet till it finds its rest in Thee."[53] The great Christian tradition assumed "the human creature's capacity to receive divine Beauty."[54] In light of modernity's tragic severing from belief in God as the transcendent source of beauty and the human experience of the beautiful, the goal of theological aesthetics lies in showing the organic unity between Beauty and the beautiful.[55] Such severing might be seen in how people in the West today typically turn to music or art to give them pleasure apart from any religious, metaphysical, or transcendental considerations. García-Rivera finds in Hans Urs von Balthasar's view of Jesus as "the aesthetic model of all Beauty" the basis for an incarnational hermeneutic that bridges the chasm between the divine origin of Beauty and its human reception, so that the glory of God might result in the praise of God.[56] The aesthetic dynamic of glory and praise revealed in the incarnation makes possible "liturgy," which the author describes as "the human art which receives Glory and returns Praise," making "the entire creation participating in a liturgy of praise" the final goal of redemption in Christ.[57]

García-Rivera finds in the theology of signs a semiotic approach to mediate between the divine and the human. A sign is "a visible signifier standing for an invisible signified."[58] Like a sacrament (Lat. *sacramentum*), a sign communicates some aspect of the mystery (Gk. *mysterion*) of God in a way that God's human creatures can receive and respond to. While Plato's notion of a higher universal form transcending worldly appearance separated Beauty from the worldly place of human ascent

---

52. García-Rivera, *Community of the Beautiful*, 9.
53. Augustine of Hippo, *Confessions*, 4.
54. García-Rivera, *Community of the Beautiful*, 10.
55. García-Rivera, *Community of the Beautiful*, 10–11.
56. García-Rivera, *Community of the Beautiful*, 15.
57. García-Rivera, *Community of the Beautiful*, 18–19.
58. García-Rivera, *Community of the Beautiful*, 30.

to it, Augustine's appropriation of Plato's form through the idea of an anagoge, or ascent of the soul to the vision of God, involved a movement toward the Creator that does not take the human creature away from creation.[59] García-Rivera sees in an incarnational theology of "sign" the unifying factor in a theological aesthetics, one in which the sign (for example, the Eucharist) signifies a divine reality that can also be participated in.[60] Signs have an objective divine origin and a subjective human receiver. However, because "human art" involves "a relationship between thought and act," the interpretation of a sign involves not only a "logical" component, but also an "ethical" one.[61]

García-Rivera is interested in how an aesthetic of ascent or praise does not end in a Platonic flight from the world, but becomes a transformative experience of divine beauty or glory that transfigures humans into what he calls a "Community of the Beautiful." Drawing from Jan Mukarovsky's argument that what makes an artistic form such as a poem beautiful is its ability to accent little elements like "rhythm and cadence" by "foregrounding" them, namely, by "the lifting up of a piece of background and, then, giving it value," the author argues that what defines the beauty of a community theologically is how God lifts up the lowly.[62] In the Magnificat, for instance, Mary praises God for bringing down the powerful and lifting up the lowly (see Luke 1:51–52).[63] The author sees Mary as a paradigm of the poor church who praises God amid her sufferings. In Christ's incarnation and his resurrection from the dead, we see God's glory revealed and his lifting the lowly out of love to bring them to the praise of God.[64]

---

59. García-Rivera, *Community of the Beautiful*, 30.
60. García-Rivera, *Community of the Beautiful*, 33.
61. García-Rivera, *Community of the Beautiful*, 34.
62. García-Rivera, *Community of the Beautiful*, 35.

63. "Mukarovsky's semiotic principle of 'foregrounding' now becomes the biblical principle of 'lifting up the lowly.' As such, it reveals what I call the Community of the Beautiful. . . . It echoes over and over again in the Scriptures. From the Creation of the Cosmos out of chaos, through the psalmist's praise in the midst of agony, the Prophet's call to the wicked, Wisdom's song to the hidden beloved, the Magi's gifts to a helpless child, even the cruel 'lifting up' the Son of Man for the sake of the world, 'foregrounding' appears as aesthetic counterpoint to the lowly settings of the Biblical narrative. For me, Mary's song gives voice to the redemptive nature of this theological aesthetics. God's Beauty embodies itself as a 'lifting up the lowly,' creating the Community of the Beautiful" (García-Rivera, *Community of the Beautiful*, 36).

64. "God born out of the lowly 'lifted up' into human existence, crucified into the darkness by being 'lifted up,' and 'lifted up' once again from the cave of his tomb reveals

In the article "Theo-Drama as Liberative Praxis," Roman Catholic theologian Roberto Goizueta argues that "the lived faith of the poor gives rise to a theological aesthetics of liberation that subverts modern and post-modern notions of the symbol as an arbitrary, interchangeable sign with no intrinsic connection to its referent."[65] Although Goizueta appreciates Balthasar's theological retrieval of the premodern idea of sign or symbol as a gratuitous revelation of divine self-giving received by the creature in faith and praise, he argues that Balthasar's aesthetics proposal is not sufficiently concerned with ethics.[66] Goizueta fears a gnostic approach that turns aesthetics into "an apolitical religious experience" of divine beauty detached from God's commitment to transform life in the world, especially among those whom the world or "dominant culture considers 'ugly.'"[67] In this sentiment, he echoes García-Rivera's desire to integrate soteriology and ethics in aesthetics through the signs of Christ and Mary as the lowly lifted up by God.

At the center of Goizueta's liberation aesthetics lies a christological "criterion of beauty," namely, "the body of a tortured, scarred criminal hanging from a cross—and therefore, the bodies of those whom Jon Sobrino calls the crucified people of history."[68] The point of aesthetics lies in moving the disciple from merely experiencing the Christ on the Mount of Transfiguration to following him down from the mount to Golgotha. As Goizueta puts it, "the transformation effected in the experience of God's glory . . . must ultimately issue not just in transformed feelings . . . but, most importantly, in transformed actions, a transformed *praxis*."[69] In the "theo-drama," the dialogical relationship between divine gift and human reception, "divine love stirs and attracts" us to reflect the glory of God in our love for others; otherwise stated, "as divine action, God's love compels our action."[70] Aesthetics is thus not ultimately concerned with modern rationalistic or individualistic utilitarian or therapeutic ends, but rather with action or discipleship inspired by the beauty of God's love in Christ.

---

an original Imagination, and aesthetics which has love and not simply delight as its aim" (García-Rivera, *Community of the Beautiful*, 37).

65. Goizueta, "Theo-Drama as Liberative Praxis," 62–76. For a fuller treatment of themes in this article, see Goizueta, *Christ Our Companion*.

66. Goizueta, "Theo-Drama as Liberative Praxis," 62–63.

67. Goizueta, "Theo-Drama as Liberative Praxis," 63.

68. Goizueta, "Theo-Drama as Liberative Praxis," 63.

69. Goizueta, "Theo-Drama as Liberative Praxis," 68.

70. Goizueta, "Theo-Drama as Liberative Praxis," 70.

Drawing from Gustavo Gutiérrez's emphasis on "the preferential option for the poor," Goizueta explains that even though God's love (or praxis) toward his human creatures is universal and gratuitous, it also has a "sociohistorical character" that allows us to extend a priority of love toward our neediest neighbors—especially in a social location in which the poor and vulnerable are dehumanized.[71] Like a mother who loves her children the same yet defends her weaker child against the attacks of the stronger one so that neither one is dehumanized, the universality of God's love precludes neutrality in order to transform broken relationships.[72] Returning to the christological criterion, theological aesthetics sees the death and resurrection of Christ "not simply as the victory of life over death but the victory of justice over injustice; it is God's vindication of an innocent victim."[73] If God's vindication of the just against the unjust in the raising of his executed Son reveals at some level who God is, then, the human response to such revelation becomes an embodiment of his divine character in a life of discipleship that involves solidarity with suffering people everywhere.

Like García-Rivera, Goizueta sees the critical role ethics plays in a theological aesthetic to prevent it from becoming a secularized, individualistic, or therapeutic aesthetic. On the one hand, a theological aesthetic has its basis in God's love, and therefore it cannot be reduced to social activism. On the other hand, it involves a human response to God's love in worship and praise, but such a response cannot be reduced to an individualistic experience or happy feeling without concern for life among neighbors in the world. Understandably, these Catholic authors' understandings of divine grace and human freedom differ from Luther's classic emphases on forensic justification (in contrast to sanative justification or infused grace) and the inability of fallen human will to find God's beauty in suffering and the cross (in contrast to the human will's graced capacity for finding God's beauty in creation). Nevertheless, a Lutheran aesthetic does share with these theologians an interest in finding a way of speaking about God's revelation of his glory in the crucified Christ that humans can receive by faith in Christ and participate in through love of neighbor. Both share a concern for grounding theological aesthetics in the centrality of God's revelation in Christ crucified and risen for

71. Goizueta, "Theo-Drama as Liberative Praxis," 71.
72. Goizueta, "Theo-Drama as Liberative Praxis," 71.
73. Goizueta, "Theo-Drama as Liberative Praxis," 72.

salvation (soteriology) and its embodiment in a cruciform way of living in the world on behalf of suffering neighbors (ethics).

An important Luther source for linking Christology and ethics, the *Heidelberg Disputation* (1518), remains a key hermeneutical source for understanding the Reformer's cruciform approach to reality or, more concretely, the nature of God's revelation in Christ and its implications for faith and life. The *Disputation* helps us understand further the theological vision that informs Luther's cruciform approach to music. The theological theses are divided into four parts. The first two parts deal with the human inability to do works of the law to achieve righteousness before God (theses one through twelve) and free will's incapacity to avoid sin (theses thirteen through eighteen). The other two parts deal with the contrast between two kinds of theologians (those who approach the knowledge of God through creation and those who do so through the cross [theses nineteen through twenty-four]) and the contrast between human love and the love of God (theses twenty-five through twenty-eight).[74]

Toumo Mannermaa makes the bold claim that the *Disputation*'s distinction between human love and God's love provides the fundamental framework that "determines the basic structure of Luther's theology."[75] In Thesis 28 of the *Disputation*, Luther writes: "The love of God does not find, but creates, that which is pleasing to it. The love of man comes into being through that which is pleasing to it."[76] Humans love those with whom they share attributes they see (or want to see) in themselves—attributes they are already naturally attracted to and therefore see as pleasing. In his explanation of this thesis, Luther identifies those attributes as "the true and the good" in people.[77] Luther objects to the scholastic theologians' understanding of human love, according to which humans are naturally inclined and driven to love others with whom they have in common the goodness they see (or desire to realize more fully) in themselves.[78]

In Thesis 19 of the *Disputation*, Luther states: "That person does not deserve to be called a theologian who looks upon the invisible

---

74. This outline of the theses basically follows Forde, *On Being a Theologian of the Cross*, 21–22.

75. Mannermaa, *Two Kinds of Love*, 9.

76. Luther, *Luther's Works*, 31:41.

77. "[T]he intellect cannot by nature comprehend an object which does not exist, that is the poor and needy person, but only a thing which does exist, that is the true and good. Therefore it judges according to appearances, is a respecter of persons, and judges according to that which can be seen, etc." (Luther, *Luther's Works*, 31:57–58).

78. Mannermaa, *Two Kinds of Love*, 10–11.

things of God as though they were clearly perceptible in those things which have actually happened [Rom 1:20]."[79] In his explanation of this thesis, Luther uses the term "the invisible things of God" to refer to divine attributes such as "virtue, godliness, wisdom, justice, goodness, and so forth."[80] These are precisely the type of attributes that humans—or as Luther would call them, "theologians of glory"—naturally seek in themselves or in others as objects of love. Theologians of glory seek after those invisible qualities of God that they find or perceive to be visible, apparent, or reflected in themselves or in others (that is, in what is seen in creation), which in turn justifies their being loved by God or their loving others. Luther reacts against the idea that human love reflects divine love, so that both humans and God seek after the true and good they are naturally attracted to in people. If that were true, God would then love people as objects of goodness who best reflect his divine attributes in a creaturely way. Like humans, God would love others to the degree that they are deemed good.

Mannermaa notes that "the theology of glory is based on Human Love."[81] Accordingly, theologians of glory focus on the beauty of their works to make them righteous before God, their free will to avoid sin, and their intellectual ability to know God through what they observe in creation. They also love those with whom they share such a high view of their spiritual capacity. When used to establish one's or others' worthiness to be loved by God, gifts from God which are "good" in themselves (that is, works, will, and reason) nevertheless become "mortal sins" or "evil" in that they drive us toward that self-realizing love which looks for what is attractive in us and others, and thus away from God's creative love in Christ toward us and in us.[82]

By contrast, theologians of the cross trust in God's works, will, and reason as revealed in the crucified Christ—a move that appears "evil" in the eyes of the world but is finally "good" for us.[83] They die to their human

79. Luther, *Luther's Works*, 31:52.
80. Luther, *Luther's Works*, 31:52.
81. Mannermaa, *Two Kinds of Love*, 28.
82. "Although the works of man always seem attractive and good, they are nevertheless likely to be mortal sins" (Thesis 3, Luther, *Luther's Works*, 31:39); "A theologian of glory calls evil good and good evil" (Thesis 21, Luther, *Luther's Works*, 31:40).
83. "Although the works of God always seem unattractive and appear evil, they are nevertheless really eternal merits" (Thesis 4, Luther, *Luther's Works*, 31:39). In his explanation of Thesis 21, Luther notes that "the friends of the cross say that the cross is good and [human] works are evil, for through the cross works are destroyed and the old

attempts to earn the love of God so that they can be raised anew as receivers of God's unmerited love in Christ. This radical trust in God makes the theologian of the cross receptive to God's unmerited love in Christ, which in turn shapes the way he or she loves others. Theologians of the cross acknowledge that human love looks for "that which is pleasing to it," and thus must be put to death in us so that the love of God "which does not find, but creates, that which is pleasing to it" might shape us to love that which is not attractive to us.[84] The love of God *for us* is the beauty of the crucified and our sharing in his death and resurrection. The love of God *in us* is "the love of the cross" which impels us to find beauty in the unlovable neighbor and in simple acts of love toward them.

> Rather than seeking its own good, the love of God flows forth and bestows good. Therefore sinners are attractive because they are loved; they are not loved because they are attractive. For this reason the love of man avoids sinners and evil persons. Thus Christ says: "For I came not to call the righteous, but sinners" [Matt 9:13]. This is the love of the cross, born of the cross, which turns in the direction where it does not find good which it may enjoy, but where it may confer good upon the bad and needy person. "It is more blessed to give than to receive" [Acts 20:35], says the Apostle.[85]

When theologians die to all their merits, they are receptive to receiving the love of Christ and thus act according to it toward others. Or to put it in terms of aesthetics, only when one dies to the beauty of one's works, will, and reason can one be raised to delight in the beauty of the crucified Christ and embody such beauty by loving that which is not beautiful in the eyes of the world. The revelation of God in the crucified Christ and our human reception of the same through our sharing in his death and resurrection shapes us in turn to die to the love of self and embrace the love of the unlovable. To say the same in the language of signs, the beauty of God's glory is revealed in the sign of the crucified and risen Christ, received by faith in the beautiful gospel sign of Word and sacrament, and lived out in the sign of a priority of love toward those whom the world sees as ugly or unattractive. For Luther, such love embraces a wide array of neighbors whom natural human love avoids, namely, those who are seen as bad, needy, sinners, evil, and enemies. To the list one can certainly

---

Adam, who is especially edified by works, is crucified" (Luther, *Luther's Works*, 31:53).

84. Luther, *Luther's Works*, 31:41.

85. Luther, *Luther's Works*, 31:57.

add vulnerable and marginal neighbors often rejected by natural human love, such as widows, orphans, the poor, the sick, and the alien.

Luther's distinction between the two kinds of theologians and the ways they operate provides a framework for an aesthetic that does not look for divine beauty in the naked glory of God or people who presumably reflect such glory (a theology of glory), but in the God who reveals his love in the crucified Christ by making sinners alive through the gospel (a theology of the cross). Reflecting on Luther's love of the cross as a form of Christlikeness rooted in the gospel, a love that goes beyond forms of human love based on friendship or shared values, Mannermaa challenges us to reach out to neighbors who are unlike us and even unlikeable. In their concern for linking aesthetics to God's vindication of the suffering Christ and lifting of the lowly, US Hispanic theologians call above all for human embodiments of beauty in solidarity with suffering neighbors. Although Luther/Mannermaa and García-Rivera/Goizueta operate with different soteriologies, they raise important questions for artists and musicians who, due to their vocation and craft, must think about the intentional embodiment of beauty in their works for the sake of serving the Lord in his church and world.

AESTHETIC GUIDELINES FOR INSTRUMENTALISTS IN WORSHIP AND DEVOTIONAL SETTINGS

We have shown that, in the Reformation tradition represented by Martin Luther, vocal and instrumental music can both express theological meaning and function theologically in the formation of theologians. Aesthetics scholar Enrico Fubini has argued that, by seeing music as a divine gift, Luther bestowed upon it a certain autonomous dignity.[86] The positive value assigned to music led on the one hand to the appreciation of its effects upon the whole person (including the affects) and on the other hand to an interest in the deep study of the artistic possibilities of instrumental music in its own right (such as those displayed in Lutheran composer J. S. Bach's development of counterpoint and harmony), even apart from other considerations such as its use in supporting a poetic or liturgical text.[87] We have also argued that Luther's christological approach to instrumental music and ethics—specifically,

---

86. Fubini, *Estética musical*, 162.
87. Fubini, *Estética musical*, 163, 184, 241, 515.

its interest in both conveying God's beauty in the crucified Christ and shaping hearers in a life of repentance and virtues that include loving the unlovable—can address the concerns of US Hispanic theologians who seek to connect the experience of God's beauty in the revealed Christ with a life of commitment toward crucified peoples today.

We can now suggest some ideas for applying the christological aesthetic laid out above to instrumentalists' self-understanding or identity and purpose or significance as performers in the context of the Christian church's worship and devotion. Instrumentalists are first and foremost *recipients of God's beauty in Christ*. This follows from acknowledging music as God's gift. They have heard the beauty of God in Christ's giving himself for us on the cross and have responded to the same in faith wrapped in song and sound. They approach their instruments as extensions of their identity as receivers of beauty, and thus identify not mainly as solo performers but as fellow worshipers who along with God's people receive and are shaped by God's gifts.[88] In highlighting this aspect of the instrumentalist's role in worship, we do not mean to belittle the musician's technique and artistic expression, but to foster appreciation for the use of his or her gifts within the theological framework of Luther's view of instrumental music as a means to the worship of God, the source of all gifts. Even as they perform music with excellence to lead or assist God's people in worship or to enrich hearers in other devotional settings, instrumentalists remain recipients of the gifts of God wrapped up in their musical offerings. By not drawing attention to themselves and their musicianship as ends in themselves, church instrumentalists embody a cruciform identity that puts God's gifts first.[89]

---

88. Although Nicholas Wolterstorff agrees that religious concerts are enriching, he argues that "at no point should the liturgy be halted to enable . . . a soloist to render 'special music.'" On Sunday morning, "the instruments really do assist the song of the people, rather than the song of the people being turned into a *sotto voce* accompaniment to the organ." He concludes by noting that even if a choir leads the congregation, they are not "praising God on our behalf. Rather, we as a people are praising God, being led in our praise . . . by the singing of the choir" (Wolterstorff, "Thinking about Church Music," 12–13). I would simply add that the "we" in Wolterstorff's last sentence includes the instrumentalists themselves!

89. One could argue that musicians inevitably draw people's attention to their ritual performance for a variety of reasons, and that the degree of attention their playing draws might be influenced by cultural factors or attitudes toward musicians. My main point is mostly one of attitude, namely, that musicians must check their ego at the door as much as possible, thinking of themselves first as receivers rather than givers of God's gifts.

Instrumentalists are also *servants of the gospel and of those who receive it*. Their purpose or significance follows from the vocation or calling they have been given, namely, to express and embody through their music the gospel sign of God's beauty in Christ crucified and risen in a way that it invites people's faith and delight in it. By placing their craft at the service of the Word, instrumentalists take on the role of a preacher or teacher of Christ. They become musical heralds and propagators of the good news.[90] My use of music painting on the double bass as a means to tell the Exodus story and set up the singing of Psalm 27 can be seen as instances of preaching or teaching God's care and salvation for his people. By becoming storytellers of the gospel, instrumentalists invite hearers to believe. Approaching their instruments as extensions of this vocational purpose involves both an objective and a subjective dimension. Instrumentalists must understand theologically the sign of the gospel they intend to communicate or embody, and they must also understand culturally the people whom they are leading or assisting in the reception of the gospel sign.

Instrumentalists are also *theologians*—that is, they look for ways to speak about, for, and to God through their instrumental offerings so that their music embodies the gospel in ways that are both biblically faithful and culturally understandable to the congregation.[91] In the language of signs, instrumentalists understand how to use their music to express the gospel and how to do so in a way that speaks to the people. Concerning the gospel sign in congregational worship, they must attend to how the instrumental music fits theologically with a particular liturgical action or time of the church year.[92] For example, in the offertory I mentioned

90. In his discussion of Georg Rhau's (1488–1548) musical contributions to the early Reformation period (the first half of the sixteenth century), Schalk notes that the prefaces to various collections of music Rhau published at this time laid out a Lutheran theology of music with the following elements: "Music is of divine origin and is God's gift to man; the end of music is the glorification of God; and music, from a Lutheran viewpoint, is to serve in the proclamation and propagation of the Word. *Thus the purpose of music is to sound forth the Gospel in the world....* All these prefaces attest to the Reformation conviction that *the singer or musician is in fact a preacher of the Gospel*" (Schalk, *Music in Early Lutheranism*, 55; italics mine).

91. Frank Burch Brown rightly speaks against the myth "that music can be treated simply as a 'package' that contains the gospel message instead of being treated as an art that embodies and interprets the gospel message by its structure and the way it sounds" (Brown, "Religious Meanings and Musical Styles," 142).

92. Thus "the character of the music [must] fit the liturgical action it serves—and fit [a] theologically correct understanding of that action" (Wolterstorff, "Thinking about Church Music," 13). He adds that "fittingness, not style, is the basic consideration to be

in the introduction to this essay, my choice to play a secular melody with a meditative tone on the double bass at a low range and with a somber timbre fitting such a tone seemed to align well with the reflective and penitent season of Lent. In other devotional settings, such as the religious concert I cited at the beginning of the essay, instrumentalists must make sure their musical decisions have a theological rationale that matches the religious story they seek to tell and invites others to partake in through either singing or listening. In that concert of programmatic music, I used a variety of techniques on the double bass, including high-pitch harmonics, fast tremolos, playing on the string with the back of the wooden bow (*col legno* technique), lyrical bowing, pizzicato (plucking), and the percussive use of the instrument's wood in order to tell the story of God's presence amid his people in the exodus. The progression of these technical elements, along with the corresponding variations on the melody of a psalm, colors, rhythms, and even silences, were intuitively and deliberatively meant to match the story. Conversely, elements of the story were arguably heightened by their musical embodiment and expression. Word and music work together to draw hearers to the story.

Instrumentalists are also *interpreters of culture*. Their musical choices should make sense to the people they serve, just as monophony and polyphony made sense to Luther's ears in the context of the musical culture of his day. This means that at times a performer will have to humbly set aside one's own stylistic preferences to make the gospel clear to the people. Other times it means that the performer will need to gently challenge people to move beyond their familiar stylistic preferences in order to make them understand, hear, and sing the gospel more richly or fully.[93] In their service to the gospel and God's people, performers read the people in their cultural setting and make musical decisions accordingly. Performers and congregations may have their favorite selections, music that is familiarly sweet to their ears, but both will also need to be stretched a bit so they might grow and mature together in their faith and love. Though everybody has individual tastes in music, all will proceed

---

introduced when thinking about music in the liturgy" (Wolterstorff, "Thinking about Church Music," 14).

93. The performer as a cultural reader must know not only church music, but also secular musical idioms. He or she must also negotiate between the old and the new, rejecting outright neither tradition nor innovation in music. Here Luther and early Lutheran musicians serve as examples for today. See Schalk, *Music in Early Lutheranism*, 182–83.

to worship in a spirit of charity, being open to musical experimentation while keeping at the center what serves the gospel.[94]

As theologians and cultural interpreters, instrumentalists also become *bearers of an inclusive catholicity*. García-Rivera's call for "lifting the lowly" as a type of "foregrounding" that brings to the front and gives renewed value to an element previously hidden in the background serves as a theological rationale for a performer's use of musical elements that can challenge people to move beyond their musical comfort zones into embracing other global expressions of the church's faith. Introducing congregants to sounds and canticles from other cultures can itself be a "countercultural" way to expand people's appreciation of the church as a catholic, universal communion.[95] As an example, using variations on a melody from a psalm in the Spanish language at the religious concert mentioned earlier, including the plucking of a Cuban *guaracha* to the psalm's chord structure, and my singing of the psalm's chorus as I played the wood of the double bass to a Panamanian *tamborito* rhythm awakened and challenged a mostly Anglo, English-speaking audience to revel in the universality of the gospel in an increasingly ethnically diverse country. Such musical choices have the capacity not only to communicate the gospel, but also to empower people to move beyond the familiar in order to live out the implications of the gospel among and with underrepresented voices.

Finally, when instrumentalists "lift the lowly" by bringing their musical contributions to the foreground, they become *bearers of mercy and justice*. They invite people to enter the world of the marginal "other" and embrace a cruciform life by pitching their tent among often forgotten neighbors. Like Goizueta's "liberative aesthetics" of discipleship, which give priority to the neediest neighbors, instrumentalists introduce people to a vision of what it means to live before the needy as "theologians of the cross" (Luther's term), embodying the love of God in us by loving the neglected and unattractive. Luther's cruciform reading of reality through the cross invites instrumentalists to lift up the lowly

---

94. One should lead with charity as one deals with musical tastes: "I will sing hymns in the style that fits comfortably with your ears and suits your tastes, and I will ask and hope that you treat me likewise" (Wolterstorff, "Thinking about Church Music," 16).

95. What C. Michael Hawn says about vocal music certainly applies to instrumental music: "Singing the songs from another culture is a counter-cultural expression of faith that calls into question the context of the normative culture in light of the transcultural message of the Gospel and the historical shape of Christian liturgy" (Hawn, "Reverse Missions," 104).

by displaying the beauty of marginal neighbors and their musical offerings—their compositions, arrangements, instrumentation, colors or timbres, and chord or rhythmic patterns. The same *tamborito* rhythm played on the double bass in my rendition of the exodus story to call attention to the catholicity of the church can also invite congregants to learn more deeply about the lives and plight of neighbors from different cultures both here and abroad. Like verbal language, musical language becomes a window into people's lives, showing not only their artistic gifts but also their struggles and joys. Musicians have the capacity to open people's eyes to opportunities for cross-cultural and intercultural engagements that foster solidarity with, encourage learning from, and enable collaborating or partnering with neighbors whose lives are often in the background. It is thus possible to see how by the Spirit's power a cruciform musical aesthetic that receives its inspiration from the proclamation of God's love in Christ can inspire a life of discipleship that reaches out to and works with "the least of these."

Earlier I suggested that musicians, as receivers of God's gifts, should not draw attention to themselves or their musicianship as ends in themselves. The same could be said of musicians as theologians who use their craft vocationally to glorify God and communicate God's gospel. Egos run high in musical circles. In this context, church musicians are reminded of their identity as servants of the gospel and of God's people. There is, however, a place for musicians as interpreters of culture, bearers of an inclusive catholicity, and bearers of mercy and justice to embody and bring to the foreground in their musical renditions the partially neglected or silenced cultural-linguistic, artistic-musical, and theological-ethical gifts God has given her church from among the nations. By their mere presence as strangers, their exceptional skill and craft, or their communal joy in music-making, musicians from all nations—especially those whose gifts are less known or appreciated—often embody the intercultural, transcultural, and cross-cultural identity of the Christian church. In this context, musicians inevitably draw attention to their ritual performance not as an affront to the gospel, but precisely as a way to celebrate the joy of the gospel in their lives and teach others to do the same with a generosity of spirit.

BIBLIOGRAPHY

Augustine of Hippo. *Confessions*. Edited by Roy Joseph Deferrari. Translated by Vernon J. Bourke. *The Fathers of the Church* 21. Washington, DC: Catholic University of America Press, 1953.

Bonds, Mark Evan. *Antiquity through the Baroque Era. A History of Music in Western Culture* 1. 3rd ed. Upper Saddle River, NJ: Prentice Hall, 2010.

Brown, Frank Burch. "Religious Meanings and Musical Styles: A Matter of Taste?" In *Music in Christian Worship: At the Service of the Liturgy*, edited by Charlotte Kroeker, 135–55. Collegeville, MN: Liturgical, 2005.

¡*Cantad al Señor!* St. Louis, MO: Concordia, 1991.

Crockford, James. "Get Happy: Luther and the Power of Musical Affect." *LOGIA* 26, no. 1 (2017) 50–52.

Forde, Gerhard O. *On Being a Theologian of the Cross: Reflections on Luther's Heidelberg Disputation, 1518*. Grand Rapids: Eerdmans, 1997.

Fubini. Enrico. *La estética musical desde la Antigüedad hasta el siglo XX*. Madrid: Alianza Editorial, 2007.

García-Rivera, Alejandro. *The Community of the Beautiful: A Theological Aesthetics*. Collegeville, MN: Liturgical, 1999.

Goizueta, Roberto S. *Christ Our Companion: Toward a Theological Aesthetics of Liberation*. Maryknoll, NY: Orbis, 2009.

———. "Theo-Drama as Liberative Praxis." *Crosscurrents* (2013) 62–76.

Granados, Jerónimo. "Martín Lutero y la música." *Cuadernos de Teología* 26 (2007) 136.

Hawn, C. Michael. "Reverse Missions: Global Singing for Local Congregations." In *Music in Christian Worship: At the Service of the Liturgy*, edited by Charlotte Kroeker, 98–111. Collegeville, MN: Liturgical, 2005.

Luther, Martin. *Luther's Works*, American Edition. Vols. 1–30 edited by Jaroslav Pelikan. St. Louis: Concordia, 1955–76. Vols. 31–55 edited by Helmut Lehmann. Philadelphia/Minneapolis: Muhlenberg/Fortress, 1957–86.

Mannermaa, Tuomo. *Two Kinds of Love: Martin Luther's Religious World*. Minneapolis: Fortress, 2010.

Prenter, Regin. *Spiritus Creator: Luther's Concept of the Holy Spirit*. Translated by John M. Jensen. Philadelphia: Muhlenberg, 1953.

Sánchez M., Leopoldo A. "Telling the Exodus Story on the Double Bass, Latin American Style." Wabash Center blog. https://www.wabashcenter.wabash.edu/2022/07/telling-the-exodus-story-on-the-double-bass-latin-american-style/.

———. "Theology in Context: Music as a Test Case." *Concordia Journal* 38, no. 3 (2012) 205–24.

Schalk, Carl. *Music in Early Lutheranism: Shaping the Tradition (1524–1672)*. St. Louis, MO: Concordia, 2001.

Wolterstorff, Nicholas P. "Thinking about Church Music." In *Music in Christian Worship: At the Service of the Liturgy*, edited by Charlotte Kroeker, 3–17. Collegeville, MN: Liturgical, 2005.

SEEKING PENTECOSTALITY

Worship Practices at Reba Place Church[1]

Nancy Elizabeth Bedford

From its beginnings in the sixteenth century, Anabaptism was "a charismatic movement—or even a cluster of interrelated movements—that never achieved uniformity. It championed a practical Christianity whose theological foundations were as often implicit as explicit."[2] This continues to be the case 500 years later. The ability to "read" the theology implicit in worship and other practices of faith alongside theological treatises or other explicit forms of written communication thus becomes a central task of theology in Anabaptist contexts. This essay will examine a number of the rich worship practices at Reba Place Church, a congregation in the Anabaptist-Mennonite tradition, in order to tease out some of the implicit and explicit theological convictions it embodies and the future directions toward which its practices may be gesturing.

---

1. By "Pentecostality," as I explain below, I refer primarily to concrete ways in which church communities try to live out the implications of the gospel of Jesus expansively and creatively with the help of the Holy Spirit.
2. Rempel, "Baptism," 300. Emphasis mine.

LITURGICAL HABITS OF THE HEART

Sunday Morning at Reba

I am writing this essay as a participant-observer of a community which I've been a part of with my family since 2003. Even before we migrated to the United States, when we were still living in Buenos Aires, several people said to us, "If you are going to live in Evanston," a Chicago suburb, "you should check out Reba Place Church. You'd like it." Somebody even gave us a clipping about the church from a Mennonite magazine. I tucked the suggestion away in a mental file. My husband had grown up nominally Catholic and made profession of faith in an Argentine Baptist church. I had grown up Argentine Baptist with strong Anabaptist leanings and was also closely linked through my work to progressive and liberationist mainline Protestant denominations in Argentina. We had been part of a small Baptist church in Buenos Aires.[3] However, we did not identify with wider trends among Baptists either in Latin America (such as the adoption of hierarchical "apostolic" polities and Neo-Pentecostal practices) or in the United States (such as the complementarian theological anthropologies of the Southern Baptist Convention included in *The Baptist Faith and Message* after the fundamentalist takeover of the 1980s).[4] We were open to worshiping in a Mennonite church, noting the ecclesiology "from below," the counter-hegemonic sensibilities, the focus on discipleship and nonviolence, and the affinities with a Latin American liberationist ethos that can often be found in Anabaptist settings.[5]

I had several criteria in mind, both positive and negative, for choosing a church home. The negative: it could not be overly large or dominated by a parking lot, it could not be a "white space" frequented almost exclusively by white folk, and there could not be any symbols of nationalism in the sanctuary (such as the US flag). The positive: it would be a community where people were committed to following the way of Jesus and where theologically robust preaching and music were central to the worship service. Above all, I wanted to find a church community where my family could continue to grow in faith and commitment to

---

3. I describe that church community in Bedford, "Little Moves Against Destructiveness."

4. For my reflections on wider ecclesiological trends in Latin America, see Bedford, "¿Toda potestad en el cielo y en la tierra?"

5. My dissertation was about this very matter. See Bedford, *Jesus Christus*. See also Rutschman, *Anabautismo Radical y Teología Latinoamericana*.

God and to our neighbors instead of being traumatized by the church as many of my friends and students had been. Our daughters were quite small during our search (the oldest was six years old, and the twins were two), so that meant find a place where children were not seen as a bother or a hindrance to worship.[6] It also meant it should be a place where their identities both as Latinas and as young women would be appreciated and affirmed as they grew up.

All of this was brewing in the back of my mind as we made our way to Reba Place Church for the first time on a cold Chicagoland Sunday morning in February of 2003. My more immediate concern was how to manage the on-time arrival at an unknown church's worship space of three small children and two adults in a somewhat presentable state. Of course we arrived late. We walked into the Meeting House, but because of the sanctuary's layout we could only see the back of the risers. We could hear, though, and were greeted by the sound of rousing Black gospel harmonies. My husband and I looked at each other in silent agreement: even before we had seen any of the people in the service, we felt drawn into the church by the music.

Reba Place Church meets in a converted brick warehouse that once was a school bus depot. It is located in south Evanston, at the intersection of Custer and Madison streets, nestled alongside the elevated tracks of the CTA Purple Line between Main and South stations. Evanston, home to Northwestern University, is a municipality bordering Lake Michigan directly north of Chicago. The Reba Meeting House is thus located in a liminal space between the urban, racially, and culturally diverse dynamics of Chicago's Rogers Park neighborhood a few blocks to the south and the exclusive, wealthy, and mostly white North Shore suburbs two or three miles to the north. South Evanston is enmeshed in a process of gentrification, but the church members are, as a rule, not wealthy. A number of them belong to Reba Place Fellowship, an intentional Christian community founded in 1957.[7] The Fellowship

---

6. For more on how this can be achieved, see Elizabeth Tamez Méndez's chapter in this book.

7. See the Fellowship website, https://www.rebaplacefellowship.org/. Membership in the church was initially linked to membership in the intentional community, but in the 1980s the option for church membership apart from membership in the Fellowship emerged. Nonetheless, the congregation's practices and ethos continue to owe a great deal to its close connection to an intentional Christian community that practices the sharing of goods in the spirit of Acts 2. For an account of the fraught but generative path of the Fellowship's first thirty years, see Jackson and Jackson, *Glimpses of Glory*.

eventually gave birth to the church and to its sister congregation, Living Water Community Church in Rogers Park.[8] Reba Place Church currently has a membership of about 135 people, with attendance on Sundays hovering between 110 and 150. Approximately one-fourth of the attenders and members are people of color.[9]

The worship space inside the Meeting House at Reba is circular. The modest lectern, communion table, and a cross, along with the piano, drums, and other accoutrements of the praise team, take up about a third of the circle. In front of them to one side, artfully blending into the brown industrial carpet, is a round section of the floor that can be opened up to become a sunken baptistry. Behind the lectern and table is a screen for projecting lyrics during worship and occasional slide presentations during the messages. There also hang banners that change in color and theme with the liturgical seasons. For example, starting at Pentecost and during Ordinary Time, one sees a red banner with stylized flames. Artisans in the congregation fashioned the wooden cross and lectern, the banners, and various other works of art, including icons in the Russian Orthodox style, a woven representation of a tree in which the crucified Jesus can also be seen, and a painting depicting the risen Christ.[10] A set of movable screens separates the backdrop of the praise team from a small, enclosed chapel, the kitchen, and an open space where tables can be set up for potlucks or other events.

The remainder of the circle consists of risers with padded chairs rather than pews. The semicircular rows rise up one behind the other and are thus set higher than the lectern, the space for the praise team, and the baptistry. There are no hidden spots in the congregation; people can glance up and see a panoramic view of the rest of the semicircle. There are also colorful flags that can be removed from the risers and

8. See https://livingwatercommunitychurch.org/.

9. Lehman, interview. As in Evanston as a whole, many of the adults are college graduates. Remarkably, ten or twelve have studied theology or philosophy at the graduate level. On the other hand, there is a strong contingent of adults who work at blue-collar and service jobs. High levels of literacy are not necessary for meaningful participation in services. The ages of attenders are fairly evenly distributed, though there are at present perhaps three times more small children than adolescents.

10. The Mennonite traditions of quiltmaking and woodworking are evident in the community, especially in marking pivotal moments of life, for example, in the custom of giving a couple a commemorative handmade quilt at their wedding or of fashioning a simple wooden casket when a community member dies, if the family so desires. Gardening, canning, and sewing are also alive and well among many church members. All these practices push back against consumerism.

waved during worship, something that small children especially enjoy. One of the front rows is reserved for wheelchairs, for there are regular attenders and members with limited mobility. Underneath each chair is a wire receptacle with a blue Anabaptist-Mennonite hymnal and a red hardcover New Revised Standard Version Bible. As in most churches, people tend to habitually sit in particular sections.

The precise order of worship on a typical Sunday is not set in stone, but the structure and elements below are usually present and come together in a way that allows for the worship service to run quite precisely from 10:00 to 11:15 AM. As a prelude, at 9:30 there is a time for fellowship around coffee and bagels in the area near the kitchen. At 10:00 the worship time begins with a gathering song performed by the praise team, usually four to six singers and a variety of instrumentalists of differing ages playing piano, drums, guitar, electric bass, and on some Sundays a violin, saxophone, banjo, or cello. At 10:03, lead pastor Charlotte Lehman (or another member of the leadership team if the pastor is not there) gives a warm welcome to members and visitors. Immediately afterward, someone reads the first Scripture passage, often a psalm. At 10:05, we pass the peace: it is lively, enthusiastic, and full of hugs. As greetings wind up, announcements begin. At 10:10 comes the gospel reading, when all who are able are invited to stand, followed by the pastoral prayer and a time of praise and worship singing that lasts for about twenty minutes.

The songs reflect the rich and complex history of the congregation. First, there is a strand of autochthonous Reba music composed through the years by people who have belonged at some point to the congregation, most notably Jim Croegaert.[11] These are mostly songs drawing from folk and Celtic influences, with lyrics that reference scriptural texts. Second are songs from the Black gospel tradition, including spirituals, more contemporary African American church music, and occasionally South African tunes. A good example of this strand is the album *Gospel Journey*, produced by an earlier iteration of the praise team.[12] A third strand is the long Mennonite tradition of singing hymns in four-part harmony, sometimes a cappella. A fourth strand, less central but nevertheless present, is contemporary praise songs, some in Spanish. The congregation loves to sing and for the most part does so enthusiastically.

---

11. See https://roughstonesmusic.com/about-jim-croegaert/.
12. A recording is available at https://www.amazon.com/Reba-Praise/e/B001LI7OEU.

At around 10:35, the offering is gathered. Baskets are set out on the very back row, and whoever feels led to do so gets up to pass them around while the congregation sings. The servers are often small children with a parent. When everyone who so desires has contributed to the baskets, the servers gather near the lectern as the congregation sings a doxology. Whoever presides over the offering collects the baskets and offers a prayer. Then the pastor comes forward, sends the preschoolers to their classes, and either asks for prayer before the sermon or prays for the preacher of the day. The sermon begins around 10:40 and runs until 11:00. After the message, the congregation engages in sharing time, which can include testimonies, prayer requests, or a response to the sermon. It is led by a "shepherd of the sharing," not by the pastor.[13] At 11:10, the pastor invites the prayer ministers to come forward; these are two or three people who are available to pray after the benediction with anyone who desires it. She then announces the Grow classes, our version of Sunday school classes that run from 11:15 to noon. These always include classes for children through middle school and a sermon discussion group for those high school age or older; other offerings such as book studies and topical discussions are interspersed throughout the year.[14] After the benediction, the pastor concludes the service by saying "Go in peace," to which the congregation responds, "Jesus is Lord."

The Lord's Supper and Baptism

The first Sunday of every month is Communion Sunday. On those Sundays, instead of a twenty-minute sermon there is a short homily and a longer sharing time. The Lord's Supper liturgy is most often from the Anglican *Book of Common Prayer*, a practice largely the legacy of longtime

---

13. This is one way in which gender dynamics in the service retain a certain symmetry. The "shepherd of the sharing" is often (though not always) a man, whereas both the pastor and the children/youth minister are women (one of them HAPA [Half Asian Pacific American] and the other Latina). Both Reba Place Church and Reba Place Fellowship went through a decades-long process with much discussion and many position papers about female leadership in the community, with parishioners first "agreeing to disagree" before finally accepting women as senior pastors and leaders. In so doing, the church moved from a complementarian understanding of gender and theological anthropology to one of mutuality, which ultimately had implications for LGBTQI folk in the church too.

14. Much of the "Christian education" at Reba takes place implicitly through community participation in our faith practices. I describe some of that process in my essay "Espíritu les enseñará todas las cosas."

member Linas Brown, now deceased, who was an Episcopal priest and held daily Eucharist in a small chapel fashioned from one of the Meeting House rooms.[15] People go forward to the communion table to receive the elements, usually by intinction. The offerings of bread, gluten-free crackers, wine, and grape juice are handed out by servers who vary from month to month. Meanwhile, the praise team sings, often songs such as "Down to the River to Pray" and "Let us Break Bread Together." While the servers hand out the elements, saying "The body of Christ, broken for you" and "The blood of Christ, shed for you" (or similar words), the pastor stands by a small cross to the side to pray with anyone who wishes it.

Communion Sundays always include a potluck meal after the service with vegetarian and non-vegetarian options. All are invited to the meal, which is an important moment for the common life of the congregation. People sit at round tables and engage in intergenerational fellowship and conversation. After the meal, many remain to put up the tables and clean the space. The commensality gestures both back toward the Lord's Supper and the remembrance of Christ's life, death, and resurrection and forward to the eschatological banquet promised in Scripture (e.g., Luke 22:16).

The invitation to partake of the Lord's Supper is usually something like: "All who are purposing to follow Jesus with their lives are invited to come to the table." Baptism is not explicitly mentioned. Most people at Reba, especially those raised in Mennonite traditions, were baptized by immersion in adolescence or later, upon a public profession of faith. However, those who were christened as infants in other traditions and who feel that their baptism was significant and sufficient are not asked to be re-baptized in order to partake in the Lord's Supper or even to become full members of the church.[16] This is one way in which ecumenical life together has shifted traditional Anabaptist practices in a post-Christendom context. Children are not turned away from the table if they were baptized as infants, they desire to participate, and their parents or guardians deem it is appropriate for them to do so. On the other hand, there is no pressure to participate and no judgment if a person does not.

---

15. A number of people in the congregation are dually affiliated with Reba and another community (mostly Roman Catholic or Episcopalian).

16. Those who continue to consider themselves practicing Roman Catholics can become associate members. The association with Bridgefolk, "a movement of sacramentally minded Mennonites and peace-minded Roman Catholics who come together to celebrate each other's traditions" (http://www.bridgefolk.net/), has been significant to many "Rebites" through the years.

Reba actively combines a strong community ethos with a robust respect for a person's individual conscience. It is understood and accepted, for example, that some people may journey for a time with the congregation but later move on to other churches, perhaps ones more "sacramental" or more "evangelical" in their practices. The particular mix of a community that tries to be "rooted in an Anabaptist tradition, catholic in spirit, evangelical in conviction, charismatic in practice, antiracist in calling, and inclusive in love"[17] is not always a long-term fit for people, but former members and attenders are often remembered, welcomed if they return for a visit, and prayed for when they are ill or otherwise in need.

Formal membership in the church entails a commitment to giving and receiving counsel while seeking to discern God's will, sharing financial resources, exploring and making use of spiritual gifts, remaining faithful in prayer, accepting the congregation's leadership with integrity, making every effort to maintain the unity of the Spirit with all members, and affirming the *Confession of Faith from a Mennonite Perspective*.[18] To affirm this confession does not necessarily mean to agree with every word in it, as it is not a binding statement and the Anabaptist tradition is not a creedal one. But it does mean respecting the values and character of the congregation as a Mennonite community of faith. Its values are reflected in its commitments, such as the centrality of the way of Jesus and the kingdom of God "above nationalism, racism, or materialism"; the nonviolent resolution of conflicts "without having to strike out in fear to defend ourselves"; the centrality of a life of simplicity and service as a witness of God's love; and the practice of a community biblical hermeneutic that trusts the Holy Spirit for help in the discernment of the meaning of Scripture for contemporary life.[19]

Baptism occurs at Reba usually once or twice a year, often in conjunction with the Easter season, in continuity with ancient Christian tradition. It usually entails a separate service, often on a Sunday afternoon if the baptism takes place in the Meeting House baptistry. If it takes place in Lake Michigan, it usually occurs early on a Sunday morning. All three of our daughters chose to be baptized in the Meeting House during the liminal time between middle school and high school. Our oldest had been requesting baptism for years after making a profession

---

17. "Reba Place Church: Who We Are."
18. "Reba Place Church Membership Questions."
19. https://www.mennoniteusa.org/who-are-mennonites/what-we-believe/confession-of-faith/.

of faith when she was four, while we were still in Argentina. However, both our church in Argentina and Reba Place Church discouraged her from getting baptized until she was older. Traditionally at Reba the "age of accountability" was about sixteen, but more recently young people in early adolescence have been allowed to go ahead with baptism. However, it is not a rite that all the young people in the church are expected to go through; many choose not to be baptized.

All three of our daughters first went through a study of materials provided by the church and were assigned baptism mentors.[20] On the days of their baptisms, they gave public testimonies of faith, telling the gathered congregation about their faith journeys. They then renounced all powers of evil, confessed the lordship of Jesus, expressed their conviction about the centrality of discipleship in a context of community, and were baptized by immersion in the name of the Father, the Son, and the Holy Spirit by pastor Charlotte Lehman. Celina Varela, the children and youth minister, and a member of the leadership team, assisted, also entering the baptistry. After emerging from the waters, the baptizands were bundled up in large beach towels with their names embroidered on them and surrounded by the congregation, who went forward to encircle them, lay hands on them, and pray for them. There is no special celebration of the Lord's Supper linked to the baptismal services at Reba; those who are baptized partake of their first communion the next time the church is gathered on the first Sunday of the month.

Another important liturgical custom of the congregation that usually takes place on the second Sunday of the month—though it is not limited to those Sundays—is a congregational dance. These emerged through the influence of Messianic Jews in the congregation. All are invited to come forward and be part of the simple dance. The dancers wind all around the worship space, up and down the risers, while the praise team and congregants who do not want to dance sing and clap. People in wheelchairs, young children, and old people dance as vigorously as the many formally trained dancers in the congregation. It is one of many opportunities the liturgical traditions at Reba offer to enact an intergenerational choreography as well as to worship God in an embodied way.

---

20. The main resource they used was Hershberger, *God's Story, Our Story*.

THE LITURGICAL CALENDAR AT REBA

Reba Place Church consciously follows the liturgical calendar. The liturgical seasons are marked in several ways: by the changing themes and colors of the banners, by the titles "24/7" (a weekly bulletin sent electronically on Fridays and available in printed form on Sundays), and by the worship emphasis. The church year begins with Advent, in the first week of December, and finishes at the end of November. Patriotic holidays in the United States such as Memorial Day or the Fourth of July are never commemorated in the services; neither are secular holidays such as Valentine's Day or Mother's Day, except perhaps tangentially.[21] On the other hand, Black History Month is consciously incorporated into the calendar each February as a way to celebrate African American heritage and Black contributions to society.

Weekly lectionary readings and sermon passages are included in "24/7" and tend to follow the Revised Common Lectionary or the Narrative Lectionary, though the pastor and leadership team often plan special sermon series and emphases that depart from the lectionary. In the fall of 2017, for example, four scientists and researchers who are part of the church but not usually on the preaching rotation prepared a series on faith and science. Among the themes were the values and research methods of scientists and what they can contribute to the faith community, the importance of humility and service to the truth, the fact that science and faith need not be enemies, and the urgency of addressing human-induced climate change. In the summer, when the Grow classes for children are on hiatus, the preaching emphasis is oriented toward them. The rest of the year during the service, school-aged children are invited to use special notebooks designed by a resident artist (Julie Larson) and the children and youth minister (Celina Varela), with space to draw and reflect on what they are hearing and seeing. Preschoolers are ushered out to special activities during the sermon.

Though the lead pastor preaches most of the time, there is an additional core group of four or five mostly seminary-trained preachers upon whom the pastor calls several times a year, each with a very

---

21. Sometimes mothers and fathers are recognized on these days through a special prayer or litany, but the celebration does not shape the whole service. In 2018, Ash Wednesday and Valentine's Day coincided, and the pastor worked that into the message, giving out both roses and ashes to remember that we are both made in God's image and will return to dust.

different style.[22] One regular preacher, Joseph Marshak, often develops monologues based on minor biblical or historical characters and delivers them in costume, providing historical and theological context. Anne Stewart, who grew up in Mississippi in the Black church tradition and is a long-time antiracism educator and former English teacher, often weaves poetry, call-and-response, and singing into her messages. My own sermons tend to be expository and exegetical, sometimes connected to my theological research at the time, as when I was writing a book on Galatians and preached a sermon series on the epistle.[23] It is worth noting that in a typical Sunday service, the segment dedicated to praise and worship through song and the segment dedicated to the sermon (or in "Menno-speak" the "teaching") each receive twenty minutes. Preaching or teaching is important, but not more so than praising, giving testimony, or enacting worship in other ways.

High Holy Seasons

The two most important liturgical seasons at Reba revolve around the poles of Christmas and Easter. For Advent and Lent we have a tradition of acting out simple plays or scenes written by amateur playwrights in the church, sometimes in conjunction with a sermon and at other times taking the place of the sermon. A series of dances also are linked to the seasons. During Advent there is a dance related to the Annunciation, portraying Mary interacting with an angel while someone plays the piano and sings "Breath of Heaven."[24] Usually the same young woman who has danced and acted as Mary in the plays becomes the Mary at the Christmas Eve service alongside a young man who plays the role of Joseph. The youngest baby in the congregation plays Jesus. Other children participate as angels, shepherds, sheep, and other animals rejoicing over the birth of Immanuel. There are also dances each week of Advent in which children and young people light the candles of the Advent wreath.[25] Our daugh-

---

22. An audio archive of some recent sermons can be found here: https://www.rebaplacechurch.org/sermons.

23. Bedford, *Galatians*. I will likewise either teach a Grow class or preach a sermon series with a small forthcoming book on Christology for Herald Press, which will allow me to get community feedback and to serve the community as a theological educator.

24. Shelly, "2013 12 11." In this clip our daughter Valeria is the angel, and her friend Briana is Mary.

25. See gonzodaddy's "Reba Church Advent" for an example of one such Sunday.

ters have participated in the plays and dances since childhood, giving them the opportunity not just to hear the story of Jesus' birth, but to perform and dance to it. The incarnational aspect of this liturgical tradition is deeply formative and theologically significant because (among other reasons) it serves to impart a nondocetic understanding of Christology: Jesus had a real, flesh-and-blood mother who had to deal with pregnancy and childbirth in adverse circumstances.[26]

Alongside the rejoicing of the Advent season with its lights, greenery, and expectation, the community has come to recognize that Christmas can be a difficult time for many people, especially given the forced cheeriness and capitalist fervor of the season in the United States. There are at least two ways in which the church tries to come to terms with that reality. One is the "Blue Christmas" service that arose perhaps a decade ago, which acknowledges lament, suffering, and depression as part of the journey of faith. Another is the "Angel Tree," which in conjunction with the church prison ministry allows people in the community to provide simple gifts for those whose loved ones are incarcerated or otherwise unable to be present during the holiday. As a rule, Advent and Christmas at Reba are not about consumption and material gifts, but about celebrating the deeper meaning of "God with us," born under conditions of poverty and vulnerability to a brown-skinned family living under the oppression of a hostile Roman empire.

Lent and Holy Week are also high points of the liturgical year at Reba. In recent years, church office manager Courtney Coates has edited booklets of meditations for Lent, written and illustrated by community members who contribute poems, devotional thoughts, and drawings germane to the daily Scripture passages.[27] On Sundays leading up to Holy Week there are plays and dances that enact the events narrated in the Gospels after Jesus resolves to "set his face to go to Jerusalem" (Luke 9:51). On Maundy Thursday, the church community meets for a meal of homemade bread and soup, a celebration of the Lord's Supper, and an opportunity for footwashing. The footwashing is usually practiced among close friends and family members and is a tender opportunity to embody Christ's gesture of service. In recent years, the commemoration of Good Friday has consisted of a service of readings, silent meditation,

---

26. There is something profoundly meaningful about the fact that the first active role a newborn will probably enact at Reba—regardless of biological sex—is that of embodying Jesus.

27. Coates has also done this on occasion for the Advent season.

and song, followed by a chance to visit interactive stations of the cross where one can touch, feel, taste, or smell metal nails, vinegar, and other palpable symbols of Jesus' ordeal and that of so many other "crucified" victims in history. A community reading of the entire Gospel of Mark has also been a regular feature of Holy Week.

After a pause on Holy Saturday, the Easter Sunday celebrations begin at dawn with an ecumenical sunrise service at Lighthouse Beach on Lake Michigan. The 10:00 AM Resurrection Sunday service at Reba is marked by song and celebration. A high point is a dance to Jim Croegaert's song "Was It a Morning like This?," which depicts Mary Magdalene's discovery of the empty tomb.[28] The service is also punctuated by the call and response "Jesus is risen!" "He is risen indeed! Hallelujah!" Balloons decorate the space, and children are encouraged to take them home at the end of the service. In the part of the world where Reba is located, spring usually starts to emerge very faintly around Eastertide, so often the very first daffodils and crocuses can be seen on Easter Sunday. It is a time of promise and excitement marking the beginning of the end of a very long winter season.[29]

In Search of Pentecost and Ordinary Time

The celebration of the work of the Spirit in the "Ordinary Time" of the church that begins with Pentecost is perhaps by definition more diffuse than the remembrances and reenactments of the birth, death, and resurrection of Jesus. As with many churches, in contrast to Christmas and Easter, Pentecost is not a date fervently awaited or celebrated with much fanfare at Reba. On Pentecost Sunday the liturgical colors of the banners change, and there are readings from Acts 2 as well as hymnody that celebrates the presence of the Spirit, but there is no cycle of plays nor a tradition of specific dances to mark the day. I found that it was difficult for my children as they grew up to learn and retain what Pentecost stands

---

28. See https://vimeo.com/97628890. It would be hard to overstate the significance of the dances that recur year after year both for the community as a whole and for the dancers who share their talents and glorify God through the movement of their bodies.

29. When I first lived in Evanston, I resisted connecting the season of spring to Easter because I am from the Southern Hemisphere, where I had related Easter to the glorious, golden autumn weather in the mountains of Córdoba, Argentina. I slowly realized, however, that to enjoy the subtext of a spring-like Easter season can legitimately be part of my contextual theology as long as Easter is not understood fundamentally as a rite of spring any more than Christmas need be connected to a snowy landscape.

for even though Reba is one of the few communities I know where many of the members who are part of Reba Place Fellowship try to put into practice the common purse, the community of goods, and the Spirit-infused life of discipleship described in Acts 2.

Perhaps one reason for the relative obscurity of Pentecost is that whereas Christmas and Easter both have explicit periods of preparation in the liturgical calendar (Lent and Advent) rooted partly in catechetical and baptismal preparation, Pentecost marks the beginning of the long and somewhat amorphous season of Ordinary Time. Positively expressed, Pentecost looks forward in hope to what the Spirit may yet do in the church and in the world. It therefore has not only a pneumatological flavor, but also a strongly eschatological one.

There are intimations that the lack of emphasis on Pentecost and the "Ordinary Time" it inaugurates in the liturgical calendar may be shifting slightly in wider Anabaptist Mennonite circles as an explicit sense of the urgent need for the Spirit's guidance in interpreting the way of Jesus in the present comes to the fore. Such an awareness is congruent with the strong pneumatology present in the movement's origins, which was arguably one of the reasons for its initial dynamism and counter-hegemonic stances.[30] For instance, the contemporary Anabaptist prayer book *Take Our Moments and Our Days* provides two volumes: *Ordinary Time* and *Advent through Pentecost*.[31] The first volume, entirely dedicated to Ordinary Time, divides each month into weeks focused on the Lord's Prayer, the Beatitudes, the Parables of Jesus, and Signs and Wonders, each imbued with a search for discernment and guidance from the Spirit. Yet even the second volume, at first glance dedicated primarily to Advent, Christmas, Lent, and Holy Week, provides two weeks' worth of Pentecost prayers in what the authors call "a thoroughly Anabaptist enthusiasm for the importance of the Spirit in the life of the church." They add: "The work of the Spirit we celebrate in this season is paradoxical, holding together Spirit and letter, law and gospel, the inner life of the spirit and the outer life of discipleship."[32] The authors of the prayer book clearly delineate the centrality of the Spirit even for a Christocentric tradition such as the Anabaptist one.

---

30. See Klaassen, "Some Anabaptist Views." Klaassen argues that one of the sources of the pneumatological vitality of early Anabaptism was a reliance on Pauline language, which deeply connects the Spirit with Christ (131–32).

31. Boers et al., *Take Our Moments*.

32. Boers et al., *Take Our Moments*, 2:792–94.

Seen in the light of eschatological expectation, one can detect hints of what is "coming to be" through the Spirit at Reba. Pastor Charlotte has pointed out, for instance, that the production of art is a central mark of the creative work of the Spirit in the congregation.[33] There are many talented artists in the church who contribute actively to the worship life of the community, providing texture and complexity to the shared life of faith through and beyond the high holy times of Christmas and Easter.[34] For her ordination, Pastor Charlotte crafted a banner decorated with the Lamb of God as a companion to a Lion of Judah banner she had previously made for the church. Both are exhibited in the Meeting House and add to the richness of christological depictions in the worship space, moving as they do beyond androcentrism and even anthropocentrism. Another important practice linked to art is that of sharing creative endeavors, be it at the "Hatch at the Patch," a monthly opportunity to present and discuss artwork in a household made up of millennials, or at occasional concerts and open mics in the Meeting House that provide a space for storytelling and musicmaking.[35]

In visiting other Mennonite churches, I have observed liturgical gestures that might be fruitfully adapted for Reba. At Hively Mennonite Church in Elkhart, Indiana, for example, during the Sunday morning service they light the peace candle with a prayer, often in both English and Spanish, along these lines:[36]

> God of Peace, Christ of Peace, Spirit of Peace,
> you are calling us to be peacemakers.
> Today we light this candle
> as a reminder of our calling.
>
> *Dios de Paz, Cristo de Paz, Espíritu de Paz:*
> *Tú nos llamas a ser hacedores de paz.*

33. Lehman, interview.

34. This can be seen, for example, in the icons of Lois Engelman, the paintings in the Meeting House and Ministry Center by Rob Larson and Josh McCallister, the lively animal mural by Anne Gavitt that decorates the walls of the nursery, and the colorful banners and backdrops for the worship space by Julie Larson, Hilda Carper, and Charlotte Lehman.

35. There are a number of young musicians connected to the Reba church community creating music in different genres, including Laytham El-Tayyab and MC Audax the Damsel. MC Audax the Damsel is one of my daughters.

36. See http://www.hivelymennonite.org/services. I've slightly altered the Spanish version.

Hoy encendemos esta vela
Como recordatorio de nuestro llamado.

The candle is lit by different people each Sunday who may offer a word about specific ways of peacemaking and justice-making in which they are involved. I could imagine such a moment becoming part of Reba worship during Ordinary Time as a way to underline the material implications of Pentecostality—of the Spirit poured out on all flesh—for our life in the world as followers of Jesus by the Spirit in the way of peace and justice.

THE URGENCY OF PENTECOSTALITY

Anabaptist scholar Stuart Murray says it is possible to divide Anabaptists today into four large groups: (1) the direct descendants of the early Anabaptists (such as Mennonites, Amish, and Hutterites); (2) denominations that emerged later but were directly inspired by Anabaptists (such as some Brethren and Baptist groups as well as the Bruderhof movement); (3) Anabaptist churches in the Global South and elsewhere that are not necessarily linked ethnically to the first Anabaptists; and (4) neo-Anabaptists, who belong to other confessions and denominations yet are heavily influenced by Anabaptist convictions.[37]

If I think of my own journey as a person of faith and a confessional theologian, I've been touched by all of these strands: by descendants of Middle European Anabaptists from Paraguay, Canada, and the United States, including some of my closest friends in primary school in Buenos Aires; by Argentine Mennonites in my high school and hometown in Córdoba province, people with whom I had discussions about the viability of pacifism; by my professors at a Baptist seminary, especially William Estep and Jan Kiwiet, who deeply engaged the inheritance of the Radical Reformation; and by theologians sympathetic to Anabaptist perspectives, such as my doctoral advisor Jürgen Moltmann. The force of all of these influences, as well as the work of Anabaptist theologians I learned about and read, from Michael and Margaretha Sattler to Thomas Finger, led me eventually to Reba Place Church, which in its ethos reflects a mixture of all four of the Anabaptist strands Murray describes.

C. Arnold Snyder, a Mennonite historian, summarizes the Anabaptist ecclesiological conception as "a church of believers, born of the

37. Murray, *Naked Anabaptist*, 184–85.

Spirit, centered on Christ."[38] Said otherwise, the Anabaptist vision is "of the church as a community of disciples, born again by the Spirit of God, discerning God's will together."[39] Such an ecclesiology presupposes on the one hand a commitment to know and deeply internalize the way of Jesus (particularly as depicted in the Gospels) and on the other hand a willingness to actualize that path of discipleship by the power of the Spirit. In other words, a healthy Anabaptist ecclesiology requires a christological pneumatology and a pneumatological Christology, lived out in community, with a strong dose of eschatological hope. Some possible distortions of Anabaptist ecclesiology as seen in its history are legalism, groupthink, and a sectarian separation from the world that leads to a lack of engagement with it (for example, quietism and passivism rather than pacifism and nonviolent conflict resolution).[40]

One key to a healthy Anabaptist church is a strong pneumatological underpinning.[41] The Holy Spirit is the only one capable of pushing the church to engage society in a missional way that avoids legalism or sectarianism and turns the characteristic gifts of simplicity, discipleship, and peacemaking in the Anabaptist community into assets that benefit others whether or not they belong to the church.

One way to conceptualize this pneumatological mark of the missional church is through the notion of Pentecostality, a trait not limited to Pentecostalism, though Pentecostalism as a movement points to Pentecostality and reminds us of it. Pentecostality is the characteristic way of being in the world that emerges whenever the church (any church of any confession) has a robust sense of the work of the Spirit in its midst

---

38. Snyder, *From Anabaptist Seed*, 20.

39. Snyder, *From Anabaptist Seed*, 21.

40. At Reba, for instance, we need to be vigilant about not letting our delight in community life morph into sectarian habits that are unintelligible and uninviting to newcomers or outsiders. Also, we should not allow a reticence to be pushy about faith in our secularized context to keep our light under a bushel.

41. In his review of Anabaptist pneumatology, Jamie Pitts notes a certain "reticence about the Holy Spirit and experience of the Spirit throughout the tradition" but also detects "the quest to know, understand, and experience the Spirit" (Pitts, "Historical Anabaptist-Mennonite Pneumatology"): "[P]art of how Anabaptist-Mennonites have sought to know, understand, and experience the Holy Spirit is by learning from other Christians. Other constitutive features of this pneumatology include a strong association between the Spirit and disciplined community, a persistent epistemological tension between Word (Jesus, Scripture) and Spirit, and an occasional emphasis on the Spirit's role in consummating history (eschatology)" (27).

and beyond.⁴² It refers to the centrality of the Spirit's sanctifying, liberating, and vivifying agency, without which the gospel message would wither and no longer be good news. This mark of Pentecostality brings me a lot of hope because it is linked to the possibility of God doing new things in the world by the Spirit in the way of Jesus. Because the Spirit is truly present, hovering over all of creation with motherly love, coaxing new life into valleys of dry bones, present in every speck of the universe yet not limited to that universe, the Spirit's flaming presence brings infinite possibilities for change and transformation, as described so vividly in the Pentecost story of Acts.

DEEPENING PENTECOSTALITY: FROM INCLUSIVITY TO EXPANSIVITY IN LOVE

Through the years I have noticed that one mark of the work of the Spirit at Reba (as in other churches) is the movement from attention to charismatic gestures (for example, speaking in tongues or raising one's arms in worship) to a wider Pentecostality that is deeply hospitable and focuses on the flourishing of people in all their glorious multiplicity and differences. Said otherwise, a sound pneumatology that accounts for Pentecostality is marked by love in ways that have concrete, life-giving implications for theology and church polity. One sees this after Pentecost in the early church as it went from experiencing signs and wonders that allowed for the gospel to be understood by Jews and proselytes who spoke many different languages (Acts 2:4–6) to allowing gentile followers of Jesus to do so from within their cultural particularities without adopting circumcision or Jewish dietary laws and instead focusing on the heart of the message of the Hebrew prophets and of Jesus, such as justice for the poor (Acts 15:4–29 and Gal 2:6–10). Such pneumatic movement requires a good deal of community discernment and dialogue; it cannot simply be imposed by a group of leaders.

42. I develop the idea of the *notae missionis*, or marks of the church's mission (ecumenicity, Pentecostality, ubiquity, and inclusivity or expansivity) in my essay "La teología de la misión integral y el discernimiento comunitario." "Ecumenicity" refers to a trinitarian model for church diversity in which different groups and denominations bring different gifts interacting perichoretically; "ubiquity" means that the church is present in the whole world, not as a franchise but in concrete, particular communities according to the Pauline principle of contextuality so that we see universality *in* particularity; and "inclusivity" or "expansivity" makes reference to a gender-expansive, holistic, integral, global, and cosmic mission.

Reba Place Church has attempted to be open to the movement of the Spirit—and thus to Pentecostality—in various ways through the years, sometimes with a degree of success, sometimes less so. It has tried to embody an antiracist ethos despite the white hegemony in US society at large and the "whiteness" of much of Anabaptist history in the United States. This is reflected in its worship practices and in the racial and ethnic composition of the congregants, though it arguably still functions most of the time primarily as a "white space."[43] It has tried to embrace pastoral leadership by women as well as men, moving from strongly androcentric and complementarian notions in its early years to ordaining and supporting a woman as lead pastor in the last decade. More recently it has tried to grapple with the challenges of heteronormativity.

Beginning in September 2017, for more than a year, the church community engaged in a respectful, patient dialogue and discernment process regarding whether to bless same-sex covenanted relationships and whether (and how) to affirm openly queer folk in leadership positions. The focus question that guided all the discussions was: "How can the response of Reba Place Church to the presence of same-sex attraction in ourselves and others best reflect God's Good News as proclaimed by Jesus?" The process included messages on the wider issue of biblical interpretation, confidential small-group discussions, outside speakers, a panel of LGBTQI Christians (some celibate, some not) who either are or have been connected to the Reba community, and an invitation to read materials on the topic from various perspectives. Also included was a service of lament for the pain the church, inadvertently or not, had caused LGBTQI people linked to the community in the past.[44] Eventually, the process led to a congregational vote overwhelmingly in favor of the church's adoption of its "inclusive in love" policy.

A small handful of attenders or members distanced themselves when the plan for the dialogue process was announced. One longtime member shared that after participating in the process she was unable to reconcile her convictions with the policy and had decided to attend another church. Most of the congregation, however, participated in the process and supported the document that emerged from communal

---

43. On the problem of theology as a "white space" in the United States, see Bedford, "Theology, Violence and White Spaces." For what I perceive as the "apostasy" of the docetic white Jesus in much of contemporary US Protestantism writ large (thus including Anabaptists), see Bedford, "Narrow Gate?"

44. Reba Place Church, "Roadmap."

discernment. The policy as adopted does not assume that all members or attenders see the issues in identical ways: "We respect individual moral sense and encourage ongoing reflection for each member of our body. With humility we resist the impulse to impose our moral insights on our brothers and sisters." Nonetheless, it strongly supports recognizing the gifts of all people in membership, service, and leadership, without regard to sexual orientation. It also celebrates the joining of any two adults in the loving, lifelong commitment of marriage or covenant union, as well as celebrating "other commitments of love through vows of friendship or celibacy." Notably, there was neither a split in the church nor a large exodus of members as a result of dealing with issues that continue to fracture denominations. As the policy puts it:

> We are united in our call to follow Jesus, to seek the direction of God's Spirit among us, and to love and respond to all humanity as created in the image of God. . . . We believe our loving relationships centered on what we have in common are bigger than our differences and strong enough to create a joyful community that bears a uniquely beautiful witness for the Gospel.[45]

One sees in this process—one that recognizes and incorporates the strengths of Anabaptist wisdom about conflict resolution[46]—a pattern of embodied Pentecostality. It shows how a congregation open to the guidance of the Spirit can move in the direction not just of "inclusivity in love," as the document would have it, but of "expansivity in love." By "expansivity" I mean practices that not only include the formerly excluded in pre-established patterns, but also begin to modify many formerly ingrained indicators of hegemonic common sense, nudging the habits and institutional contours of community life further in the direction of the good news of the gospel.

As a theologian interested in pneumatology—that is, the beliefs and practices that revolve around a deep consideration of the Holy Spirit—my participation at Reba provides me with an inductive path into pondering the ways of the Spirit in the midst of the messiness of life and the imperfections of a congregation that is living in this time of "Holy Saturday," enmeshed in the travails of a suffering world, while hoping and acting for its renewal and transformation. Our life together gives me hope that we can learn to "do a new thing" with God's help. As

---

45. Reba Place Church, "Inclusive in Love."
46. Mennonite Church USA, "Agreeing and Disagreeing in Love."

a professor of many students who identify as queer, I am grateful to be able to say, "You are deeply welcome at my church community, anytime, alongside those whom you love."

If we look at what love seems to mean for Jesus in the Gospels, three things seem immediately to jump out. First, God is the source of our love and takes the initiative in loving us. God's very nature is love, and the closer we come by the Spirit to the God who calls us into the rhythms of the divine economy, the more God's loving nature rubs off on us. Second, our own love is to be expressed not only to God, but to fellow creatures, even to our enemies and not least to ourselves. Love is not reserved for our closest friends or favorite people, but is a practice that moves us in unexpected directions, changing how we live in the world and how we perceive ourselves and others. Third, love is not an abstract noun, but a verb; it is something we do and show and live and breathe. Love is always connected to justice (Luke 11:42). It is not primarily a feeling, though it does entail emotion. It is a way of life with material, concrete consequences.

Jesus acted out the meaning of love in his preaching, teaching, healing, and casting out of demons, by denouncing injustice, standing up to the principalities and powers, and refusing to return evil with evil or violence with violence, by sharing meals and laughing alongside his friends and disciples, and by recognizing the insights of children, women, lepers, and outcasts of various kinds. He empowered his followers to see and live in the world differently. His fierce love crisscrossed all that he said and did. To speak of Pentecostality is to highlight and imagine ways in which, with the help of the Spirit, we take love beyond the discursive level and act it out concretely and expansively in accordance with the good news of the gospel, even in our imperfect, muddling, confounding, yet inspiring communities of faith.

BIBLIOGRAPHY

"About Jim Croegaert." Rough Stones Music. https://roughstonesmusic.com/about-jim-croegaert/.

Audax the Damsel [YouTube channel]. https://www.youtube.com/channel/UCV-XQvZmXxYsV7KV-icn48Q.

Bedford, Nancy Elizabeth. *Galatians*. Belief: A Theological Commentary on the Bible. Louisville: Westminster John Knox, 2016.

―――. "La teología de la misión integral y el discernimiento comunitario." In *La Iglesia Local como Agente de Transformación*, edited by René Padilla and Tetsunao Yamamori, 47–74. Buenos Aires: Kairós, 2003.

―――. "Little Moves Against Destructiveness: Theology and the Practice of Discernment." In *Practicing Theology: Beliefs and Practices in Christian Life*, edited by Dorothy Bass and Miroslav Volf, 157–84. Grand Rapids: Eerdmans, 2001.

―――. "El Espíritu les enseñará todas las cosas (Juan 14:26): La iglesia local como sitio para la educación teológica." In *Otra Educación Teológica es Posible*, edited by Nicolás Panotto and Matthias Preiswerk, 27–35. Buenos Aires: Libro Digital, 2017.

―――. *Jesus Christus und das gekreuzigte Volk: Christologie der Nachfolge und des Martyriums bei Jon Sobrino*, Concordia Reihe Monographien 15. Aachen: Verlag der Augustinus Buchhandlung, 1995.

―――. "A Narrow Gate? Proceeding along the Way of Jesus by the Spirit." *Mennonite Quarterly Review* 92 (October 2018) 43–55.

―――. "Theology, Violence and White Spaces." In *Envisioning the Good Life*, edited by Matthew Croasmun, Zoran Grozdanov, and Ryan J. McAnally-Linz, 149–62. Eugene, OR: Cascade, 2017.

―――. "¿Toda potestad en el cielo y en la tierra? Usos y abusos del poder en la misión de la iglesia." In *¿El poder del amor o el amor al poder? Luces y sombras del ejercicio del poder en las iglesias evangélicas*, edited by Harold Segura, 39–62. Colección FTL 35. Buenos Aires: Kairós, 2012.

Boers, Arthur Paul, et al. *Take Our Moments and Our Days: An Anabaptist Prayer Book: Ordinary Time* Vol. 1. Scottdale, PA: Herald, 2007.

―――. *Take Our Moments and Our Days: An Anabaptist Prayer Book: Advent through Pentecost* Vol. 2. Scottdale, PA: Herald, 2010.

Bookwalter, Genevieve. "Shout Out: Hassan El-Tayyab, peace activist and musician." *Chicago Tribune*, December 7, 2017. https://www.chicagotribune.com/suburbs/evanston/ct-evr-shout-out-el-tayyab-tl-1214-20171207-story.html.

Bridgefolk [website]. https://bridgefolk.net.

gonzodaddy. "Reba Church Advent—2009." YouTube video, January 26, 2010, 5:38. https://www.youtube.com/watch?v=laGsdYTDtec.

Hershberger, Michele. *God's Story, Our Story: Exploring Christian Faith and Life*. Scottdale, PA: Mennonite Publishing Network, 2003.

Hively Avenue Mennonite Church website. http://www.hivelymennonite.org/.

Jackson, Dave, and Neeta Jackson. *Glimpses of Glory: Thirty Years of Community: The Story of Reba Place Fellowship*. Elgin, IL: Brethren, 1987.

Klaassen, Walter. "Some Anabaptist Views of the Doctrine of the Holy Spirit." *Mennonite Quarterly Review* 35 (1961) 130–39.

Laytham, Monica. *Becoming Home*. 2016. https://monicalaytham.bandcamp.com.

Lehman, Charlotte (lead pastor, Reba Place Fellowship). Interview by Nancy Elizabeth Bedford, May 16, 2018.

Living Water Community Church website. https://livingwatercommunitychurch.org/.

Mennonite Church USA. "Agreeing and Disagreeing in Love." http://mennoniteusa.org/resource/agreeing-and-disagreeing-in-love/.

―――. "Confession of Faith in a Mennonite Perspective." https://www.mennoniteusa.org/who-are-mennonites/what-we-believe/confession-of-faith/.

Murray, Stuart. *The Naked Anabaptist. The Bare Essentials of a Radical Faith.* Fifth Anniversary Ed. Harrisonburg, VA: Herald, 2015.

Pitts, Jamie. "Historical Anabaptist-Mennonite Pneumatology: A Review of Confessional, Catechetical and Devotional Materials, 1525–1963." *The Conrad Grebel Review* 36 (2018) 24–53.

Reba Place Church. https://www.rebaplacechurch.org/.

"Reba Place Church Membership Questions." https://docs.wixstatic.com/ugd/c640b0_a44fb643feb4471389d255f830b57bc1.pdf.

Reba Place Church. "Roadmap for the RPC Dialogue & Discernment Process Re Same-Sex Covenant Relationships/Marriage." https://docs.wixstatic.com/ugd/c640b0_337e0ea79fc7478788d765123a2b2068.pdf.

Reba Place Fellowship. https://www.rebaplacefellowship.org/.

Reba Praise. https://www.sonicbids.com/band/rebapraise/.

Rempel, John D. "Baptism: Communicating Grace and Faith." *Pro Ecclesia: A Journal of Catholic and Evangelical Theology* 25, no. 3 (Summer 2016) 300–314.

Rutschman, La Verne. *Anabautismo Radical y Teología Latinoamericana de la Liberación.* San José, CR: SEBILA, 1982.

Shelly, Glen. "2013 12 11 breathofheaven dance." YouTube video, December 8, 2013, 5:29. https://www.youtube.com/watch?v=xQGhKH9N8HA.

Snyder, C. Arnold. *From Anabaptist Seed: The Historical Core of Anabaptist Related Identity.* Kitchener, ON: Pandora, 1999.

LITURGY, DAILY LIFE, AND PERFORMANCE

An Experiential-Reflective Approach to Congregational Practice

Júlio Cézar Adam

This essay was written for the Calvin Institute of Christian Worship event called *Strengthening Public Worship Practices: How Theological Disciplines Can Enrich and Deepen Congregational Life* and aims to answer precisely this question from the Brazilian context using the example of a historical Protestant church and the experience of an academic seminar on liturgy called *Experimental Seminar: Ritualities— Creative Research*. The goal of both the experimental seminar and this reflection is to bring liturgy and life closer together, thus facilitating the transformative effects of worship—an encounter between God and God's people—on persons and congregations that participate in worship services in their local contexts and cultures.

In the first of this essay's three parts I will discuss the context of Christian worship in Brazil, focusing on the worship services of the Evangelical Church of the Lutheran Confession in Brazil, and present the reasons that have led to the development of a practical-reflective seminar on Christian worship. In the second part I will introduce some major theoretical topics, such as the understanding of worship and liturgy, the relations of the worship service with the body, theater, and performance, and the concepts of inculturation and postcoloniality. Then, in the third section, I will offer a more detailed description of the development of *Experimental Seminar: Ritualities—Creative Research*, pointing to its potential for the making of liturgy and for the enrichment of congregational participation in Christian worship.

THE CONTEXT OF CHRISTIAN WORSHIP IN BRAZIL[1]

The Historical Context

The Brazilian context is marked by the presence of religion and the church, and worship is one of the main expressions of that mark. The first action undertaken by the Portuguese after they invaded Brazil's territory in 1500 was to hold Mass. This episode highlights two forces that would shape the development of culture and religion in that context. The first is the entanglement of religion and conquest legitimized by the political regime, i.e., worship associated with political power. The second is the impossibility of dialogue with other autochthonous forms of culture and religion, meaning that Christian worship delimits a new, exclusive, and hegemonic space in the religious field.[2] These two characteristics can still be seen today.

One of the consequences of the Portuguese colonization is that while Roman Catholicism prevailed in that context, forms of syncretism with indigenous religions and later with religions of African origin have marked Brazil's religious context for centuries, producing a unique and effervescent cultural and religious environment. (The contributions brought centuries later by Protestant and then Pentecostal traditions would not, however, become part of that religious hybridity even when denying the latter.)

In Brazil one can experience daily the effects of that religious diversity and effervescence. One might almost say that here one can experience an excess of religion that extends beyond the religious realm itself. Religion is part of culture, of society, of intimacy, of politics and the economy, of pop culture, of daily life. Besides the surprising emergence of new churches and religious movements in recent decades, the phenomena of syncretism,

---

1. For more about the Brazilian and Latin American contexts, see the essays in this book by César Lópes and Dinorah Méndez.

2. On the role of worship in colonization, see Bosi, *Dialética da Colonização*, 11, 15, 19, 26.

religious mobility, religious bricolage or hybridity are also current religious trends. The worship service is the main stage where these trends converge and where they are formulated and expressed.

Brazil's predominant Christian denominations and currents might be classified like this: There is a predominance of classical and Romanized Catholicism and of popular syncretic and hybrid Catholicism on the one hand, and, on the other hand, of Pentecostalism and Neo-Pentecostalism with their individualized, emotionally laden religious practices that have a moral and economic appeal (prosperity theology). In the middle—or at the margins—one finds Protestant and evangelical churches of missionary or immigratory origin that entered the Brazilian religious scene starting in the nineteenth century. The model of worship brought by these churches, particularly those brought by missionary projects, had an exclusive character and were opposed to Brazil's popular and Romanized versions of Catholicism.

In the historical Protestant churches these more conservative trends have over time given way to a posture that is more open to ecumenical and interreligious dialogue and has moved toward a sociopolitical commitment, but in the Pentecostal and Neo-Pentecostal churches exclusivity and opposition have been intensified.

The Evangelical Church of the Lutheran Confession in Brazil (IECLB), which at present comprises 1 percent of Brazil's population, belongs to the so-called historical Protestantism and has its origin in the immigration of Germans to Brazil that started in the first half of the nineteenth century. The liturgy that developed in this church was both literally and symbolically brought over in the immigrants—baggage, transplanted from the German to the Brazilian context and later translated to Portuguese, reflecting regional and confessional (Lutheran, Reformed, and United) differences from its original context. Unlike the churches arising from contemporaneous mission movements, the IECLB organized itself as an ethnically German church that wanted to maintain the Evangelical Lutheran traditions of its members and had in the worship service a privileged space for this undertaking. For more than a century the worship service successfully maintained the culture of its German and Lutheran origins.

In the 1970s the IECLB underwent a paradigmatic change, deliberately trying to be a Brazilian church by facing the social challenges of its context and getting closer to other churches. But its liturgy, even though translated into Portuguese, still remained very similar to the Protestant worship services of decades ago in Germany (Prussia and Bavaria).[3] It was only in the 1990s, instigated by liturgical renewal movements throughout the world through mainly the World Council of Churches and the Lutheran World Federation, that a judicious process of liturgical renewal began in the IECLB, with the goal of making worship more relevant, lively, ecumenical, contextual, and inculturated.[4]

This liturgical reform took place over a period of about ten years and culminated in 2000 with the publication of the *Book of Worship* in 2000,[5] the first liturgical model emerging from the IECLB in the Brazilian context. This liturgy preserves the traditional evangelical Lutheran confessionality, but it also recovered ecumenical principles from the Liturgy of Lima, such as the Eucharistic Prayer and the regularity of Holy Communion in the congregation's main worship service, and inculturated elements, such as liturgical songs and hymns. Furthermore, critical aspects of liberation theology were given a certain prominence, including the idea that the worship service belongs to its congregation, the development of liturgical teams, and liturgical shaping. The *Book of Worship* proposes a model for liturgical order but acknowledges the principle of liturgical shaping by individual congregations. Against this background, the worship service is understood as an encounter that brings together God and a group of people as well as these people as a community. The subject of the worship service is God. God reaches out to the congregation (Matt 18:20), and God in fact orders that worship take place (1 Cor 11:24–25: "Do this . . ."). The encounter is an action by God. People respond and accept God's invitation. In this encounter they hear God's will (the Word of God), commune at God's table (the Lord's Supper) and have fellowship among themselves. The people direct prayer, worship, and praise to God, show their willingness to accept the commitment of faith, and leave the worship service to give witness to their faith and to serve the Lord in their individual contexts.[6]

---

3. IECLB, *Livro de Culto*, 166–67.

4. On the liturgical renewal in the IECLB, see Kirst, "Renovação litúrgicas," and Adam, "Liturgical Formation."

5. IECLB, *Livro de Culto*.

6. IECLB, *Livro de Culto*, 13.

The Present Situation

In spite of this important development towards renewal, one still perceives today somewhat apathetic congregational participation in the liturgy, worship services still centered on the pastor, very rational liturgies, an excess of words and texts, a preference for liturgies imported from the Northern Hemisphere, and a rejection of elements from Brazilian culture, such as musical instruments, rhythms, or certain symbols and alternative vestments. Situations of social vulnerability or issues of a political nature receive little or no attention in the liturgy, as Cesar Lópes notes in "Learning Empathy," his study of worship in the Independent Presbyterian Church in Brazil. This apathetic and conservative participation can also be observed in various other historical Protestant churches and in the Roman Catholic Church.

The Anglican liturgist Jaci Maraschin, when talking about liturgies in historical churches, claims that "our liturgies are in general Apollonian (from Apollo and in contrast with the dynamism of Dionysus) as they are still based on the logocentric form of communication and are governed by rules, codes, and ideas."[7] According to Maraschin, we are still bound to our books of liturgy, hymnals, and traditions; our liturgies are heavily clerical; our sermons are moralistic and tend to be fundamentalist; and our liturgies are still masculine.[8]

While we observe liturgical apathy in historical churches, Pentecostal and Neo-Pentecostal worship services, many of them outside the liturgical tradition of the church, attract large numbers of people and are also celebrated enthusiastically, involving people in a more holistic and corporeal way and incorporating Brazilian cultural and religious elements. In this same context, expressions of popular culture—Carnival, soccer, concerts, or films, for example—also attract and involve thousands of people from different generations. In both Pentecostal worship services and in these cultural expressions, the use of the body in joyful, relaxed, and festive forms of movement and dance is obvious. In the IECLB, despite movements of liturgical renewal, such lively and enculturated worship services are not often seen in congregational practice. At times, the relationship between worship and life seems to be somewhat distant.

---

7. Maraschin, *Da leveza e da Beleza*, 25.
8. Maraschin, *Da leveza e da beleza*, 28.

The Experimental Seminar Proposal

The *Experimental Seminar: Ritualities—Creative Research* is primarily intended to bring the IECLB liturgy closer to local life and culture. It emerged concretely as an alternative form of teaching, learning, and researching liturgy through experience and bodily practice, particularly for students in theological schools and seminaries. It also explores ways to involve the whole congregation—not just ministers and liturgists—in liturgical celebration. It aims to respond to worship issues in not only the IECLB, but other historical churches in Brazil and elsewhere. The seminar is the result of a partnership between three teachers of liturgy and theater in Brazil and Canada: Dr. Ângelo Cardita, professor of liturgy at the Laval University in Quebec, Canada; Dr. Ismael Scheffler, professor of theater at the Federal Technological University of Paraná in Curitiba, Brazil; and Júlio Cézar Adam, the author of this text and professor of liturgy and homiletics at the Lutheran School of Theology (Faculdades EST) in São Leopoldo/RS, Brazil.

We envisioned an experiential-reflective seminar to study and research liturgy with worshiping congregations, but based on practice, daily life, action, and movement instead of on texts and theories. We started with theological students, but the second time we included congregation members. We provide space and time for bodily movement, for expression, for feeling the body, and for experiencing how the body lives daily life and finds forms and gestures to express itself in culture. If the focus is the Eucharist, for example, the seminar first explores ways in which people feed themselves, remember, give thanks, and create communion in daily life, noticing how these experiences can be expressed through the body, in space and in time, and through resources, symbols, and metaphors. This in turn helps participants reflect on how to shape a worship liturgy.

The seminar was held twice, in 2016 and in 2018, at Faculdades ESTin São Leopoldo/RS, Brazil, with theology students and congregation members. At both opportunities we created spaces for experimentation, lived experience, and reflection about how to make the liturgies of Christian congregations livelier, more enculturated, and more related to people's daily lives, with more active congregational participation reflection on the postcolonial paradigm. We are trying to find ways to document these seminars to share with a wider audience. We also continue to experiment—a foundation of our proposal. Its development will be described in more detail in the final section of this essay.

THEORETICAL AND THEOLOGICAL ANALYSIS AS THE BASIS OF THE EXPERIMENTAL SEMINAR

Worship and Liturgy

The attempt to bring life and worship closer together starts from a certain view of worship and liturgy. We understand the worship service as the encounter between God and God's congregation and the liturgy as the set of elements and forms that enable that special encounter.[9] The liturgy emanates from the biblical and ecclesiastical traditions and becomes incarnate in the congregation's life and culture in a permanent dynamic of creation through the Word of God.[10]

This dynamic of Christian worship is a representative or symbolic action (*darstellendes Handeln*)[11] of the whole gospel, a public communication of the Christian experience within the worship service. In other words, Christian worship recapitulates, updates, and disseminates the whole history of God with God's people recorded in the Bible and in the very tradition of the people of God, namely, the church.[12]

As pointed out by H.-G. Heimbrock, the central function of Christian worship is to awaken and nourish the Christian faith: "Ultimately, Christian worship does not aim to reach anything, but it intends to be 'representative action,' it intends to give expression to human joy at God's liberation—holistic expression if possible."[13] Therefore, every liturgical celebration means letting oneself become open to and surprised by something bigger than any human action, regardless of how just, worthy, or obligatory that action may be. Thus any form of objectification for one's own purposes, however noble and necessary they are, violates the essence of Christian worship. But this does not mean that the worship service is held in a cultural, social, and corporeal vacuum. The worship service is only possible due to its corporeal and cultural human dimension, which is always present in the essence of liturgy itself as an incarnational service of God rendered through the lives, stories, bodies, and senses of concrete persons.

---

9. Kirst, "Liturgia."
10. Wainwright, "Fundamentação sistemática-teológica."
11. Schleiermacher, *Praktische Theologie*, 70.
12. von Allmen, *Culto cristão*, 21.
13. Heimbrock, *Gottesdienst*, 9.

The definition of "worship service" offered by Lutheran theologian Peter Brunner[14] through exploring the German word *Gottesdienst* corroborates the above idea. The word *Gottesdienst* enables one to say that the worship service is a service rendered by God to the congregation and at the same time a service by the congregation before God. According to this view, the worship service is always a response to what God did and does in Jesus Christ. The congregation's service before God is loving service to neighbors through a faith awakened and maintained by God. It is always God who acts in both movements.[15] What the heart means to the body is what worship means to the church: all action by the church circulates, coming from worship and returning to worship.[16]

God's action in the worship service will always engender a response in people, in the congregation and in the world, that goes beyond its primary function as an action and service of God that creates and maintains faith. Dietrich Rössler calls this secondary outcome "side effects."[17] Based on these side effects of the worship service, Peter Cornehl describes four functions of Christian worship.[18] The worship service conveys more than just information. It also includes *expression* through the rites, symbols, and hope. Furthermore, the worship service is a place of *orientation* or *guidance* through the gospel narrative's representative action. It is also a space of *affirmation* of the faith that undergirds the congregation and a time of *integration* in which the congregation is constituted as God's family.

Ernst Lange proposes four other functions of worship: identity, distance, celebration, and feast.[19] The worship service creates *identity* in the people who celebrate it, functioning as a mirror in which the congregation sees and recognizes itself. This is not simply a cultural or social identity, but an identity that comes from the outside, given by God's self through Jesus Christ. It is through Christ that the congregation recognizes itself. Christian worship also creates *distance*. Although the worship service is intertwined with the reality of its context, it is a consecrated moment that creates a space for distancing, for evaluation of the context and of oneself, of one's disfigured identity, and of contact with the alternative, the utopian,

14. White, *Introdução ao culto cristão*, 15.
15. White, *Introdução ao culto cristão*, 15.
16. von Allmen, *Culto cristão*, 53-54.
17. Rössler, *Vernunft der Religion*, 17–18.
18. Cornehl, "Theorie des Gottesdiensts," 181–84.
19. Lange, *Predigen als Beruf*, 85–90.

which Lange calls a counter-world. This is a force of resistance to and subversion of the order. The worship service is organized around *celebration*. It creates a space to celebrate human existence in its most authentic and profound incarnation, Jesus Christ, the reason for the feast. Finally, Christian worship is a *feast*, a playful activity before God, a possibility of subversively inverting the crudeness and cruelty of reality.

The worship service is not theater or human performance but a representative action of the gospel both performed into the congregation's life and starting from it. But because worship involves the lives of concrete persons and cultures, theater and performance can help us understand the role of corporeity, intimacy, movement, expression, play, and drama in the worship service.[20]

A study by Israel Flores Olmos of the testimony of immigrants in the liturgy of worship in the Protestant Church of Andalusia reinforces the function of the liturgy to create bonds among individuals and communities with the history of salvation. For this reason, research projects and studies on this interrelationship have been of great importance for our experiment.

Performance, Body, and Rite

Considering this view on worship and its relation to daily life, a significant issue always in the background of the experimental seminar was the practical, living, corporeal, social, and cultural dimensions of the liturgy. The liturgy in the ordo of the Roman Catholic church was born from practical experience, a corporeal and symbolic expression of lived experience, such as the bath that cleans and refreshes the body at baptism, the meal at the Lord's table, the chance for people to hear, see, smell, taste, and feel at the Eucharist. Thus, rites are related to practical life and are designed to solve social and individual dramas (Victor Turner). As time passed, the ritual practices became crystallized, formatted in such a way that they may appear to be relics seemingly unrelated to the concrete daily life of the worshiping congregation.

In the liturgical reality of many Brazilian churches, the body is often forgotten, particularly in Protestant congregations. Sometimes it seems that we attend worship services with only our head, our reason—even in Brazil, where culture frequently finds its expression in the body, in

---

20. Schilson and Hake, "Christliche Gottesdienst," 9.

movements, in emotions. Aldo Vannucchi, a Catholic scholar, emphasizes the need to consider the body and symbolic and ritual expression in the worship liturgy:

> We are not pure spirits. We think, love, believe, pray; we are also saved with our body. Or to put it better: we are also body. Thus, if the liturgy, by an impossible hypothesis, intended to neglect our existential corporeity, it would not say anything to us nor would it be a moment of encounter, through Jesus Christ, with the Father, in the unity of the Holy Spirit, because the real Christ is the Word made flesh, born from Mary, "taking the form of a servant, being born in the likeness of men."[21]

Speaking about the body in the worship service is not something generic and abstract but is directly related to life lived in the body, the space of pleasure and pain, desires and miseries, hunger, thirst, and fear, tiredness and joy. Speaking about the body in the liturgy means to speak to the concreteness, individuality, and diversity of life. But the body and corporeal, theatrical, and performative expression are not ends in themselves. We want to look for the theological-liturgical meaning starting from the body, with the worship service and liturgy as the space where the whole theology of God's incarnation takes place as a symbolic, representing action.[22]

> Without the realism of the incarnation, the whole liturgy resembles a theater, a theater of bad taste, since, after all, going to the theater is something optional, while attending the liturgy is proclaimed as something obligatory. It is not by chance that in Latin America the concept of sacrament itself is so much ideologized at the service of the established order and reduced to a magical efficacy. If we do not take God's incarnation in Jesus seriously, then evidently all sacramental life will become only ritualism, rather than a sign and means of Christian liberation.[23]

The underlying critique is that, after the emergence of the printing press and modernity, the sacrament ended up becoming in many cases a simple reading of the ordo—that is to say, the ritual practice that birthed the ordo has been replaced by the ordo. In the case of Brazil, this clinging to the ordo and to tradition also reflects a certain Eurocentric colonial

---

21. Vannucchi, *Liturgia e libertação*, 16.
22. Baronto, *Laboratório Litúrgico*, 33.
23. Vannucchi, *Liturgia e libertação*, 40.

dependence, as indicated above. Thus the worship service becomes a disincarnate ritualism distant from life and concrete bodies.

To speak of concrete bodies means to shape liturgy from concrete bodies in the liturgy—bodies of women, adolescents, young people, Black people, Indigenous people, LGBTQ people, the elderly. Each body is expressed in the liturgy of the body of Christ from a particular or collective history, an experience of control or of permission, a feeling of fear or of desire.[24] The Experimental Seminar can help people not only to "learn how to perform the rite" (or to stage or establish a scene), but to learn while participating in a rite. This is the catechetical role of the liturgy, as described by Ione Buyst:

> The paschal mystery of Jesus Christ is celebrated with sensory signs that have necessarily to do with the human person's corporeity: encounters with brothers and sisters, greetings, embraces, spoken or sung prayers, listening to the reading of Scripture, singing of psalms, hymns, and songs, the Supper, bathing with water, anointing, . . . walking in a procession, kneeling down, sitting or standing up. These actions are actually symbolic because they link two realities, two persons—in this case, Christ and his people.[25]

For this reason, it was important to include a theater scholar in our Experimental Seminar. Theater and dramatic arts, besides having countless points of affinity with the liturgy,[26]—such as corporeal practices, spatial experiences, dramaturgical thinking, involvement of actors, and others—can be used not only as pedagogical resources, but to help one become aware of one's own life, of the body and its space in the liturgy. Performance is very important to us too. Not only does it have common bonds with rite, but "performance is basically a language of experimentation . . . aiming to liberate human beings from the ties that condition them and art from the commonplaces imposed by the system. . . . Performance deals in a ritual way with the basic existential questions."[27]

That is why a proposal from the Liturgical Laboratory, developed by a group of Catholic liturgists and reported in a book by Luiz Eduardo

24. Shoop, *Let the Bones Dance*, 2–5.
25. Buyst, *Como estudar liturgia*, 22.
26. On the relation between liturgy and theater, see Friedrich, *Liturgische Körpe*, and Meyer-Blanck, *Inszenierung des Evangeliums*. Studies that problematize the relationship between the holy and theater are Artaud, *Teatro e seu duplo*; Innes, *Holy Theatre*; Brook, *Teatro e seu espaço*; and Scheffler, "Características do sagrado."
27. Cohen, *Performance como linguagem*, 45.

Pinheiro Baronto, is important to us. The Liturgical Laboratory was an interesting and peculiar reference: "The Liturgical Laboratory consists in a technique that took up elements from two basic sources: the religious pedagogy of Hélène Lubienska de Lenval and the psychodramatic methods of Jacob Levy Moreno. In a later refinement of the experience, the holistic view was also used as a basis to re-signify the proposal."[28] The Experimental Seminar draws heavily from the Liturgical Laboratory's proposal, but the Seminar does not start from a particular liturgical element as the Laboratory does, but risks starting from the experience of daily life itself and explores bodily expression in itself, thus allowing for greater freedom in shaping the liturgical rite.

Another study underlying the Seminar is one by David Plüss on the worship service as text staging (*Textinszenierung*).[29] According to this study, the Protestant worship service is not just a discursive, communicational, and catechetical event, but also a performative, ritualistic, and representational one. In this respect its relationship with the theories of ritual, theater, and performance are thus very important. Plüss's study, however, focuses on observing the already existing Protestant worship as text staging, whereas our Experimental Seminar starts from the body of daily life, with performance and experimentation serving as a means to recreate and transform the worship service itself.

Inculturation and Postcoloniality

As described in the first section of this essay, worship services in Latin America and Brazil are characterized either as part of the program of Iberian colonization or as part of the maintenance of the ethnic identity of minority groups, as in the case of the German immigrants and the IECLB. In both cases the worship service, liturgical ordo, hymns, liturgical calendar, and worship space were transplanted to the Southern Hemisphere. Local cultures and daily life did not often enter liturgical agendas, which were often restricted to the translation of texts into local languages. Even liberation theology, which developed as a contextual theology closely connected to the local sociopolitical reality, mainly in

---

28. Baronto, *Laboratório Litúrgico*, 15.
29. Plüss, *Gottesdienst als Texinszenierung*, and Adam, "Liturgia e performance."

the biblical, systematic, and ecclesiological areas, dealt very little with liturgical issues, as if worship were unrelated to context.[30]

Driven to a large extent by the liturgical reform of the Second Vatican Council and the World Council of Churches, in the 1980s and 1990s the Brazilian Protestant churches started a process of liturgical renewal that enculturation would strongly impact. In the case of the IECLB, the studies on worship and culture by the Lutheran World Federation[31] were highly relevant to the process of liturgical renewal. There was an awareness of the negative effects of the "culture of the other," of the Northern culture perceiving itself as the standard culture and of its domination over local, autochthonous, Indigenous, African, and popular cultures. Inculturation is not enough; it is necessary to ask *how* to inculturate, *what* to inculturate, and *for what* and *for whom* to inculturate.[32]

Enculturation is a process through which the church's liturgy relates to and interacts with the local culture, allowing the gospel to become incarnate in the culture, life, and history of the liturgical community of a given time and place. The immediate goal of enculturation is enabling a congregation to have a worship service that reflects its culture so people can adequately hear and experience the gospel. What is enculturated is obviously the gospel of Jesus Christ. Lutherans believe this gospel comes to the church through concrete elements: the Word of God and the sacraments. These elements, inherited from a broad and long process of contextualization, become a "form" or "order" (ordo): Word, baptism, and Eucharist. Although the ordo results from this incarnational process—a process of enculturation—the ordo itself gets enculturated over and over again. In other words, enculturation starts from this already established ordo,[33] but does not see itself as something closed or final.

When the Experimental Seminar tries to establish contact with daily life and culture, it is to a large extent trying to shape an enculturated liturgy, which is sometimes difficult in historical churches that are still very much influenced by the colonial paradigm. Therefore, besides

30. Buyst, "Teologia e liturgia." Outstanding exceptions are the liturgies that took a different direction, such as those of Central America, the Misa Criolla (Creole Mass) in Argentina, and the Missa dos Quilombos (Mass of the Quilombos), Missa da Terra Sem Males (Mass of the Land without Evil), and the Romarias da Terra (Land Pilgrimages) in Brazil.

31. Lathrop, "Shape of the Liturgy," and Chupungco, "Two Methods of Liturgical Inculturation."

32. Adam, "Worship with a Brazilian Face," 240.

33. Lathrop, "Shape of the Liturgy," 67.

the exercise of enculturation, a new concept has entered the scene during the past decade: postcoloniality (or decoloniality) is a new way of perceiving local and global reality on the basis of its differences, subtleties, fragmentariness, alterities, ruptures, and social, cultural, sexual, political, and religious alternatives instead of only on the basis of what is already established and standardized.

> [S]peaking of postcoloniality means to challenge and deconstruct the dynamics of identification pursued by the colonial forces by exposing their own weaknesses through the heterogeneities inscribed in that subject, with the purpose of making visible the intrinsic bifurcations that characterize the global context, which enable its constant malleability, transformation, and openness to new forms of sociocultural construction.[34]

Thus, postcoloniality intensifies the gaze at culture, daily life, and the body, highlighting particularly those aspects that do not fit into the homogeneous standards of prevailing systems and absolute truths and are, for this reason, seen as weak, fragile, and vulnerable. This new gaze will have an effect on the enculturation of the liturgy, not only by seeking dialogue with the specificities and nuances of local cultures, but by thinking about the liturgy as a space of sociopolitical transformation, something that Claudio Carvalhaes calls the "liturgical turn."

> The liturgical turn continues with the traditioning, challenging interpretations, questioning not only liturgical thinking and church practices, but also its [sic] many orders, symbols, forms of liturgical creation, understanding of bodies and sexualities, vocabularies, uses of the Bible, liturgical resources, forms of access to holy things, relations to economics and other fields, and so on.[35]

THE EXPERIMENTAL SEMINAR: RITUALITIES —CREATIVE RESEARCH

Overview

The Experimental Seminar: Ritualities—Creative Research was held twice, both at Faculdades EST in São Leopoldo/RS, August 16–18, 2016 and May 2–4, 2018. Each time, around fifteen people gathered over

---

34. Panotto, *Religión, política y poscolonialidad en América Latina*, 34–35.

35. Carvalhaes, *Liturgy in Postcolonial Perspectives*, 8. Also of importance to liturgy are these works: Barros: *Celebrar o Deus da vida*; Jagessar and Burns, *Christian Worship*; and Lartey, *Postcolonializing God*.

three afternoons: the three organizing professors, groups of graduate students in theology (both master's and doctoral) at Faculdades EST, and non-academic participants—musicians, liturgists, ministers, and members of faith communities. Most participants were Lutheran, some were Roman Catholic, and there was a roughly equal number of men and women. What they had in common was their interest and involvement in rituality, Christian liturgy, church and liturgical music, and theater in academic research and/or practical congregational activities with the purpose of bringing worship and life closer together.

One of the seminar's premises is that it should start from practice, daily life, action, and movement rather than from texts and theologies. The seminar should be something experimental, constructed daily among the organizers and the participants. Thus, we had to create space and provide time for bodily movement, for expression, for feeling the body, and for experiencing how the body lives daily life and finds ways and gestures to express itself. We consider that human beings alienated from their bodies—bodies that are domesticated by society—are inserted into contexts of the Christian tradition where corporeity is often undervalued.[36]

A Closer Look

The work methodology has three parts: (1) practical experiments oriented toward "creative research," (2) developing a relationship with elements of the liturgy of Christian worship, and (3) moments of reflection on action, using as a reference previous knowledge and experience as well as studies on rituality, corporeity, theatricality, performance, and liturgy. In the first part, participants engaged in practical experiments, based on the bodily and relational disposition to or readiness for playful and creative action, through a somatic exploration of ritual gestuality, liberating it from both the representation of meanings and social or religious functionalism. In the second part, the participants took parts of the liturgy, related them to similar expressions in daily life and culture, and experimented with their execution through bodily expression and performance. In the last part participants discussed theoretical approaches to corporeity, rituality, and spatiality, and the experience was recorded, indicating possibilities for use in a congregation's worship liturgy.

---

36. There are at least three layers that must be considered as difficulties for Christian academic experimental work: overvaluing the spirit vis-à-vis the body; the excessively "serious" and functionalistic adult and academic context; and adult bodies that have been neglected and repressed over the years.

While not an exhaustive list, below are some of the primary realizations participants and organizers had as a result of the seminar's exercises:

1. *Practical experiments for becoming aware of one's body.* At the beginning of the seminar and of each session, participants worked with their bodies and with movement through exercises, dynamics, games, observation of their own bodies, interaction with other participants, and movement within the space, highlighting rhythm and perceptions of space, one's own body, and the bodies of others. Exercises are recapped and refined, and new exercises are introduced according to the group's need and readiness.

   At the beginning of the seminar, for instance, before spoken introductions, we propose to get to know each other through movement, encountering our own bodies and the bodies of others in a particular space. This is a special time for moving the body, perceiving it, and preparing it through simple stretching exercises and moving the articulations of the limbs, the spine, the hips. This initial moment already shows the participants' readiness, their physical limitations (such as spine problems, shoulder problems, limitations of stretching), and their level of social inhibition (perceived in the spontaneous comments made while moving, being observed, and observing others move).

   Continuing this initial moment or at the beginning of other sessions, the coordinator intensifies the exercises of perception and movement through bodily interaction with mutual back massages. Here again one can see sociocultural readiness or inhibition. Thus, the exercises help recover self-esteem, develop a broader awareness of the body, reflect on gender issues, and value certain parts of the body.

   Next, continuing what was done previously or at the beginning of another session, the coordinator helps the group perceive with greater attention the place of the seminar's work, creating a more relaxed attitude through exercises designed to make them familiar with the environment while continuing to awaken an ability to observe by strengthening individual and collective concentration. These exercises consist of walking around the room, observing the structures (the characteristics and state of the walls, ceiling, columns, windows, doors, and floor), the dimensions (length, height, depth), the luminosity, the furniture, the objects, and the empty areas. This may simply involve walking around the room, without any interaction among the participants and, according to each person's curiosity, touching surfaces and objects to better perceive them.

The coordinators were struck by the change that takes place when people deal with their bodies, with movement, with the other, and with the space as the exercises are executed. At the beginning one can see the participants reacting in a contained manner, laughing about unusual movements, and perhaps feeling ashamed of their own bodies, but later in the seminar one can see their enhanced ability to perceive themselves and others, a playful expression, and more explicit and conscious interaction. This development is very important for what comes next.

2. *Body, movement, and liturgy, or life in the liturgy.* Having participated in the bodily experimentation exercises, the second part of the program, which can be developed over one or more sessions, is designed to reflect on the rites related to a particular part of the worship liturgy. Here we put into practice one of the seminar's main goals: to think about liturgy and the worship service starting not with the ordo, the set of elements and forms, or from tradition, but with life itself, with the body.

At the first seminar, in 2016, we focused on the opening liturgy, specifically the welcome and greeting. In the large group, we reflected on rites and gestures surrounding the beginning of something. How do we begin something? Is it possible to go back after we begin something? These were two of the questions we raised. Refining the reflection, we talked about rites and gestures at the beginning of the year, at the beginning of a friendship, at the beginning of a theater play. When does the beginning begin? Does the play, for example, begin when the curtain is raised? What about the worship service? When and how does it begin? What are the bodily, physical, and temporal dimensions that are mobilized by the initial rites of our liturgies? In the case of Christian worship, we think that the trinitarian invocation or greeting, the sound and music of the bells and the prelude, the entrance of the liturgy team, the silent prayer in front of the altar or table by the person leading the liturgy, or the congregational gestures of standing up, silence, or welcome are rites that mark the beginning.

After this reflection, we broke into small groups. Each group was supposed to express in a bodily manner—making use of the various discoveries and experimentation of the previous moment and without using words—a moment of the worship service's beginning. Each group presented its performance; the others could comment. Then we brought the different expressions together in a larger rite. Concluding, we talked about how we might incorporate performance into the worship liturgy in our congregations.

The profound meaning of what we had done struck everyone. It was very simple but at the same time very meaningful. It had intensity of movement, coming close to poetic movement (Jacques Lecoq). We challenged participants to write down what we had done along with their own reflections.

Another liturgical rite that we explored in 2016 was the Eucharist. We wrote the word "Eucharist" on the blackboard and looked for terms associated with it, such as unity and communion (uniting), commensality (eating, drinking, smelling), thanksgiving (thanking), memory (remembering, reminding). In small groups, participants looked for a rite in daily life that represented one of those terms. Using the bodily experiences from earlier exercises, examples the rites of daily life were presented through bodily expression and without words (sounds were allowed).

After some preparation and experimentation, the groups presented small performances: going to the grocery store and preparing food (commensality); a *chimarrão*[37] service (communion and union); gestures of thanks by an artist after a performance (thanking); and looking through a photo album (memory). One can see how daily life and culture were relevant in these constructions. Next, we adapted the daily rites into a liturgical eucharistic rite. One of the questions we raised concerned the boundary between rite and daily life. The Eucharist is a meal (daily life and culture), but at the same time a rite, a liturgy (representative action).

In the 2018 seminar we dealt only with the liturgy of the Word, particularly Scripture readings. Bodily exercises and experimentation involving speech, reading, and discourse provided essential resources for this part. It was also important to note different kinds of discourse present in culture: political discourse, newscasts,

---

37. *Chimarrão* is a typical Indigenous tea drunk in southern Brazil.

graduation speeches, eulogies, and different forms of preaching, such as Catholic, Protestant, and Pentecostal discourses. Individually and in groups, we read Psalm 102 and Mark 7:24–30, creating "scores" for the readings to help interpret the content.

3. *Reflection on liturgical practice or the congregation's participation in the liturgy.* Just as each seminar and each session began with bodily movement, the seminar and each session ended with moments of reflection and recording of what we did and what it meant. Participants observed how much we are stuck in fixed structures and act according to patterns and how difficult it is to get out of what is established when celebrating the liturgy. It is very difficult to recover the essence of a rite without breaking with the rite itself, which is precisely what we were trying to do in the seminar. We also considered how to ensure that a liturgical rite or symbolic gesture is both special and related to daily life without becoming itself an empty ritual disconnected from daily life and culture.

We also wondered about the role of the liturgical tradition we received through colonization and migratory transplantation in our context. We asked to what extent tradition is dynamic and to what extent it is static. We concluded that every tradition only makes sense if it can be revived. Ângelo Cardita, for example, gave the example of singing hallelujahs. In the worship service we sing hallelujahs over and over again, sometimes even using the same song, and yet they have a different, present, and living meaning in each service. This reflection led us to the topic of enculturation and postcoloniality. The liturgy becomes alive and meaningful in people's lives when it is enculturated, becoming incarnate in the life of the worshiping community.

We also reflected on rites and their functions. Rites have to do with repetition and rhythm. They do not change easily. Their fixed structure gives freedom to those participating in them precisely because of the life contained in them. Based on J. Le Goff's observations, we discussed the mechanical elements of rites, the dynamic nature of gestures, and the poetic aspect of gestures and rites (the sacred, transcendent element that makes the rite a unique mystical experience). In this context, the worship service's functions of expression, guidance/orientation, affirmation, and integration

(Cornehl) and identity, distance, celebration, and feast (Lange) helped us in our reflection.

POSSIBILITIES FOR FUTURE LEARNING

It should be remembered that the seminar is experimental. It is not designed to teach time-tested and established practices, nor is it a workshop. Rather, it is a laboratory risk field in which—like all laboratories—every experimentation, although guided by previous studies, can fail. But this does not annul the possibility of learning. One fundamental element of our research would be delineated only at the moment participants met. We might have expected a certain group composition due to the venue (Faculdades EST) having theological students, most of them Lutherans, but the individual experiences, the views on liturgy, the degree of openness to novelty, and the physical and cultural readiness would only be presented when a group with its own dynamics was formed—that is, a congregation is defined by its specific collection of individuals and their personal relationships with themselves, with the divine, and with human alterity.

Generally, participants evaluated both editions of the seminar positively, and it was evident that the seminars' success depended on the willingness and openness of the cohorts. The evaluations can be summarized in four categories:

1. *The relation of the liturgy to daily life.* Participants noted that the seminar activities helped them better reflect on elements, gestures, and postures of daily life. They observed that the liturgy often seems to be something distant from daily life. One participant said, "Usually, in the worship services I don't get the meaning of what is done, nor is there a relation to what I take seriously in my life" (D). Another participant reinforced this idea: "It is important to reflect on the elements of daily life by relating them to the 'holy.' When talking about daily life, we feel freer. In the rite, we change our attitude and become more formatted. Through the reflection on daily rites, the seminar enabled us to discover other ways of making the liturgy."

2. *The body expresses itself and communicates in the liturgy.* Just as daily life is important to consider in liturgy, the body, physical contact, and movement are also important. Participants observed that we are not usually aware of our bodies in the liturgy. Particularly in

the Protestant realm[38] we are more concerned with words, with the content, than with the body, movement, and performance even though they also involve communication. As one participant put it, "We are usually concerned with what we're going to say and not with the body." Another participant noted that the body does communicate and especially the body of the liturgist invites worshipers to something. This should be better explored, he said, because "most often the liturgist doesn't invite with the body." A fundamental question for future seminars is that of how gender and race are reflected in the liturgy. We must include women and people of color in preparing and conducting future seminars.

3. *The liturgy is something to be experimented with.* One participant mentioned the importance of silence in the liturgy: "I realized how difficult it is for us to be silent in our liturgies." The seminar created space for experimentation. "When one experiments, one risks getting things right," someone else said. We have traditionally been afraid to experiment in the liturgy, as if it were not an appropriate space for experimentation. One participant said that in the seminar she felt she was doing something truthful, enabling her to have an experience of being present and giving her a feeling of lightness. In contrast, she said, "In individualistic society people are 'absent'; they are not involved in the rite." One participant realized that experimentation made a different liturgical hermeneutic possible: "We talked about the liturgy from our own point of view, from the point of view of the congregation, and not from the minister's point of view." The same person raised the question of whom the liturgy serves. The possibility of experimentation is the seminar's major contribution because through experimentation we realized that we do not always have to shape and celebrate the liturgy in the same way. It is easier to propose something when we experiment with possibilities.

4. *It will be difficult to take what we experienced in the seminar to congregational worship.* Although the seminar highlighted daily life, the body, and experience in liturgy, some participants acknowledged that it was a laboratory, something uncommon, and

---

38. This is different in Pentecostal churches, where the body is given more space and the liturgy is marked by the movement, dance, and expression of the whole person and community.

that it would be very difficult to take the experiences made there to regular worship services. As one participant put it, "What we experienced in the seminar was very cool. The experience with the Eucharist may not be taken to a parish Mass, but it could be taken to smaller groups, in the families, prayerful Bible reading, groups." It is important to emphasize that the seminar was not designed to provide a recipe for liturgy but to teach participants to incorporate something else into the rites that we already have.

The participants' evaluations corroborated our suspicions and also the goals of the Experimental Seminar: Ritualities—Creative Research: that daily life, culture, the body, and experience are interesting points of departure for ritual and liturgical reflection.

The experimental seminar is just that: an experiment. It emerged from wondering if liturgy could be more related to the life and culture of the congregation taking part in the worship service. Each participant tried to analyze this question from their particular context. As far as the IECLB is concerned, the seminar has a great potential for promoting liturgical renewal in the church by bringing the worship service closer to life and Brazilian culture. The next step will be trying it out in a congregation, with a liturgy team, or with a youth group.

BIBLIOGRAPHY

Adam, Júlio C. "Liturgia e performance entre representação e comunidação: um breve relatório." *Tear—Liturgia em Revista* 40 (2013) 3–8.
———. "Liturgical Formation, Liberation Theology and Latin American Culture." *Studia Liturgica* 47, no. 1 (2017) 1–13.
———. "Worship with a Brazilian Face." In *Worship and Culture*, edited by Gláucia Vasconcelos Wilkey, 239–61. Grand Rapids: Eerdmans, 2014.
Artaud, Antonin. *O teatro e seu duplo*. São Paulo: Martins Fontes, 1993.
Baronto, Luis Eduardo Pinheiro. *Laboratório Litúrgico: Pela inteireza do ser na vivência ritual*. São Paulo: Salesiana, 2000.
Barros, Marcelo. *Celebrar o Deus da vida: Tradição litúrgica e inculturação*. São Paulo: Loyola, 1992.
Bosi, Alfredo. *Dialética da Colonização*. São Paulo: Cia das Letras, 1982.
Brook, Peter. *O teatro e seu espaço*. Petrópolis, Brazil: Vozes, 1970.
Buyst, Ione. *Como estudar liturgia: Princípios de ciência litúrgica*. 2nd ed. São Paulo: Paulinas, 1990.
———. "Teologia e liturgia na perspectiva da América Latina." In *Eu sou o que sou*, edited by C. Favreto and Ivanir A. Rampon, 38–76. Passo Fundo, Brazil: Berthier, 2008.

Carvalhaes, Claudio, ed. *Liturgy in Postcolonial Perspectives: Only One is Holy.* New York: Palgrave Macmillan, 2015.
Chupungco, Anscar J. "Two Methods of Liturgical Inculturation." In *Christian Worship: Unity in Cultural Diversity*, edited by S. Anita Stauffer, 77–94. Geneva: LWF, 1996.
Cohen, Renato. *Performance como linguagem.* São Paulo: Perspectiva, 2013.
Cornehl, Peter. "Theorie des Gottesdiensts." *Theologische Quartalsschrift* 159 (1979) 178–95.
Friedrich, Marcus A. *Liturgische Körper: Der Beitrag von Schauspieltheorien und -techniken für die Pastoralästhetik.* Stuttgart/Berlin/Köln: Kohlhammer, 2001.
Heimbrock, H. G. *Gottesdienst: Spielraum des Lebens: Sozial- und Kulturwissenschaftliche Analysen zum Ritual in praktisch-theologischem Interesse.* Kampen and Weinheim: Kok and Deutscher Studien Verlag, 1993.
Igreja Evangélica de Confissão Luterana no Brasil. *Livro de Culto.* São Leopoldo, Brazil: Sinodal, 2003.
Innes, Christopher. *Holy Theatre: Ritual and the Avant Garde.* Cambridge: Cambridge University Press, 1981.
Jagessar, Michael, and Stephen Burns. *Christian Worship: Postcolonial Perspectives.* London: Routledge, 2014.
Kirst, Nelson. "Liturgia." In *Teologia prática no contexto da América Latina*, edited by Christoph Schneider-Harpprecht, 119–41. São Leopoldo: Sinodal/ASTE, 1998.
———. "Renovação litúrgicas: experiências recentes na IECLB." *Tear—Liturgia em Revista*, São Leopoldo, 24 (2007) 5–16.
Lange, Ernst. *Predigen als Beruf: Aufsätze zu Homiletik, Liturgie und Pfarramt.* 2nd ed. München: Kaiser, 1987.
Lartey, Emmanuel. *Postcolonializing God: An African Practical Theology.* London: SCM, 2013.
Lathrop, Gordon. "The Shape of the Liturgy." In *Christian Worship: Unity in Cultural Diversity*, edited by S. Anita Stauffer, 67–75. Geneva: LWF, 1996.
Lópes, César Márques. "Learning Empathy: Removing Lament from the Null Curriculum." In *Worship through Latin American Eyes*, edited by María Eugenia Cornou and Noel Snyder, 150–74. Eugene, OR: Cascade, 2026.
Maraschin, Jaci. *Da leveza e da Beleza: Liturgia e pós-modernidade.* São Paulo: Aste, 2010.
Méndez, Dinorah B. "Contextualizing Evangelical Worship within Mexican Religiosity." In *Worship through Latin American Eyes*, edited by María Eugenia Cornou and Noel Snyder, 106–30. Eugene, OR: Cascade, 2026.
Meyer-Blanck, Michael. *Inszenierung des Evangeliums.* Göttingen: Vandenhoeck/Ruprecht, 1997.
Panotto, Nicolás, *Religión, política y poscolonialidad en América Latina: Hacia una teología posfundacional de lo público.* Madrid/Buenos Aires: Miño y Dávila, 2016.
Plüss, David. *Gottesdienst als Texinszenierung: Perspektiven einer performativen Ästhetik des Gottesdienstes.* Zürich: TVZ, 2007.
Rössler, Dietrich. *Die Vernunft der Religion.* München: Piper Verlag, 1976.
Scheffler, Ismael. "Características do sagrado nas propostas teatrais de Antonin Artaud e Jerzy Grotowski." Master's thesis, Universidade do Estado de Santa Catarina, Florianópolis, 2004.
Schilson, Arno, and Joachim Hake. "Der christliche Gottesdienst ist zwar kein Kultdrama oder Theater, doch immer suchte und fand er seine eigene Form

auch in Transformation und Abgrenzung von beiden." In *Drama "Gottesdienst": Zwischen Inszenierung und Kult*, edited by Arno Schilson and Joachim Hake, 9. Stuttgart: Kohlhammer, 1998.

Schleiermacher, Friedrich. *Die Praktische Theologie nach den Grundsäzen der Evangelischen Kirche*. Berlin: O. Reimer, 1983 [orig. 1850].

Shoop, Marcia W. Mount. *Let the Bones Dance: Embodiment and the Body of Christ*. Emerging Theology Initiative. Louisville: John Knox, 2010.

Vannucchi, Aldo. *Liturgia e libertação*. São Paulo: Loyola, 1982.

von Allmen, Jean-Jacques. *O culto cristão. Teologia e prática*. 2nd ed. São Paulo: Aste, 2006.

Wainwright, Geoffrey. "Fundamentação sistemática-teológica." In *Manual de Ciência Litúrgica* 1., edited by H. C. Schmidt-Lauber et al, 104–35. São Leopoldo: EST/Sinodal, 2011.

White, James F. *Introdução ao culto cristão*. São Leopoldo: Sinodal, 1997.

SECTION II

Crossing Borders

SONGS FROM OTHER HEARTLANDS

Church Music in the Global South

MARCELL SILVA STEUERNAGEL

FROM NORTH TO SOUTH

In 1910, over twelve hundred representatives of various denominations, missionary societies, and mission boards met in Edinburgh, Scotland, to discuss strategies for evangelization on a global scale. According to Brian Stanley, "Many of the conference participants clearly shared the firm belief . . . that Christianity stood on the threshold of a global expansion of millennial dimensions."[1] The very fact that these delegates convened in Scotland to discuss the matter, coupled with the lofty rhetoric that set the tone for this World Missionary Conference, indicates how, in the minds of these participants, there was little question that Christianity must spread from North to South, and from West to East. All that was needed was a final push, says Stanley, to achieve the goal: "Through the redoubled missionary endeavors of the non-Roman churches of the west, the world was on the eve of a new transfiguration destined to inaugurate the kingdom of God in its fullness and glory."[2] For these delegates, the heartlands of Christianity spread across the

---

1. Stanley, *World Missionary Conference*, 2.
2. Stanley, *World Missionary Conference*, 2.

Euro-American axis.[3] However, the assumption that Europe and North America are the heartlands from which Christianity emanates to other parts of the globe no longer mirrors the demographic realities of its constituency. Christianity has moved south. This "North/South inversion"[4] has been a focus of investigation in theology and missiology, religious and cultural studies, diaspora studies, and ethnomusicology and congregational music studies. Within the context of this alteration, the question of how Christians in the Global South worship gains importance even as this new reality challenges Christian worship practices considered normative within the old paradigm. I approach this inversion from North to South from the perspective of the study of church music, asking: How has this shift changed the way worshiping Christians in the South see their own repertoires and worship practices in relation to their Northern counterparts? Amidst this change, how have negotiations of identity, culture, and belief led to the development of models of music ministry that "deviate" from Northern patterns? This essay investigates these questions, seeking to discern commonalities and contrasts in musical worship practices of Christians outside of the Euro-American axis in relation to their Northern counterparts.[5, 6]

3. This idea of the "heartlands" of Christianity is used by a number of scholars to denote a remote geographical center, from which the Christian faith and its missionaries are sent forth, that would retain the religious and cultural essence of Christian civilization.

4. I use the term "inversion" to point to the dual dynamic of shrinking numbers of self-identified Christians in the Global North even as statistics point to the growth of Christianity in the South. According to a 2011 report by the Pew Research Center, "In 1910, about two-thirds of the world's Christians lived in Europe, where the bulk of Christians had been for a millennium, according to historical estimates by the Center for the Study of Global Christianity. Today, only about a quarter of all Christians live in Europe (26%). A plurality—more than a third—now are in the Americas (37%). About one in every four Christians lives in sub-Saharan Africa (24%) and about one-in-eight is found in Asia and the Pacific (13%)" (Pew, "Global Christianity").

5. I use "Euro-American axis" to describe the historical fulcrum of Christendom, which includes Western Europe and, more recently, Anglo North America.

6. It is important to emphasize here that this analysis is not a hymnological analysis in two important aspects. The first is that hymnology as a discipline, especially within theology and historical musicology, has customarily gravitated toward the analysis of lyrics and written texts as the focus of religious music-making. My scholarly stance is to move away from the idea that the textual content of congregational song is its primary theological focus while other questions of performance and context remain secondary to comprehending the "meaning" of church music. While my conceptualization of the theological work that occurs through congregational singing does indeed include textual theological content, it also strives to recognize the multimodal nature of congregational music performances: musical styles, questions of embodiment (such

Although little has been written specifically about models of church music developing in the Global South and the ways in which these practices are serving congregations in their local contexts, scholars have examined the relationship between the inversion of the church's demographic epicenter and the impact of this transformation on mission and ministry.[7] Therefore, the first portion of this essay frames an investigation of worship practices in the context of this literature. The second half employs methods from the ethnographic toolkit,[8] particularly interviews, to investigate local realities. By comparing responses from selected worship leaders in the Global South (Brazil, India, Mozambique) with each other and with the aforementioned literature, I look for resonances and contrasts in the way these interviewees talk about their practices and models of worship as related to music ministry. I also point to the ways in which the contexts in which these leaders perform their roles influence said practices. But first, we turn to an account of the North/South inversion of Christianity.

---

as dance and expressive gestures), sociopolitical resonances and connections, modes of mediation, and others. Since this essay is an investigation of religious music-making in relation to worship practices in the Global South, I do not focus primarily on text-related theological questions, but on the structural and systemic shifts that surround, inform, and shape music-making in these contexts.

7. Throughout this essay I use expressions such as "inversion" and "reversal" to signify the shift of Christianity's numerical epicenter from the North to the South. This should not imply that Christianity has absconded from Europe or North America, but it does recognize the declining numbers reported by churches in these regions.

8. While I do recognize that ethnography, in its fullest methodological sense, relies on a careful combination of field-related research components such as observation and interviews, it must also be recognized that the use of ethnography has spread to many disciplines in the humanities that are beyond the clear boundaries of anthropology or sociology. At the intersection of ethnomusicology and church music scholarship, for instance, ethnographic methods are used to varying degrees and in a wide variety of methodological combinations. It is in this latter sense that the term "ethnography" is used here, in full recognition that to move from an initial advocacy of legitimacy for other heartlands as founts of Christian musics to a comprehensive study of these sources would require a much more structured and exhaustive type of ethnographic research. In other words, while conducting interviews certainly can fall within the purview of ethnography, interviews themselves are but one tool within the ethnographic toolbox and must be recognized as such.

"FROM THE WEST TO THE REST": CHRISTIANITY GOES SOUTH

Paul Borthwick narrates an encounter with an American missionary couple in Nigeria who expressed surprise at his connection to a local missionary agency instead of an American organization: "Our conversation revealed the differences between their paradigm and mine. They were sent by a US-based ministry that defined 'gospel-preaching churches' as non-Pentecostal and non-charismatic, male-led, emotionally quiet, hymn-singing and (implicitly) led by white missionaries."[9] For this couple, being American missionaries in Nigeria was a "package deal" that brought with it not only evangelistic aspirations but underlying assumptions about worship practices. I argue that this anecdote illustrates how the impetus for Euro-American missionary endeavors might be connected to the prescription of worship practices in the missionary field.[10] I offer here two considerations in an attempt to deconstruct some of these assumptions. These considerations will then frame our investigation of developing worship practices—in this case, particularly musical practices—in the Global South.

First, Borthwick's anecdote demonstrates a common dissonance, or tension, between the idea of the Christian faith as a civilizing force emanating from a heartland to "uncivilized," exotic lands, and the recognition of the diversity of worship practices in the global church that seem to resist homogeneity. In other words, what Borthwick describes is a potential "cognitive dissonance" between what missionaries might construe as appropriate worship practices for their fields of work and the expressions of piety that these cultural contexts afford. To account for this potential diversity, some of the scholarship addressing global expressions of the Christian faith has shifted towards an idea of world "Christianities." This change in language acknowledges, among other things, that "wherever Christianity has established roots, it has become a locus of musical expression" in terms of the unique theological, ecclesiological, and worship practices that develop in each locality in which the Christian faith takes hold.[11, 12]

---

9. Borthwick, *Western Christians in Global Mission*, 21.

10. I do not mean to suggest that this is true only in the case of modern Euro-American missionary efforts.

11. Reily and Dueck, *Oxford Handbook of Music and World Christianities*, 1.

12. The language of "Christianities" resonates with postcolonialist/decolonialist

The tension between terms like "Christianity" and "Christendom" highlights that these are more than general terms to describe the global church; they also reveal the way sectors of the church (along with its members, theologians, politicians, and musicians, to name but a few) think about themselves and their roles in space and time. Philip Jenkins, in *The Next Christendom*, recognizes that "for many modern readers, the term 'Christendom' carries undesirable implications. The English word 'Christendom' is archaic, and of its nature refers to a bygone era in which the Christian religion represented the central justification and organizing force of society."[13] Although Jenkins defends his use of the term, I argue that the term "Christianity," or even "Christianities," better expresses the kaleidoscopic variety of worship expressions and practices of Christians around the world. Thus, while the idea of Christendom aligns with a centrifugal narrative of Euro-American/Northern Christian missionary and cultural influence from heartland to fringes, or "from the West to the rest," I strive to recognize these myriad Christianities as a type of constellation instead of a central headquarters with satellite operations. This effort carries with it the need to better describe the diversity of church music practices around the world. From Latin America to Africa and throughout Asia, people worship in very different ways.[14] I argue that

---

stances of scholarship in the humanities that attempt to move away from pre-established narratives of Christian history and identity. Jenkins discusses the issue in the framework of "Christendom" versus Christianity (*Next Christendom*, 26–29). Rajashekar argues that "a Eurocentric reading of history tends to trace the story of Christianity from Paul to Philippi and to Rome and on across Europe to the conversion of Constantine and the barbarians. Seldom did such a reading look beyond Constantinople into Asia or pay attention to Christianity that looked neither to Rome nor Constantinople as its center" ("Lutheranism in Asia," 62). It is in this spirit of "paying attention" that many of these usages of "Christianities" are acknowledged. This is true not only of resources such as Reily and Dueck's *Oxford Handbook of Music and World Christianities* and Macmillan's *Christianities of the World* series, but also of academic programs. The University of Cambridge, for instance, features a research area called "World Christianities" (https://www.divinity.cam.ac.uk/researchareas/research-areas/wc#section-3), while the Divinity School at the University of Chicago recently sponsored an event called Global Christianities: New Directions for the 21st Century (https://divinity.uchicago.edu/global-christianities-new-directions-21st-century).

13. Jenkins, *Next Christendom*, 26. Jenkins's work continues to be one of the main sources in this conversation, along with the work of Lamin Sanneh.

14. I do not want to imply that there is no variety in Euro-American worship, but only that the variety mentioned goes beyond the purview of the normative typology of worship in the North, which can be characterized (at least from the perspective of tradition) by an emphasis on choral music, a strong presence of organ and keyboard as the preferred instruments of church music, and a preference for hymnody that arises

there is no reason why these worshipers should be burdened with the notion that their worship practices are, in a sense, "deviant" from those of a bygone heartland to which they might bear a historical or denominational/theological connection.

The second consideration is the role of the missionary as a "middleman" in the negotiation of what worship practices may or may not be considered acceptable for worship. Within narratives of Christian missions,[15] missionaries have played a crucial role in connecting headquarters and front lines in an entangled web of evangelistic efforts and the development of Western colonial networks.[16] For most of the history of modern Christian missions, the missionary has been a mediator and a cultural ambassador not only of a gospel, but also of the cultural baggage this gospel was fraught with even as it was introduced through missionary activity. Moreover, it appears that a large portion of church music around the world has been curated through these Northern missionary efforts. Hawn says:

> Though Christian song has been transmitted across language groups and cultures since the apostolic era, the first wave of global song in the modern era was the hymns that accompanied the European, and later the North American missionaries to the ends of the earth, translated into many languages and accepted broadly by the peoples of the world as sung expressions of the Christian faith.[17]

Here, C. Michael Hawn recognizes two vital dynamics. The first is that transmission of song is as old as the church itself and that cross-fertilization is part of the DNA of Christianity due to the missionary drive at the core of its theology. In other words, cross-pollination of worship practices will occur whether one wants it to or not. The second dynamic Hawn points to is that this Euro-American repertoire is the first "global"

---

from, or at least aurally fits within, the Euro-American canon of "classical" music and sounds according to commonly accepted Western standards of musical theory and performance practices.

15. One resource that investigates the development of the very concept of *missio dei* in connection with the entangled expansion of the West and its Christianity is Kollman, "At the Origins of Mission and Missiology." Kollman's work also provides nuance to the idea that colonial enterprise and missionary activity necessarily acted in collusion; he describes tensions between the European systematization of the missionary enterprise and the political interests of colonial projects.

16. Westhelle, *After Heresy*, xii.

17. Abbington, in Hawn, *New Songs of Celebration Render*, 209.

repertoire of the church thanks to these missionary efforts. The song of the church is intertwined with its history, and missionary endeavors leave sonic footprints on foreign beaches that are not erased when they leave. In this sense, "Top 10" selections from the Euro-American North linger in hymnals and song collections in the South; Luther's famous "Ein Feste Burg," for instance, has more than a dozen Portuguese translations still in use throughout Brazil.[18] But the demographic inversion of the church significantly alters this configuration and modifies the role and place of the missionary. For Hiebert, missionaries operating within this new reality are "in-betweeners" in a complex lattice of cultures, religions, churches, denominations, academy, and practice.[19] Hiebert steers away from the depiction of a missionary as an overseer sent by a central office with power to edit cultural expression, describing her instead as one intermediary within a web of social, cultural, and political interactions.

These two considerations shed light on the contrast between the reality of the church today and the one assumed by the participants of the World Missionary Conference in Edinburgh in 1910. The balance has shifted, as Jenkins states: "Christianity has in very recent times ceased to be a Euro-American religion and is becoming thoroughly global. . . . In 1900, the overwhelming majority of Christians were non-Latino whites; in 2050, non-Latino whites will constitute only a small subset of Christians."[20] Jan Pranger agrees, saying that "today, the majority of Christians live in Africa, Asia, and Latin America, and thus outside of what traditionally are considered to be the Christian heartlands of Europe and North America."[21]

What are the implications of this new reality for the worship practices of the church in general and for church music in particular? Ogbu Kalu affirms that "the growth of Christianity in the Global South, and in Eastern and Central Europe . . . have influenced global processes to scramble the old modes of Christian expressions, ministerial formation, theological education, and missionary structures and strategies."[22]

---

18. The dynamic I am describing here resonates with Bevans's "translation model" of contextual theology in *Models of Contextual Theology*, which in turn echoes Kaplan's "translation" mode of adaptation of Western Christianity to African idioms in *Indigenous Responses to Western Christianity*.
19. Hiebert, "Missionary as Mediator," 297.
20. Jenkins, *Next Christendom*, xi.
21. Pranger, "Lutherans in the World Church," 11.
22. Kalu, "Globalization and Mission," 35–36.

Kalu recognizes the many implications of this reversal because they affect the church's standard repertoire of responses, techniques, and methods for dealing with the complex interactions between Christ and cultures.[23] Another consequence of this dynamic is the reversal of missionary flows. James W. Aageson and Arland Dean Jacobsen suggest that in this new reality, "the flow of missionaries may well be reversed. As Lutheran churches in Europe and North America continue to lose membership, both Europe and North America themselves become mission fields."[24] If this flow is reversed, it follows that the cultural flows that accompany missionary endeavors can also change directions. This raises the question: how will practices from the Global South affect the music of the church in the North?

Furthermore, and in order to give further nuance to the three scenarios we describe here, an account of worship practices within the context of this reversal must consider two milestones: the establishment of the World Council of Churches (WCC) in 1948 and the impact of the Second Vatican Council beginning in the 1960s. The WCC afforded a platform on which the call for a truly global and ecumenical hymnody could be made, creating space for "the ecumenical wave" of the WCC's formation.[25] The proceedings of the Second Vatican Council further amplified this new configuration, impacting the music of the church more than its own proponents could have imagined. Marini suggests that the impact of Vatican II "exceeds in breadth and depth all other major reforms of the past, including the one attributed to St. Gregory the Great and the reform of the sixteenth century."[26] Regarding the music of the church, an important contribution of Vatican II was to "unleash" vernacular language in worship, setting in motion a process that became irreversible. E. Elochukwu Uzukwu, speaking about Catholic worship in Africa, states:

> Despite the hesitancy of the Church leadership and the slow movement toward African rites, indications are that there is no going back from the emergence of local liturgies in Africa. Certain key gestures in various African regions, thanks to the

---

23. These interactions appear to be, I argue, more complex than those described by H. Richard Niebuhr's typology in the mid-twentieth century (Niebuhr, *Christ and Culture*. See also Ottati, "'Christ and Culture'" and Yeager, "View from Somewhere").

24. Aageson and Jacobson, *Future of Lutheranism*, 4.

25. Hawn, *New Songs*, 210.

26. Pilcher et al., *Vatican Council II*, 2.

reforms of Vatican II, have become widespread all over Africa. These include the use of the vernacular language; the adoption of local liturgical hymnody accompanied by drums, gongs, and other native instruments, hand clapping, rhythmical swaying, and dancing; and the increasing visibility of local liturgical art and architecture. These elements have started to demarcate liturgical life in the African region.[27]

The further this irreversible process moves along, the more distance it affords for non-Western scholars and practitioners to analyze their previous modes of interaction with the Vatican (in the Catholic case) and with their Euro-American overseers (in the Protestant case). Muchimba, another African scholar, goes so far as to qualify the forced adoption of Western standards of music making on African Christians as "spiritual colonialism."[28] Carlos Mariátegui agrees: "The missionaries imposed not only the Gospel; they imposed the service, the liturgy."[29] In any case, the inevitability of these changes has transformed the way practitioners and theologians approach music-making in the church, as Uzukwu's critique demonstrates.

Today, the Christian religious landscape is different from that of the world that witnessed the establishment of Vatican II and the WCC, as Mark Noll describes: "The Christian church has experienced a larger geographical redistribution in the last fifty years than in any comparable period in its history, with the exception of the very earliest years of church history."[30] The consequences of this change, according to Noll, are these:

> The contemporary multiplicity of world Christianity reveals itself in a rainbow of variations throughout the world. . . . In a word, today's Christian situation is marked by multiplicity because of how deeply the Christian message, fully indigenized in local languages, has become part of local cultures. The new shape of world Christianity offers a mosaic of many, many varieties of local belief and practice. Immigration, the modern media, global trade and the ease of contemporary travel have stirred this mixture.[31]

---

27. Uzukwu, *Worship as Body Language*, 270–71.

28. Muchimba, *Liberating the African Soul*, 55.

29. My translation of Mariátegui, "Misioneros no impusieron el Evangelio; impusieron el culto, la liturgia," in *7 ensayos*, 144.

30. Noll, *New Shape of World Christianity*, 21.

31. Noll, *New Shape of World Christianity*, 26–27.

If Noll's description is accurate, scholars and disciplines interested in the study of religious music-making in general and of Christian worship in particular are faced with a new challenge. Previous models and practices of ministry—especially those configured within the previous North/South alignment of centrifugal flow, which might be dubbed "normative" models when the weight of missionary influence behind them is recognized—may be inadequate to address contemporary challenges in ministry and in scholarship. If new modes of cultural interactions (what Arjun Appadurai calls "new conditions of neighborliness"[32]) are the norm, these previous models may not adequately address these global realities. Moreover, it is almost certain that new practices will also affect the music of the church in the North in the future. As Kalu observes,

> This inculturating potential cautions us against homogeneity because hearers interpret with the lenses of their indigenous worldviews. Such a perspective privileges indigenous agency: the initiative and creative responses by local actors. Third-world contexts are not a tabula rasa on which foreign culture—extra space bearers—wrote their scripts. Hidden scripts abound at the level of infrapolitics.[33]

If there is no *tabula rasa*, these traditional models, when applied in a context radically different from their own, elicit fresh connections due to local actors, different modes of mediation, and infrapolitical dynamics unforeseen at their points of origin. This is what Peter Vethanayagamony argues:

> Christianity was once the religion of the confident, technologically advanced, and rising affluent, and sometimes those things were seen as a mark of God's favor. Christianity, now increasingly, is associated mostly with rather poor people and with some of the poorest countries on earth. Just like the Pauline mission, their mission is powerless in worldly terms and therefore dependent on the Holy Spirit. It not only lacks economic and political might; it also lacks the big organizational structure of the modern missionary movement.[34]

What happens when the "big organizational structure" Vethanayagamony describes is removed? Such transformations modify the role

---

32. Appadurai, *Modernity at Large*, 29.
33. Kalu, "Globalization and Mission," 31.
34. Vethanayagamony, "Mission from the Rest to the West," 65.

of music in the worshiping life of the church because the context of the church is itself different. In the same vein, Jenkins relativizes Northern approaches to dealing with culture: "Because of the long Western dominance of Christianity, debates over faith and culture often focus on attitudes to specifically European matters. . . . The more we look at the Christian faith in its European guise, though, the more we can see this too represents a kind of inculturation, albeit an old-established example."[35] His words attest to the fragmentation of this connection between Euro-American culture and increasingly autonomous religious landscapes around the world.

Thus, as the church moves south and grows in unexpected directions, new challenges must be addressed from fresh perspectives. Jenkins argues that "much of the most spectacular Christian expansion in recent decades has occurred not within either the Protestant or Catholic realms but in new independent denominations."[36] These new independent denominations contrast significantly with "older groupings." In fact, even within these traditional holdings, the music of the church is changing. Understanding how churches in the Global South—albeit significantly different from each other—deal with the challenge of developing local expressions of worship and models of ministry as they negotiate particular mixtures of new and old religious scenarios becomes crucial not only for these congregations, but also for churches in the North who seek to address issues of diversity, multiculturalism, and changing demographics in relation to their own worship practices.

The aforementioned comparisons can be used to investigate changes on a global scale. In the next section, the three local realities that we glimpse through our interviews of Global South communities can help practitioners and scholars think about larger shifts in the worship practices of the church at large, even if local realities differ radically amongst themselves. Jenkins argues that "it is not absurd to compare churches in very dissimilar societies, provided that they share significant features that distinguish them from the traditional Christian heartlands. . . . Christians in the newer churches operate on assumptions very different from believers in the United States or Germany."[37] In order to understand the nature of these changes, we now turn to three accounts of musical worship practices in three different continents.

35. Jenkins, *Next Christendom*, 136.
36. Jenkins, *Next Christendom*, 76.
37. Jenkins, *Next Christendom*, 9.

PORTRAITS OF WORSHIP FROM THE GLOBAL SOUTH

Three scenarios are presented here, each from a distinct corner of the Global South: Brazil, India, and Mozambique. These research sites share several commonalities even as they are distinct from one another. While all of them are removed from the traditional Euro-American heartlands of Christendom, each of these bears connections to the North. The respondent from Mozambique was trained at a Bible college in Asia with ties to the American nondenominational church-planting movement; the Indian worship leader identifies his church as nondenominational with an evangelical stance;[38] and the Brazilian respondent hails from a church with historical ties to European Evangelical and Reformed traditions. Consequently, all of these worshiping environments have some kind of connection with, broadly speaking, Protestant traditions.[39] It is important to acknowledge how these connections may have helped to shape the worship practices in each of these contexts. In addition, these scenarios offer a glimpse into how nontraditional influences also begin to shape worship practices: the respondent from Mozambique speaks of the influence of Brazilian worship practices, reflecting missionary endeavors in the South that do not necessarily pass through the Euro-American axis (at least not directly), and the Indian respondent mentions Christian contemporary worship music celebrity Chris Tomlin, demonstrating a new flow of influence in the study of church music: that of influences mediated through mass media, mainly through digital means.

I conducted a written interview with a worship leader in each of these scenarios. The questions in the interview centered around the practice and theology of music in the life of the church, practical and logistical

---

38. It is important to distinguish his use of "evangelical" from American Evangelicalism (see next footnote). In this regard, when I refer to American Evangelicalism, I do so with a capital "E" to distinguish it from other forms of evangelicalism in the global south.

39. I refer to "Protestant" traditions instead of "evangelical" traditions for two reasons. First, it allows for the many ways in which Pentecostal worship practices have also contributed to some of these cases. That influence appears more explicitly in the Mozambican case because of its connection to the American Evangelical nondenominational tradition. The worship practices of the Brazilian Lutherans in this study could also be described as "Luthercostal"; while they recognize the Lutheran tradition, they also incorporate swaying, hand-raising, and other practices that do not typically fit into the North American description of mainline Lutheran worship. Second, it is therefore crucial to understand that, even when these interviewees refer to evangelicalism, they are not referring to North American Evangelicalism but to their own constructions of what it means to be evangelical in their worship.

considerations of music ministry, and questions about the philosophy of church music that grounded each of these practices. Other questions investigated their relationship to Northern missionary efforts in their countries and to global Christianity. All three responded to the same set of written questions, and these original interviews were complemented with follow-up communication via email or social media.[40]

The first interview was with a female worship leader in her thirties. Located in the very south of Brazil, hers is a century-old Lutheran congregation with roots in the German tradition introduced to Brazil via nineteenth-century immigration.[41] The congregation has a strong musical program in both traditional and contemporary styles. The second interviewee was a male worship leader in Bangalore, India. He serves on the pastoral team of a nondenominational congregation within India's evangelical tradition and has historical ties to Northern missionary efforts. His is an urban congregation that negotiates traditional Indian and modern Western influences in worship; the worship leader mentioned jazz, grunge, and sitars in his interview. The final interviewee is a male worship leader in Mozambique, a national pastor of his denomination with oversight over the musical practices of several local congregations. Serving at a church planted through Brazilian missionary efforts, he has developed a ministry that is intentionally moving toward African expressions of worship. This church places itself within the Pentecostal tradition and has ties to American-influenced church planting movements in Asia.

Overall, these respondents acknowledged the global changes scholars describe. All interviewees agreed that Christianity is more diverse than it was a century ago, and they recognized the connection between these transformations and relevant themes in scholarship such as globalization, the rise of communication technologies and the information revolution, and mass media. Nonetheless, some changes are unique. The Mozambican worship leader, for instance, describes how previously "faith was taught as a lifestyle and not as an instrument of material possession."[42] This is a reaction to the conflation of charismatic

---

40. I am personally familiar with two of the three scenarios (India and Brazil), having participated in services at these two churches myself. In the Mozambique case, I depended upon extra details and clarifications from the interviewee and from another ethnomusicological sources familiar with the context.

41. For more on this history, see Steuernagel, "Church Music through the Lens of Performance."

42. Email interview with author, March 23, 2017. All translations from Portuguese are mine.

expressions and prosperity theology prevalent throughout the African continent. Comparing the results of these three interviews with each other and with the scholarly commentary addressed in the previous section highlights a series of connections. Four resonances stand out, all related to worship practices and the models of church music ministry ancillary to these practices. In some cases, these resonances fragment into contextual particularities of each case, but they are all connected by similar constraints, as we shall see.

The first resonance is the volunteer nature of worship practices in these contexts. In all scenarios, volunteers supply most of the music for worship. In the Brazilian case, the worship leader describes how "at present, all musicians are volunteers except for me and the choir director."[43] In the case of Mozambique, the interviewee works to recruit, train, and pastor musicians for the local church, all volunteers. In the Indian scenario, the same pattern occurs. Moreover, when financial investment in music ministry does happen, it goes toward hiring people who can develop and leverage volunteer networks; in other words, the focus is not on "pay to play" but on multiplying (in many cases scant) resources in a way that enhances community life and creates integration between belonging and service. I suggest that this reflects the financial challenges of most churches in the Global South—a challenge echoed in the literature and to which we will return in this essay as the issue of resources comes to the fore through the interviews.

A second resonance among interviewees is the emphasis on a broad spectrum of participation in the musical worship practices in these congregations, featuring participants with different levels of musical ability and from different generations. The Indian worship leader says he has both "working professionals and students on the team."[44] Moreover, in the Brazilian scenario, there seems to be an intentionality behind this intergenerational environment: "Working with different instrumental groups helps in the musician's learning process and puts older and more experienced musicians in contact with younger players, an exchange that I consider important." This variety applies both to musical ability/training and experience. While none of these churches offers a formal avenue for musical training, education is tied to ministry work. The Brazilian leader illustrates how these processes

---

43. Email interview with author, March 21, 2017. All translations from Portuguese are mine.

44. Email interview with author, March 15, 2017. Interview conducted in English.

of involvement in ministry can develop organically: "On account of my artistic aptitude, one of the first things with which I got involved in the context of our local congregation were the choir and leading worship. Based on this experience, I went on to discover a calling that became my profession." The narrative in India was similar:

> I first got involved when as a young boy. I was called out of Sunday School to play the guitar for the hymns in church. This was a new church and I was the only musician available! I always tell people . . . I learned how to play the guitar in church! I have zero musical education. Completely self-taught. I play by ear. In the early years of my guitar playing, I would play alongside my uncle in church. His guitar would be plugged in, but mine wasn't. I would watch his finger formation, as he played different chords, and would go home and try the same.

In these accounts, learning happens in the process of making music. Nevertheless, even as this pedagogy of "learning by doing" is valued, there is recognition that further development is required, and in fact specialized education is needed to further ministry development: "I don't usually teach music classes anymore," says the Brazilian leader. "There is no time for it, and near our church, in a five-block radius, there are two good music schools to which I recommend students." For her, members of the worship ministry need to learn both on and off the platform. This description points to an outsourcing or complementarity of music education, which still happens in integration with practice in church. In other words, the introduction to music-making and practical experience with worship happens in the church, while specialized training may (and, by the tone of interviewees, should) occur elsewhere.[45]

A third cluster of resonances arises here that fragments into particularities connected to how these churches negotiate missionary influence and/or the influence of Northern/Western models of ministry and worship practices. Analyzing these portraits can help us understand how these negotiations happen. In the case of the Mozambican church, there is a strong connection between the planting of the church by Brazilian missionaries and the establishment of a music ministry, illustrated by the Mozambican leader's account of his path to ministry: "I got involved in music ministry because of a Brazilian missionary . . . that was part of

---

45. I would further suggest that increasingly this education also includes an online component, such as tutorial videos on YouTube, instead of formal music education environments. Again, financial restrictions come into play.

the mission team that came to plant the church of which I am a member today." While this missionary connection is in effect a "horizontal" one between countries in the Global South, the causal relationship between the missionary effort and the worship expression of the church mirrors other discourses that describe the influence of the Euro-American church on its southern affiliates. As this leader describes it, "the [music] ministry was initially developed by Brazilian missionaries, and because of that we adopted a style of music that was typically Brazilian, along with Hillsong." But he goes on, stating:

> Later, following the advice of other musicians, also foreigners [along with ethnodoxologists], we saw the need to go back to an Afro style of music, which currently accounts for nearly sixty percent of the music sung in church. This has brought greater understanding of the gospel and the person of Christ for all ages and, consequently, greater involvement by the church in worship and spiritual development, including the gradual growth of the church.

Therefore, even as the worship leader recognizes this missionary connection, he contrasts Euro and Afro styles in discourse and emphasizes the need to develop an African expression of worship. Similarly, just as Uzukwu and Muchimba describe the "moving away" from Tridentine worship practices in the post-Vatican II Catholic case of African churches, the Mozambican worship leader describes a process of separation that occurs through intentional experimentation. This example in turn illustrates Hawn's idea that cultural exchange in the Christian church is as old as the church itself and continues to occur today as it did in previous times.

This contrast between Euro and Afro styles is paralleled in the Indian case, located as it is within the ancient cultural heritage of the Indian subcontinent. Here, a tension between East and West surfaces. The Indian worship leader tells how

> a lot of us who have grown up in urban India, especially the bigger cities, have a strong Western music influence/upbringing. I grew up listening to my dad play his jazz LPs. I didn't know any other music as a child! While the Indian film industry was churning out hits that would sweep the country, many Christian families would not even watch Indian movies (or any movies, for that matter!), so I was not exposed to this kind of music. It was only when I left India in 1993 for higher studies as a 22-year-old [that] I started appreciating Indian culture and

music. . . . If you walked into my dorm room in the Philippines, you would smell incense and hear sitars (whenever I was taking a break from Pearl Jam and Soundgarden!). But the common musical language in our particular church is Western music. We will do a few Hindi and other regional language songs now and then, but it's mainly Western worship music.

. . . However, we have a wide variety of music. . . . We still do the old traditional hymns, [and] we mix some of the older choruses with the newer songs of today. We try to choose songs that have lyrical depth and are not just mournful, superficial love songs to God, where the focus is more on the person than God![46]

I feel that because I have a stronger Western musical influence and upbringing than most people in my congregation, those who enjoy music in regional Indian languages might be missing out, because that means stepping out of my comfort zone, which I don't do too often when it comes to music in church. A lot of us also rely only on the West for new worship songs . . . [even though] there is so much amazing talent within India.

A tension surfaces between the underlying sense of obligation the leader experiences towards congregants who prefer a more indigenous style of worship, who "enjoy music in regional Indian languages," and the Western influence pervasive especially in India's urban centers.

Overall, the negotiation over foreign and indigenous styles of worship in these churches seems to crystallize into poles: one of similarity/integration, and the other of contrast/differentiation. These ministries navigate the tension in varied ways, but the tension is there and must be dealt with through intentional shifts, as in the case of the Mozambican church, or by piecing together different repertoires from different traditions, as in the Indian case. The Brazilian worship leader, on the other hand, described significant integration between foreign and domestic styles of music. Her use of Brazilian music seems to be connected to practical pastoral concerns,[47] and her considerations related to the vocal properties of Portuguese, which call for a nasal quality and different melismatic patterns than English. Toward this goal of integration, she

46. This critique by the Indian worship leader appears to echo a common trope against "bad" contemporary worship music—namely, that the lyrics of much of this repertoire tend to be more repetitive and less substantive than the texts of classic Euro-American hymnody.

47. Follow-up conversation with author, March 25, 2017.

spends significant time curating repertoire, attending to considerations of language and song in her particular context of worship, and investing financially in a vocal coach that helps her to model this integration in performance practice.[48]

A fourth resonance appears as these leaders describe their challenges in the areas of recruitment and training for worship ministry. We have examined the issue of musical education, but this challenge also relates to theological education needs in these contexts. The first challenge appears in the tension between a congregation's regular need for music and the inconsistency/unavailability of its volunteer base, the first resonance we encountered: "I believe the greatest difficulty is in working with people who are serving on a volunteer basis," the Brazilian worship leader said. "It is not always possible to rely on a volunteer's faithfulness. Besides, the lack of musical education in schools in general hampers the recruitment of musicians, along with the idea that 'if it is done from the heart,' God will accept anything." This description expresses the trope of lack of resources in all interviews but amplifies the issue: it is not only finances, but a lack of education that creates difficulties for participation in music ministry.

In other words, financial constraints, musical education, and theological education all connect to create specific challenges for church music ministry. The need for theological education is connected to the scarcity of financial and educational resources, which condition and shape local worship practices in various ways. The Mozambican worship leader mentioned the need for continuing education:

> The main difficulties I encounter in the development of my ministerial goals on a local level is the lack of books and other literature.... The greatest challenges for the development of church music in my country is the lack of well-trained musicians with the availability to travel to many parts of the country, especially because of the absence of financial resources and transportation capabilities for extended trips. In addition, the lack of books or manuals/brochures about contextualized music and Biblical worship [is a difficulty].

While these changes may appear unique to the Mozambican context, opinions on the need for musical and theological education seem to depend on the ecclesiology of the congregation. The Indian worship

---

48. For more on this integration, see Steuernagel, "Church Music through the Lens of Performance."

leader connected the church's theological stance to its ecclesiological organization:

> We are nondenominational, but evangelical in our stance. We don't have one pastor in charge, but rather a pastoral team. I am a part of this team, and I am responsible for the music. I wouldn't call myself a "worship pastor" because worship is not only the four or five songs we do during the first half of the service. Worship is life.

For the Brazilian worship leader, the connection between education and the church's needs is configured differently: "Musical education is foremost in order for any activities to be well-performed, so that the congregation doesn't get confused during our celebrations. While musical education deals with form, theological education deals with content." When set against the backdrop of Lutheran theology and ecclesiology, the educational and congregational focus of her comments reveals her theological alignment. In the Mozambican church, theological and musical training are connected:

> In my opinion, musical and/or theological education for those involved in the music ministry of my church is important because it not only guarantees greater comprehension of a Biblical music ministry, but also assures greater development of the musical skill (singing and playing) and guarantees continuity for new musicians so (they) can contribute with greater textual understanding (both of music and of God's Word) and instrumental [in the sense of musical instruments] to the development and edification of the church.

In the Indian church, however, a different perspective translates into different requirements for participants in the ministry:

> I believe a strong walk with Jesus and a passion for music with a decent level of musicianship is what is most important. I do not consider myself theologically or musically trained, but I believe I still have a positive influence not only over the musical growth of my team, but also their walk with God. So no, I don't think theological and musical education is essential. We don't use song sheets, chord sheets, etc. We jam, man. I believe God loves it when we jam for Him!

I suggest that, in this case at least, another factor comes into play: classical Indian music, whether Hindustani or Carnatic, values improvisation as an essential skill. Thus, the idea that "God loves it when we jam for Him" connects easily to the larger culture as well as to the ethos of Western pop/rock, both of which tend to favor improvised expressions over through-composed, notated music (albeit in extremely different ways).

These local congregations, spread out as they are on the map, reflect how Christianity's shift to the Global South has created room for worship practices that may diverge from any construed normative northern practices, such as a preference for through-composed musical forms,[49] even as they call attention to the complex interactions between missionary legacy and action, cultural, social and political considerations, and other factors that affect how congregations worship. While a comprehensive investigation would have to consider many other scenarios and impel methodological considerations toward full ethnography, a few considerations can be outlined here through the correlation between literature and interviews.

CONCLUSION: MANY HEARTS, ONE SONG

The first section of this essay investigated ways in which the church's move southward has implications for the worship practices of congregations both in the Northern and Southern hemispheres, bringing to the fore questions that arise from this North/South inversion as the main focus of this investigation. In the second section, glimpses into local realities of church practices were compared to each other in the context of this southward shift. Finally, in lieu of a typical conclusion, I offer here four considerations that point toward further study, contributing to scholarly conversations and practical experimentations around questions of how to strengthen worship practices.

First, I suggest that Christian worldviews are shaped by the culture that surrounds them even as they influence that culture, both in terms of theological thought and ecclesiological practice. Such a claim derives from previous conversations in contextual theology, such as Stephen Bevans's argument that "reality is not just 'out there'; reality is 'mediated by meaning,' a meaning that we give it in the context of our culture or our historical period, interpreted from our own particular horizon and in

---

49. Hawn suggests this connection in "Sequential and Cyclic Musical Structures and Their Use in Liturgy."

our own particular thought forms."⁵⁰ It is a claim that resonates with the cases examined here and with Jenkins's conclusion that "as Christianity moves southward, the religion will be comparably changed by immersion in the prevailing cultures of those host societies."⁵¹ This is certainly the case in our ethnographies in terms of intentional strategies, such as the shift to Afro styles in Mozambique and the integration of German heritage and local musical styles in the Brazilian case, both of which describe voluntary tweaks to the worshiping life of these congregations directly related to context. Furthermore, these interconnected dynamics of change also occur unintentionally, as these congregations enact adaptations to context that are not always preconceived and can seem minute, but that slowly mutate their worship into unique expressions of faith.

Second, I point out that financial and logistical shortcomings effectively undermine traditional music ministry practices such as large, well-equipped rehearsal spaces and choral libraries, which have been normative modes of developing musical worship practices (at least in part) in mainline Protestant denominations in the North. Furthermore, because most of the educational capital in these areas remains within the Euro-American context, there is a gap between the educational, financial, and logistical needs of these congregations and the availability of resources. Noll describes how most of the scholarship drive in theology remains within the educational systems of the North.⁵² Craig Ott outlines several hindrances to what he calls a "level playing field" for global theological work, including the fact that because non-Western theologians "rarely have the financial resources" to participate in international theological conversations, they "generally have less opportunity to reflect, research, write, consult, and participate in theological dialogue."⁵³ Based on the cases analyzed here, I argue that the same is true in relation to the development of worship practices in Global South congregations, especially if this development—as is the case with music-making—requires investments in education, rehearsal and performance spaces, audio and video equipment, and other needs. As we will see, all respondents mentioned financial limitations as a main deterrent to further development. The tension these authors describe emphasizes the dissonance between contexts where Christianity is growing and the traditional centers that still retain

50. Bevans, *Models of Contextual Theology*, 4.
51. Jenkins, *Next Christendom*, 7.
52. Noll, *New Shape of World Christianity*, 28.
53. Ott and Netland, *Globalizing Theology*, 310.

the majority of financial and intellectual capital. This contrast is sure to come to the fore as these issues are negotiated on a global scale.

Third, I argue that worship practices of the Global South are impacted by theological variations of increasing order and intensity. This is an irreversible process that feeds back into itself because of the interconnectivity of global communications and the increasing diversity of the church. Noll says, for instance, that "global South Christians retain a strong supernatural orientation and are by and large far more interested in personal salvation than in radical politics," compared to their Northern counterparts.[54] Jenkins further observes that "these trends must make us think carefully about the character of what we consider normative or typical Christianity. Not just is the 'normal' Christian in the modern world no longer Euro-American; she is unlikely to bear much resemblance to American mainline Protestantism."[55] How do Christians worship within the environments that Jenkins and Noll are describing? The intentional management of intergenerational musicians in Brazil and the improvisatory nature of congregational worship in India are musical responses to particular contexts. In short, diversity becomes the norm instead of the exception.

Fourth, I emphasize that the ways in which these practices may influence Christianity on a global scale, particularly when these influences feed back into the North, are relevant to this discussion of worship practices. Asian scholar Pongsak Limthongviratn argues that "the perpetuation of a Western view is often irrelevant to Asian cultures."[56] Jenkins articulates this position even further:

> If in fact the bulk of the Christian population is going to be living in Africa, Asia, or Latin America, then practices that now prevail in those areas will become ever more common across the globe. This is especially likely when those distinctive religious patterns are transplanted northward, either by migration or by actual missions to the old imperial powers, to what were once the core nations of world Christianity. When we look at the Pentecostal enthusiasm of present-day Brazil, or the indigenous

---

54. Jenkins, *Next Christendom*, 9.
55. Jenkins, *Next Christendom*, 10.
56. Limthongviratn, "Focus and Issues in the Lutheran Church in Asia Now and Tomorrow," 54.

churches of Africa, then quite possibly we are getting a foretaste of the Christianity of the next generation.[57]

Aageson and Jacobson echo Jenkins's and Limthongviratn's views, speaking from within a particular denominational stance:

> As Lutheranism becomes more fully indigenized in the Two-Thirds World, their worship and music will evolve, and their creativity will enrich North American worship and music. Through worship and music, East and West, North and South are inching closer to one another.[58]

Such diversity will only increase as religious organizations in the Global South bypass the North in partnerships (as in the Mozambique-Brazil connection), theological reflection, and ministerial practices. Ott describes these transformations:

> Political, technological, and economic globalization is making local cultures increasingly interconnected and interdependent. A locality is rarely monocultural and may even reflect an amalgam of premodern, modern, and postmodern worldviews. This means that even specific local theologies have much more in common with one another.[59]

These commonalities will not necessarily reflect Western paradigms and may arise on alternative axes. As we have seen in Mozambique, new influences will not necessarily be North American or European, but will continue to surface even as other countries, such as Brazil, increase the number of missionaries they send into the South *and* into North America and Europe.

In conclusion, I agree with Jenkins when he argues that the attempt to force models aligning with traditional assumptions of missionary work will most likely be met with disapproval in the Global South: "Churches that try and enforce practices from 'back home' on unwilling locals are going to be displaced by more flexible groups. Adaptation as such is essential and attracts little criticism, so long as the fundamental truths of a faith are not compromised."[60] Further research is needed to understand the impact of these changes on Christian worship practices

---

57. Jenkins, *Next Christendom*, 134–35.
58. Aageson and Jacobson, *Future of Lutheranism*, 3.
59. Ott and Netland, *Globalizing Theology*, 313.
60. Jenkins, *Next Christendom*, 135.

on a global scale; research can add to decolonialist perspectives that go beyond the practical temptation to provide "resources" to these churches in the South that are merely diluted replications of Northern strategies. The conversation (both practical and scholarly) around the worship practices of world Christianities must mature to move beyond "how-to" manuals for developing ministry and local practices toward the recognition of the increased order of complexity that the many scholars cited here point to. New problems must be identified and addressed, such as the ethical and theological conundrums that come wrapped in transnational worship projects; problems of translation, theological meaning, and framing in a digitally multilingual and mediated world; and the complexity of musical and religious cross-pollinations that characterize global cultural flows today. What is clear is that stock responses to these burgeoning challenges will not be sufficient to address the needs of local churches even if these techniques have been effective in the past, partly because they cannot contribute to conversations that want to move beyond standard colonial narratives of missionary efforts in order to understand changes in the church today. Thus, scholarly investigation becomes even more essential to the future of worship practices in a world that experiences multifarious expressions of Christianity, themselves a result of the missionary efforts of those based in "traditional heartlands" of Christendom. These supposed traditional heartlands cannot in good conscience—and must not—establish any kind of liturgical, theological, or expressive normativity for churches in other heartlands.

BIBLIOGRAPHY

Aageson, James W., and Arland Dean Jacobson, eds. *The Future of Lutheranism in a Global Context*. Minneapolis: Augsburg Fortress, 2008.

Appadurai, Arjun. *Modernity at Large: Cultural Dimensions of Globalization*. Minneapolis: University of Minnesota Press, 1996.

Bevans, Stephen B. *Models of Contextual Theology*. Rev. and expanded ed. Faith and Cultures Series. Maryknoll, NY: Orbis, 2002.

Borthwick, Paul. *Western Christians in Global Mission: What's the Role of the North American Church?* Downers Grove, IL: InterVarsity, 2012.

Hawn, C. Michael. *Gather into One: Praying and Singing Globally*. Grand Rapids: Eerdmans, 2003.

———, ed. *New Songs of Celebration Render: Congregational Song in the Twenty-First Century*. Chicago: GIA, 2013.

———. "Sequential and Cyclic Musical Structures and Their Use in Liturgy." In *Gather into One: Praying and Singing Globally*, 224–40. Grand Rapids: Eerdmans, 2003.

Held, David, Anthony G. McGrew, and David Goldblatt. *Global Transformations Politics, Economics, and Culture*. Cambridge: Polity, 1999.
Ingalls, Monique Marie, and Amos Yong, eds. *The Spirit of Praise: Music and Worship in Global Pentecostal-Charismatic Christianity*. University Park: The Pennsylvania State University Press, 2015.
Jenkins, Philip. *The Next Christendom: The Coming of Global Christianity*. 3rd ed. New York: Oxford University Press, 2011.
Kalu, Ogbu, Peter Vethanayagamony, Edmund Chia, and Chicago Center for Global Ministries, eds. *Mission after Christendom: Emergent Themes in Contemporary Mission*. 1st ed. Louisville: Westminster John Knox Press, 2010.
Kaplan, Steven, ed. *Indigenous Responses to Western Christianity*. New York: New York University Press, 1994.
Kollman, P. "At the Origins of Mission and Missiology: A Study in the Dynamics of Religious Language." *Journal of the American Academy of Religion* 79, no. 2 (June 1, 2011) 425–58.
Krabill, James R., et al. *Worship and Mission for the Global Church: An Ethnodoxology Handbook*. Pasadena: William Carey Library, 2013.
Mariátegui, José Carlos. *7 ensayos de interpretación de la realidad peruana*. Caracas: Biblioteca Ayacucho, 1995.
Muchimba, Felix. *Liberating the African Soul: Comparing African and Western Christian Music and Worship Styles*. Colorado Springs: Authentic, 2008.
Niebuhr, H. Richard. *Christ and Culture*. 1st Harper Torchlight ed. New York: Harper, 1956.
Noll, Mark A. *The New Shape of World Christianity: How American Experience Reflects Global Faith*. Downers Grove, IL: IVP Academic, 2009.
Ott, Craig, and Harold A. Netland, eds. *Globalizing Theology: Belief and Practice in an Era of World Christianity*. Grand Rapids: Baker Academic, 2006.
Ottati, Douglas F. "'Christ and Culture': Still Worth Reading after All These Years." *Journal of the Society of Christian Ethics* (2003) 121–32.
Pew Research Center. "Global Christianity: A Report on the Size and Distribution of the World's Christian Population." December 19, 2011. http://www.pewforum.org/2011/12/19/global-christianity-exec/.
Pilcher, Carmel, et al., eds. *Vatican Council II: Reforming Liturgy*. Vatican II series 2. Hindmarsh, Australia: ATF, 2013.
Rajashekar, Paul. "Lutheranism in Asia and the Subcontinent." In *The Future of Lutheranism in a Global Context*, edited by James W. Aageson and Arland Dean Jacobson, 61–76. Minneapolis: Augsburg Fortress, 2008.
Stanley, Brian. *The World Missionary Conference, Edinburgh 1910*. Grand Rapids: Eerdmans, 2009.
Steuernagel, Marcell. "Church Music through the Lens of Performance: The Embodied Ritual of Sacred Play." PhD diss., Baylor University, 2018.
———. "History and Structure of Hymns of the People of God, Vol. 1." *Vox Scripturae* Volume XXIV, no. 1 (2016) 181–97.
Uzukwu, E. Elochukwu. *Worship as Body Language: Introduction to Christian Worship: An African Orientation*. Collegeville, MN: Liturgical, 1997.
Westhelle, Vitor. *After Heresy: Colonial Practices and Post-Colonial Theologies*. Eugene, OR: Cascade, 2010.
Yeager, D. M. "The View from Somewhere: The Meaning of Method in *Christ and Culture*." *Journal of the Society of Christian Ethics* (2003) 101–20.

CONTEXTUALIZING EVANGELICAL WORSHIP WITHIN MEXICAN RELIGIOSITY

with Special Reference to Theology
in Congregational Singing

Dinorah B. Méndez

A common complaint in Mexican churches is that after a century and a half of an Evangelical presence in the country, many theologies, hymnody, and practices are still imported. But there is also in Mexico a lack of theological reflection, composers of national hymnody, and other conditions that would contribute to the creation of Indigenous worship practices. Arguing that old hymns are foreign, many churches have simply adopted new worship styles and contemporary hymns without noticing that most of them are also imported or copied from other places. Even worse, some of these changes have been made without serious reflection; though the changes have a sound biblical foundation, they do not consider the cultural context, making it difficult to produce a contextual theology that would make worship practices and, in turn, the gospel more relevant in Mexican culture.

This study[1] is divided into several sections. First, there is an overview of features of the Mexican religious context relevant to worship

---

1. Méndez, *Evangelicals in Mexico*. Much of this study is based on the author's

issues. This is followed by a brief summary of cultural influences on worship practices among Evangelicals in Mexico, both influences coming from the national culture and those perceived as coming from the missionaries' cultures. This description is provided as the framework to emphasize the need to contextualize Evangelical theology in Mexico. The study of Christian hymnody is suggested as a tool for contextualization. Thus, the essay analyzes how hymnody can communicate the gospel in the Mexican context using the key features highlighted in the first section. The purpose is to explore if and how, through congregational singing, Evangelical churches are able to communicate their theology in relation to cultural concepts in such a way that conceptual bridges are built, in turn creating a local and contextual theology that can present the gospel relevantly and meaningfully. This will produce mature churches that are able to learn from their experiences and grow in the fulfillment of their mission.

OUTSTANDING FEATURES OF THE MEXICAN RELIGIOUS CONTEXT

Mexico's religious context is diverse and complex. This study will focus on "popular religiosity," meaning the religious practices and spiritual beliefs of the majority of the population. Popular religiosity in Mexico is heavily identified with Roman Catholicism. Nevertheless, some of its foundations and practices are not Catholic or even Christian because we are dealing with a *mestizo* complexity, a kind of religious syncretism presenting a body of beliefs and practices that seem to be only colored but not defined by Christianity. This popular religion is considered syncretistic because it arose from two religions that clashed over five centuries and gave rise to a new religious development containing some of the beliefs and practices of each of the two original religious forces: Indigenous and Spanish.[2] We will focus on the religious context of syncretistic Catholicism due to its predominance among the *mestizo* population in the country by trying to understand some of its most salient characteristics.

For this essay on worship issues, we will focus on three important characteristics of the Mexican religious context: a sense of mysticism,

---

previous doctoral research, which was wider and supported by field research. However, this essay reduces and focuses that work on worship themes.

2. Deiros, *Historia Religiosa de América Latina*, 117–23, 128, 147.

a sense of festivity or celebration, and a sense of community. These are not the only characteristics of popular Mexican religiosity, and they are not exclusive to this religious system. However, these characteristics are highlighted for three reasons: first, these characteristics were present in the two source religions, Indigenous and Spanish, that gave birth to the new religious system being studied; second, not only were these characteristics typical of the two source religions mixed in the sixteenth century, but they are also predominant features in the resultant religious system today; and third, they manifest themselves in an intermingled and almost integral way,[3] interacting and relating among themselves.[4]

In a study to explore specifically the contextualization of worship practices, the particularities of the Mexican spirituality expressed through these salient aspects are relevant, and a brief description of each is required.

A Sense of Mysticism

The terms "mysticism" and "mystical" have been used to designate something hidden or related to a mystery. In philosophy, for example, "mystical" refers to phenomena that cannot be explained rationally.[5] Thus, in the most general sense, one might define mysticism as an effort to understand reality apart from the intellect, at or beyond the limits of reason.

Mysticism, even when classified as philosophical mysticism, always has religious connotations. In one sense, it is the essence of what religion really is. The mystic experience is a truly religious experience that appears in all religions and with similar characteristics. One may say that mysticism is an attitude through which a person seeks to or pretends to unite with the divine directly, without intermediate or external assistance. In other words, mysticism goes beyond external forms of religion to receive a direct understanding of God. The goal is to be in personal union with the divine, and everything else becomes secondary.[6]

In view of these descriptions, one might say there are necessarily two evaluations of mysticism. On the one hand, taking it to be the

---

3. Pobleto, "Evangelización de la Cultura," 155–56.
4. Escobar, "Reino de Dios," 129; Paz, *Laberinto de la Soledad*, 90; Padilla, "Sincretismo Religioso," 46–47; Toro, *Compendio de Historia de México*, 311.
5. Cardona, *Pequeño Larousse Ilustrado*, 674; Delahoutre, "Mística," 1199.
6. Berr, *Ascenso del Espíritu*, 14; Osorio, *Misticismo y Locura*, 91–102.

essence of all religion whose purpose is for individuals to commune with the divine may be understood as a moderate or balanced application of mysticism to any religion. Thus, mysticism has a place even in the Christian faith.[7] On the other hand, an attitude in which mysticism is taken as a mysterious or illuminated way to understand not only the divine but also all reality could be seen as an exalted understanding of mysticism. In this latter kind of mysticism the individual does not try to balance all human characteristics, including especially the intellectual aspect, but rather relies almost uniquely on sensorial experiences.

In Mexico, a sensation of a supernatural presence and a need for the transcendent are typical. The sensation of making contact with the occultic or mysterious is one of the elements of mysticism that has predominated in popular syncretistic religion in the country.[8] For example, the popular belief persists that everything that seems to lack an explanation has its origin in Satan and the demons. Many myths exist in which evil spirits and demons have an important role. Some still believe that churches—that is to say, the buildings themselves—provide protection against these spirits.[9] Additionally, mysticism is present in common worship practices with images of a suffering and dead Christ, worship of the dead, devotions to Mary, the worship of miraculous saints, the use of medallions and small cloth charm sacks, prayers, and the practice of consulting fortune tellers and healers.[10]

Mysticism is, therefore, one notable characteristic in the popular religiosity of Mexico that appears primarily linked to concepts and practices of magic and superstitions in connection with the supernatural world. In this sense, it seems more appropriate to refer to this characteristic as superstition rather than a sense of mysticism, as appropriate mysticism is a quality of religion that seeks a direct relationship with divinity. In the case of popular Mexican religiosity, however, it seems that superstition is emphasized more than just the mystical element.

---

7. In his discussion on mysticism in religion, David Cook affirms that religions have some element of the mysterious. Particularly in the Christian religion, the theme of the transcendent God is a central mystery. However, in Cook's opinion, for Christian mystics this is no problem, for the mystery is not to be answered or explained, but contemplated in humble investigation. See chapter 2 in Cook, *Thinking about Faith*, 29–40.

8. Canclini, *Tras el Alma de América Latina*, 128–30.

9. Deiros, *Historia*, 110–111; Alvarez, *Protestantismo Latinoamericano*, 115.

10. Dana, *Manual de Eclesiología*, 125; McAleer, *Aspectos Culturales*, 6.

A Sense of Festivity or Celebration

The basic definition of "festival" or "fiesta" is a time when one leaves the routine. It is a break from the daily grind and an entrance into the unexpected and its surprises. On these fiesta days, activities are not primarily about their usefulness but about their symbolic values. One lives moments in which the rules, customs, and habits are set aside.[11] The fiesta provides an occasion to be able to lift one's eyes above the transient and perishable toward permanent things.[12]

Some sociologists[13] consider the fiesta a ritual act. One need not be religious in order to live the fiesta or celebrate. The human spirit requires physical rest, but also a variety of intellectual, emotional, and aesthetic activities. This is what the fiesta gives and is about. Furthermore, from the social point of view, those fiestas that might be cataloged as profane provide important dates, happenings, and personalities in the trajectory of the community. Thus, the fiesta is more important than one might think, not only religiously, but also in its social and economic aspects.[14]

However, religious celebrations, different from the simply secular ones, reach superior and intense quality levels due to their objectives and centering on the divine. The distinguishing mark in these instances is that the divine life has descended upon and is with those who are participating. The divine makes its presence real and is in some way recognizable during the festival. In addition, the entire community takes part and has communion with itself through the fiesta. All the members form the whole for the fiesta. Whatever its particular focus, character, or meaning, fiesta means communal participation. This characteristic distinguishes it from other phenomena and ceremonies. The fiesta is a social act based upon the participation of those who attend.[15]

The key to evaluate the structure of Mexican celebrations is found in considering the reasons for celebrating and the origins and significance of the festivals so as to identify the organizers and participants. The answers reinforce the role of the person in the bosom of the family,

---

11. Equipo Seladoc, *Religiosidad Popular*, 93.

12. Maldonaldo, *Introducción a la Religiosidad Popular*, 113–14.

13. Eliade, *Sagrado y lo Profano*, 52–53; Tolosana, "Aragón Festivo," 43–83; Caro Baroja, *Carnaval*; Van Gennep, *Les Rites de Passage*; and Pannet, *Catolicismo Popular*.

14. Maldonado, *Introducción a la Religiosidad Popular*, 97–99, 114.

15. Maldonado, *Introducción a la Religiosidad Popular*, 97–99, 114–15.

in union with others, and outline the conduct that is expected from that person in the community.[16]

In Octavio Paz's classic book *El Laberinto de la Soledad*, in which he analyzes the Mexican character, Paz notes that Mexicans, otherwise cataloged as lonely beings, love festivals and public meetings. The Mexican people are a people of celebration. In very few places in the world is it possible to observe such large religious festivals, with their colors, their dances and ceremonies, fireworks, their folk dresses, and all that relates to their food and pastries. The Mexican calendar is full of festivities and provides innumerable opportunities to celebrate. The festival provides an opportunity for the Mexican to open up dialogue with the divinity, with the country, and with friends.[17]

In Mexican festivities, one can encounter the country's great diversity and cultural richness. In many celebrations, it is easy to identify the merging of the Indigenous and Catholic heritages. It seems that in Mexican festivals the spirit of the people is revealed. These celebrations are one of the customs that can help us depict myriad facets of the Mexican people. Mexican celebrations reflect and represent racial mixture; Indigenous and Spanish people have mixed not only their genes, their food, and their languages, but their religions and festivals as well. The pre-Columbian and Hispanic pantheons both found their equivalents and, at times, similarities in the other's celebrations. In this way, almost all Mexican festivities add to their Catholic names some pre-Columbian reminiscence.[18]

A good example of a Mexican celebration is the Day of the Dead, or the Celebration of the Faithful Dead, that combines worship at the family altar with collective worship at the cemetery. It is necessary to offer food to the dead and living alike to participate in the banquet. As with all Mexican celebrations, the Day of the Dead is vital. The day is not sad; neither does it only celebrate death. It is a happy and festive day that celebrates life. For this reason the offerings are edible. The festival has been considered of such transcendence that surrealist writer André Bretón said: "This power of (re)conciliation of life and death is without a doubt the most attractive that Mexico has."[19]

16. Iturriaga, "Las Fiestas Mexicanas," 175.

17. Paz, *Laberinto*, 42–48.

18. Iturriaga, "Fiestas Mexicanas: El espíritu de un pueblo" and "Las Fiestas Mexicanas."

19. Iturriaga, "Las Fiestas Mexicanas"; Equipo Seladoc, *Religiosidad Popular*, 175

Other types of festivities are related to family. These celebrations mark certain rituals in the cycle of life: baptism, communion, marriage, and death.[20] These religious fiestas exist as sacramental ceremonies that have gained singular importance in popular Catholicism.[21] All of these have a strong base in community or family. In general terms, the family is the chief protagonist in these sacramental popular fiestas.[22]

Through such festivities, the Mexican participates and communicates with others and with his own values. It is a paradox that a country immersed in poverty and other problems features such numerous and happy festivities. It is like an explosion or outburst. Death and life, jubilation and lamenting, the song and the howl, live together in the festival. There is nothing more exhilarating than a Mexican fiesta, but there is also nothing sadder. The night of celebration is also a night of mourning. If in daily life the Mexican covers up one's true self, in the whirlwind of the festivities this self is brought out. Mexican festivals seem to function as violent ruptures with the old or with the established, as if in order to express themselves, the Mexicans need to break with themselves.[23] Mexican festivals are like Mexicans themselves: Indigenous and Spanish. The Mexican fiesta is the space where the popular syncretistic religious process is shown in its entire splendor and with all its contradictions.

A sense of community

The word "common" is derived from the same Latin root as "companion." In general, it signifies that which touches a community or a group of people together. The members of a community live life together, eat together, and are companions. "Community" signifies being together and united by common ties.[24]

Basic human necessities are in evidence when individuals organize, relate to one another, and form groups. One basic need is for personal identity, which is connected to questions of collective belonging. Each person has social relations with family and friends, plus many social

---

(translation mine).

20. Iturriaga, "Las Fiestas Mexicanas."
21. Pannet, *Catolicismo Popular*, and Bamat and Wiest, *Popular Catholicism*, 314.
22. Maldonado, *Introducción a la Religiosidad Popular*, 104–8.
23. Paz, *Laberinto*, 42–48; Riding, *Vecinos Distantes*, 11–13.
24. Vila, *Diccionario Etimológico*, 108.

activities like study and work. Everyone needs to feel a part of social groups. People who lack a sense of belonging to a community or project tend to lose a feeling of well-being and to believe that stable values from the past are fragmenting. They lose security and personal stability due to feeling alone or feeling strangled by the surrounding group.[25]

In spite of the risk of presenting a contradiction, it is necessary to specify that while religion is personal and individual, it is inseparably communal.[26] Religion in all climes and ages has formed an integral part of the social fabric. Generally it is rooted in the traditions of the group. For this reason, the influence of religion in society and politics has almost always been very powerful.

Manifestations of collective religiosity are many and varied. Multitudes are present in religious sanctuaries, church buildings, and parochial structures. On other occasions, smaller family gatherings in homes display communal religious celebrations. Pilgrimages and other diverse religious ceremonies include both the whole community and the nuclear family. Rites of passage like baptisms, first communions, and marriage ceremonies all have a strong communal character.[27]

A sense of community can be seen in many popular devotions, which are collective religious forms where participants help one another. Thus, they have a corporate function of solidarity within the society. To find the roots of a popular religiosity with a strong sense of community, one only has to look at the heritage of the Indigenous society in Mexico. In that culture, religion ruled practically all aspects of life, individual and social. A sense of community was very important for Indigenous people. The most important characteristic of such societies was cohesion.[28] On the other hand, it is more difficult to see a sense of community in the Spanish heritage of the Mexican context because it values an intense individuality, seen when one analyzes the way in which Spanish people tried to come together in common enterprises. Some scholars say only two things the Spaniards began as common projects seem to have been accomplished: their passion for their country, Spain, and their religious passion for the church.[29]

25. Ruitenbeek, *Individuo y la Muchedumbre*, 32–40.
26. Deiros, *Historia*, 106.
27. Deiros, *Historia*, 102; Maldonado, *Introducción a la Religiosidad Popular*, 107.
28. Yañez, *Enciclopedia de México*, 411.
29. Some authors who support this idea of intense individualism in Spaniards even in common enterprises are Mackay, *Otro Cristo Español*, 22–25; Gutiérrez-Marín,

Mexicans today seem to show both of these contrasting characteristics. Sometimes, Mexicans appear to be closed beings that preserve and maintain themselves as individuals distant from the world and all others. However, this is only one side of the coin. There are moments when Mexicans open up and reveal themselves. This is characteristic of their Indigenous heritage, which considers the family to be the principal line of security for the individual, promotes loyalty, and establishes strong bonds within the neighborhood or in friendships.[30]

Popular communal expressions of Catholic syncretistic faith in the country, such as the sacraments, are carried out in community or at least in the company of loved ones or people close to the family. In these instances, Mexicans satisfy their need for a sense of community in their religious practices. However, other practices within the same popular religiosity are mixed expressions in which a sense of community is experienced together with the individual dimension of life, such as in the Mass and in the practice of confession. Such apparent contradictions can be considered marks of Mexican people of mixed heritage.[31]

It seems that in the context of popular Mexican religiosity, a sense of community must be viewed with balance, because the Mexican cannot escape his or her heritage and, in this case, seems to maintain a tension between the Indigenous and the Spanish heritages. Thus, corporate religious practices in Mexico express solidarity and a certain amount of fraternal meaning. They are a manifestation of senses of identity and belonging.[32]

A final word with reference to the aforementioned relevant elements chosen from the Mexican popular religious context is to clarify that in this religious system many expressions can contain more than one of the selected aspects. In other words, in analyzing one particular religious expression one could find in it a sense of mysticism while at the same time note that it is a festivity celebrated in community. This is important because this particularity of all of these elements interacting in many of the expressions adds one more reason to confirm them as constitutive traits of Mexican religiosity.

Finally, a word on how Evangelicals in Mexico have interacted with the features of the popular religious context outlined here is important.

Místicos Españoles, 23–31; Deiros, *Historia*, 230–31; and Paz, *Sor Juana Inés*, 270–89.

30. Riding, *Vecinos Distantes*, 16–18; Paz, *Laberinto*, 26–38.
31. Mackay, *Otro Cristo Español*, 20–37.
32. Equipo Seladoc, *Religiosidad Popular*, 185–86.

It would be especially interesting to investigate in which ways Evangelicals perceive such features and how they have related to the religious context through them. This topic deserves further and deeper study; however, it may be said that the Evangelical perspective in relation to these key characteristics of the Mexican popular religiosity is varied. On one side, it may be said that Evangelicals reject all the popular religious context as contrary to the gospel, but on the other hand, it would be possible to study if some traits of that context have been adopted to different degrees by different groups.[33]

Therefore, this brief analysis reveals that there exist possibilities to study the process of contextualization of Evangelical faith in Mexico using these relevant contextual features as the frame of reference.

INFLUENCES ON WORSHIP PRACTICES AMONG MEXICAN EVANGELICALS

In the past few decades, churches in Mexico have become increasingly responsive to changes in their worship style. It has been heard, mainly at pastors' meetings, that these changes are meant to contribute to culturally relevant worship that stems from the mainstream worshiper's experiences. It is important to affirm that there is no one unique style of liturgy among Evangelicals because there are many types of Evangelicals. Before examining the fact that many evangelical churches in Mexico have started to adopt new styles of worship and analyzing if this is helping to contextualize the gospel, it is necessary to take a brief look into Evangelical worship practices in general and their possible cultural influences.

Influences from Mexican Culture

Our account of Mexican popular religiosity makes it clear that the context into which the Evangelical faith has been inserted and developed was the result of the Spanish Conquest. The clash among the Spanish and Indigenous cultures was violent, marked by "the sword and the cross."[34] This produced a forced process of evangelization, which, in-

---

33. McAleer, *Aspectos Culturales*, 1–6.

34. Mackay, *Otro Cristo Español*, 37. The sixteenth-century conquest of a major part of the American continent on behalf of the Catholic kings of Spain is widely documented. It is recognized to have been both a political and a religious enterprise.

stead of bringing about authentic conversions to the Christian faith, engendered a syncretism between existing Indigenous religious beliefs and practices and the newly introduced Roman Catholic ones. We still see this combination or religious mixture in the salient features discussed above. *Mestizo* people since the Conquest were able to adopt the new ideas externally while internally keeping their own existing ideas. It seems that Evangelicals still have to deal with this issue, as people who convert and come to our churches may change some of their practices and show externally Evangelical behavior while privately preserving ideas from their former way of life.

Examples of this cultural influence are many: people coming from popular Catholicism to Evangelical churches reproducing their religious behavior of attending worship services once a week as they once celebrated weekly Mass; seeing baptism as family religious festivity; looking at the pastor or minister as they saw the Catholic priest; and seeing the temple or church buildings and some objects, such as the pulpit, as having a kind of mystic value.[35]

There are many other examples of Mexican cultural influences on Evangelical worship practices, but this overview will suffice for the purposes of this essay. However, it is important to mention that because of this mixed-origin *mestizo* culture, that Mexicans today tend to have an ambivalent attitude toward their identity. On the one hand, depending on the circumstances, they seem to overreact against foreign influences in a kind of exaggerated nationalism (though this does not necessarily mean they hold an entirely positive view of their Indigenous or Spanish origin). On the other hand, there is a contradictory attitude, probably because of a rejection of their own origins, that looks to imitate other cultural models. This ambivalent attitude should be analyzed when looking at the adoption of new worship styles for Evangelical churches today.

Influences from Missionaries' Cultures

Evangelical faith was a religious ideology brought to Mexico by foreigners. Thus it has generally been classified pejoratively as "foreign" in an attempt to distortedly dismiss it as a catalyst for the extension of North American imperialism and to portray non-Catholics as anti-nationalistic

---

35. See study in Méndez, "Esfera Socio-Religiosa," 120–25.

traitors to the country.³⁶ Certainly Evangelical faith is foreign to the extent that it originated in a foreign country, like other ideologies that have come into Mexico. Even Roman Catholicism came from a foreign country. However, Evangelical faith has taken root and grown in Mexican territory, and nowadays Mexican Evangelicals can easily reference the religion of their parents and grandparents.³⁷

Notwithstanding, it is necessary to acknowledge that Evangelical missionaries transmitted their faith using models of their culture that obviously differ from the Mexican cultural context. From the missionaries' perspective, their own culture was considered theologically correct and therefore transmitted as such. This contributed to shaping communities they established according to their own cultural models. Through all forms of liturgy, hymnody, written works, programs, strategies, institutions, and even seemingly insignificant details such as vocabulary and clothing, the missionaries' faith was projected as an imported product.³⁸ Yet while Evangelical faith was foreign in the beginning, it has become Mexicanized and is on the way to becoming progressively "Latin Americanized."³⁹

It will be interesting to see if Evangelical faith has influenced popular religiosity or if, as has been predicted, the Mexican popular religiosity is so strong that Evangelicals have been influenced in some way by the surrounding culture. Perhaps the influence has been mutual.

OPPORTUNITY FOR GROWTH

The Need to Contextualize Evangelical Theology in Mexico

It is important to ask to what extent Evangelicals have been able to contextualize their faith and theology in the Mexican culture in which they have been implanted. Since Mexicans' popular religiosity, as stated above, is characterized by syncretism, it is necessary to emphasize a contextualization

---

36. Bastián, *Historia*, 10–11.
37. Bastián, *Historia*, 178–87; Martínez-García, *Secta*, 9; Mackay, *Otro Cristo Español*, 255–62.
38. Deiros, *Protestantismo*, 31–32.
39. Bastián, *Historia*, 11–12.

process committed to the integrity of the gospel while at the same time addressing the relevance of the message in the cultural context.[40]

To help us understand how Evangelicals have transmitted their theology, this particular study focuses on the possible relation between Evangelical theology and the key characteristics of Mexico's religious background discussed in the first section, particularly in relation to aspects of worship. We will now concentrate on one cherished element of our Christian worship: hymnody. The idea is to examine hymns and songs as a vehicle of theological communication in the context of congregational singing, analyzing potential relationships between theological concepts and key features of Mexican religiosity.

The purpose of this examination is not only to provide an academic contribution on Mexican culture and its religion, no matter how fascinating this topic may be. Neither is this a simple exercise in contextualization, even if it is relevant and necessary. The idea here is to provide a practical application for solving a real need. Its purpose is to explore useful tools for Christian ministry. Thus, people committed to or involved in Christian worship ministries in local churches, especially those who deal with hymnodic considerations, will be able to enrich their understanding of the material and use it in meaningful ways. Similarly, pastors, evangelists, and seminary professors will enlarge their ministries by using local hymnody as a new resource to touch the lives of many. Missionaries could also learn to appreciate and respect native hymnody in their places of service. These are only a few examples of the practical usefulness of this study.

Study of Theology in Christian Hymnody as a Tool of Contextualization

A variety of disciplines must be brought together in order to understand Christian worship. Susan J. White, for instance, says that theology is necessary to understand worship as a religious phenomenon; biblical studies are required because the Bible is the authority for the faith and experiences of Christians; Christian history is needed to understand worship through the development of Christianity; and the social

---

40. Schreiter, *Constructing Local Theologies*, 151–55.

sciences must be included because worship is also a human activity.[41] In this essay, we write from the theological perspective.

Moreover, we recognize in this essay that Christian worship is that worship is individual as well as collective, that private and public approaches are necessary and interdependent components of worship, and that these aspects rely on each other.[42] The idea is that each believer participates in public worship by bringing his or her own personal relationship with God to worship. At the same time, corporate worship provides the environment for mutual edification and spiritual enrichment among those worshiping together, and in doing this, one's personal relationship with God and one's individual worship is affected.

To justify the selection of hymnody, it is necessary to clarify that there are as many different lists of essential Christian worship elements as there are authors studying these matters. The importance of each element depends very much on the point of view of each scholar. Among these elements, hymnody is mentioned repeatedly, though sometimes with different names or in different ways, such as "praise," "music," "hymns," "songs," "singing," or even "prayers."[43] However, it is also necessary to limit in some way the wide range of devotional musical expressions within Christianity. There are different ways to classify the types of music used in Christian worship (e.g., congregational singing, choral music, solo or small group music, and instrumental music). This essay will limit itself to hymnody as practiced in the context of congregational singing. One reason for this selection is that singing is one of the few elements of worship considered to have a clear origin in the apostolic era.[44] Another reason is that congregational singing of hymns is currently regarded as inseparable from Christian worship with very few exceptions, although this does not mean that it is considered most important in or central to worship or synonymous with it.[45] Thus, the main impetus for addressing hymnody in the context of congregational singing is to allow a theological study of the words of that hymnody,

---

41. White, *Groundwork of Christian Worship*, 1.

42. White, *Introduction to Christian Worship*, 34–35.

43. Wiersbe, *Real Worship*, 109; Bartley, *Adoración*, 8; von Allmen, *Worship*, 162, 169.

44. See Eph 5:19; Col 3:16; Heb 13:15; and 1 Cor 14:15, which show that consideration of music in the church must begin precisely with congregational singing. See wider discussion in Mitchell, *Ministry and Music*, 17–20.

45. Routley, *Christian Hymns*, 1.

looking for their interaction with the predominant concepts found in the more general religious context of Mexican religiosity.

Obviously, music is unavoidably inherent to hymnody, and due to its characteristics and effects it fulfills an important communicative dimension in social interactions. In fact, the combination of words and music in Christian hymnody has been of immense help in committing the word of God to memory because music enhances the power of those words.[46] On the other hand, while music communicates its message nonverbally, words—the other half of hymnody—provide verbal and conceptual communication. Because this study focuses on theological concepts, limiting ourselves to the words or lyrics of hymnody is appropriate because through them the concepts communicated can be analyzed. In fact, there has been historical concern about whether and how words in hymnody adequately communicate Christian beliefs. The communicative power of hymnody has been recognized, but so has the risk of communicating incorrect ideas.[47] Our study seeks not only to analyze the theological ideas transmitted through hymnody but also to look at how messages of hymnody are transmitted differently depending on the context, and particularly at how the theological content of Evangelical hymnody may be related to predominant concepts of the Mexican religious context.

As stated above, hymnody consists of hymns and songs that combine words and melodies. The hymnody under consideration here is used in congregational singing precisely due to its corporative character. Therefore, it is important to mention the various functions scholars ascribe to hymnody in order to identify its potential use as a tool for communicating theology in a specific religious context. For example, hymnody can function according to a lyrical theme, such as proclamation, prayer, thanksgiving, or praise;[48] a liturgical purpose, such as preparation for worship or responses of worshipers; or in one of the church's tasks, such as worship, teaching, communion, or proclamation.[49] J. Nathan Corbitt and Brian C. Castle present different uses or functions depending on the context in which the hymnody is used or the occasion for which it is performed.[50] The Bible offers a typology of hymns,

---

46. Wilson-Dickson, *Story of Christian Music*, 45.

47. See, for example, the review of the nature and function of Christian hymns in Northcott, *Hymns in Christian Worship*, 5–15.

48. Westermeyer, "Functions of Music," 99–101.

49. Webber, *Worship Is a Verb*, 186.

50. Corbitt, *Sound of the Harvest*, 16–21; Castle, *Sing a New Song*, chs. 6 and 7.

spiritual songs, and psalms (Col 3:16–17). Regardless of these different functional descriptions, there is a general agreement that, due to the richness and variety of hymnody texts, they can serve diverse purposes and therefore also result in diverse effects. Warren Wiersbe says: "I am convinced that congregations learn more theology (good and bad) from the songs they sing than from the sermons they hear. Many sermons are doctrinally sound and contain a fair amount of biblical information, but they lack that necessary emotional content that gets hold of the listener's heart." But music, he says, "reaches the mind and the heart at the same time. . . . and for this reason can become a wonderful tool in the hands of the Spirit . . . [but] naïve congregations can sing their way into heresy before they even realize what is going on."[51] Consequently, hymnody is not only a powerful medium of communication but an important tool to shape the beliefs of singers. In other words, it is pertinent to examine hymnody as a factor of theological communication in Christian worship and in a sociological setting.

It follows that if through hymnody it is possible to transmit theological concepts, it would be possible to analyze any relationships between the concepts selected as key issues in the Mexican religious context and the Christian hymnody used by Evangelicals in this country.

ANALYSIS

Using Hymnody to Communicate the Gospel in Relevant Ways in the Mexican Context

The ability of hymnody to communicate its message in a community makes clear its importance in presenting the contemporary relevance and significance of Christian faith in a social context. In fact, hymnody has changed and adapted according to the context in which it has been practiced. It has influenced cultural settings, but at the same time been influenced by those settings. The Evangelical hymnody considered in this analysis include ancient hymns translated into Spanish, contemporary songs also translated from English, a few songs originally by Mexican composers, and some popular sung psalms. We include here an investigation of sample hymnody from each category; some songs are provided at the end of this essay.

51. Wiersbe, *Real Worship*, 136–37.

Now we must consider whether the previously discussed key characteristics of the Mexican religious context (a sense of mysticism, a sense of celebration, and a sense of community) can be used to reflect on the theological content of Evangelical hymnody. We want to see if these characteristics are reflected in the sample hymnody's lyrics and to look for theological content interacting with those concepts.

A Sense of Mysticism

The mystical aspect in hymnody as well as in all other elements of worship is the desire for communion with God or for understanding divine mysteries. Even a search for refuge or stability can be expressions of mysticism.[52] This means that even though Christian worship involves rational experiences, it also involves experiences that are not always completely understandable. It is here that Christian mysticism finds its place, because the experience of God is a personal relationship transcending the intellectual and material worlds. Hymnody, then, can be useful to express this mystical experience in Christian worship. Expressions of this reality can be found in familiar hymns: "There is a place of quiet rest near to the heart of God," or "I am His and He is mine."[53] Familiar hymnody used by Evangelicals in Mexico was analyzed to identify mystical expressions.

The main idea related to mysticism found in the sample of analyzed hymnody was the spiritual relationship between the believer and God. Some emphasis was on life in heaven, where God is worshiped by saints and angels. There were also images of God beside or inside the believer in a mysterious way, even as an inner light; descriptions of people's souls crying out for the presence of God; and images of the assembly of believers worshiping God forever. The victory of God over evil powers was also mentioned. The intimate relationship of love between God and worshiper was emphasized. Therefore, a sense of mysticism was identified in lyrics from the sample of hymnody used by Evangelicals in Mexico.

---

52. Segler and Bradley, *Christian Worship*, 66.
53. Wiersbe, *Real Worship*, 180–81.

A Sense of Festivity or Celebration

A sense of celebration, or *fiesta*, as it is called in the Spanish language, is a special feature of Spanish hymnody studied in recent decades.[54] This vibrant spirit in the text and melody seems to be an inherent characteristic of Spanish-language hymnody; it promotes excitement and a spirit of joy and hospitality that makes strangers especially welcome.

A sense of *fiesta* was evident in the hymnody used by Evangelicals in Mexico, but interestingly it most often came from references to the joy and celebration of eternal life in heaven rather than in the present life. There are images of victorious celebration when Christ comes back and worshipers celebrate their salvation in heaven. There are several references to singing as evidence of the joy in the Christian life and indirect references to the joyful gathering of worshipers giving praise to God. The psalms encourage all nations, all instruments, and all worshipers to sing and to praise God with a joyful spirit.

Yet the *fiesta* theme is in tension with another aspect of the religious character of Latino people: a sense of sacrifice. The reality of suffering and misery in the cultural context gives relevance to expressions of lament as well as the expectation of hope and liberation from afflictions. When discussing *fiesta* in the Mexican context above, I noted, "There is nothing more exhilarating than a Mexican fiesta, but there is also nothing sadder." The Mexican lives paradoxically with a sense of festivity that contrasts with the realities of suffering, poverty, and misery. In the hymnody more frequently used by Evangelicals, this is expressed with an emphasis on a future hope—joyful celebration in the presence of God, free of present afflictions—rather than on festive joy in one's present reality.

A Sense of Community

A sense of community is promoted in Christian worship and in hymnody through their corporate quality. Corporate worship—the worship of a fellowship in communion, in unity—does not supplant individual worship, but is a complementary practice. Especially when sung as a congregation, hymnody can produce corporate feelings and enhance individual sensibilities.[55] Therefore, this sense of community was also identified in texts

54. Hawn, "*Fiesta* of the Faithful," 11–13. This author has contributed especially to the study of *fiesta* in worship as a particular characteristic of Hispanic people.

55. Segler, *Christian Worship*, 66–67.

from the studied sample of Evangelical hymnody in Mexico. Among the images of community found in our sample of hymnody are the church as the body or the army of Christ and the believers worshiping together here and/or in heaven. Some expressions appear in plural terms, such as "our God" or "let us praise." However, many contemporary songs are individual or have singular expressions with no explicit reference to the communal character of the Christian faith.

Indeed, even though the hymns emphasized a sense of community, we also found a strong emphasis on the individual character of the Christian life. Our analysis points to a view balanced between the collective and the individual character of the faith.

REFLECTIONS

Our investigation revealed a relationship of affinity between the content in Evangelical hymnody and the key religious concepts of the Mexican context outlined in this essay. This idea is undergirded by hints of such concepts in the texts of the sample of more familiar hymns, songs, and psalms used by Evangelicals in Mexico. The sample was taken from case studies of more than twenty different confessions. Neither the participants in the study nor the hymnody sample provide hard data meant to prove numerically any theory. However, even in these case studies, a sense of mysticism, a sense of *fiesta*, and a sense of community were identified in the hymnody. Therefore, it was valid to ask whether such hymnody could potentially communicate the theological concepts contained in their texts to people in this particular context using these key concepts.

Our analysis suggests several conclusions. For example, hymnody with messages addressed directly to God and expressed in plural or collective terms also contained much Christian doctrine, coincident with the Evangelical emphasis on beliefs rather than on experiences or feelings. This means that this kind of hymnody may be able to communicate a wider range of theological concepts using the key traits of the context as conceptual bridges. On the contrary, the sample hymnody showing affinity with a sense of mysticism included very few references to the other key aspects and was written in singular, very personal terms. This kind of hymnody can communicate more Christian experiences and feelings than beliefs. The importance of these reflections is that all types of hymnody are necessary to give expression to the full range of beliefs, experiences, and feelings in the Christian faith, and the hymnody sample we studied reveals that Evangelicals in Mexico can use this important element of their Christian worship to relate with the key characteristics of the Mexican religious context in such a way that their faith may be contextualized.

These findings affect the contextualization of the Christian faith in Mexico, but it seems that Evangelicals may still not be conscious of the ability of hymnody to communicate faith using these cultural concepts. This conclusion comes from an exclusively positive approach: the enculturation of the gospel could be viewed as excessively optimistic because it could be seen as proposing that Evangelicals should use the cultural religious context without any criteria of selection as conceptual bridges to communicate their faith. However, one must remember that the context the Evangelical faith has inhabited since its inception has been an opposite view: as an extraneous faith coming to attack the native religion and culture of the country. On the other hand, from the perspective of Evangelicals themselves, they appear to have a negative approach toward Mexican culture in their countercultural model of the relationship between Christianity and context. Therefore, to conclude that it is possible for the Evangelical truth to be transmitted through one of its important liturgical elements, hymnody, while taking into consideration cultural concepts, seems a very useful and needed balanced approach to contextualize the gospel in Mexico.

CONCLUSION

All these reflections support the idea of the usefulness of Christian hymnody as a tool for contextualizing Evangelical faith in Mexico. It is possible that Evangelicals over the years have unconsciously used their hymnody to transmit their faith, but there is evidence that this use has been almost unintentional. It is also possible that, upon future study, one might conclude that there have been diverse uses of hymnody depending on the denominational background of Evangelical churches, especially when contrasting historic churches and Pentecostal denominations.

The importance of this study appears precisely in the fact that, if churches are changing their worship styles, including their hymnological preferences, the theological shape of these churches and future Evangelicals in general could shift based on these transformations. If hymnody conveys theological content, then, changes in hymnody could produce changes in theology and thus changes in the future identity of Evangelicals in Mexico, as well as in their relationship to their own context. Our conclusion is that the adoption of different worship styles and changes in the hymnody used are not unimportant or superficial but have complex effects on the congregational life of churches, their growth, their expression of the Christian faith, the fulfillment of their mission, and their relevance in the Mexican context.

APPENDIX: EXAMPLES OF HYMNODY

Holy, Holy, Holy (hymn)

Holy, Holy, Holy, Lord Omnipotent,
my lips will always give you praise.
Holy, Holy, Holy, I worship you reverently.
God in three persons, blessed Trinity.

Holy, Holy, Holy the numerous choir,
chosen saints worship you without ceasing.
Full of joy and with golden crowns
give before the throne and the crystal-clear sea.

Holy, Holy, Holy, the big multitude of angels
who obey your holy will
adore before you covered by your flames,
before you that you have been, you are, and you will be.

Holy, Holy, Holy, even though you are watching,
it is impossible to contemplate your glory.
You are the only one that is holy, and no one is beside you
in perfect power, purity, and love.

Holy, Holy, Holy, the glory of your name!
We see it in your works, in the sky, earth, and sea.
Holy, Holy, Holy, every man worship you,
God in three persons, blessed Trinity.

God Is Here (contemporary song)

God is here, as certain as the air that I breathe,
as certain as in the morning the sun rises,
as certain as when I sing he can hear me.

You can notice him beside you in this moment;
you can feel him inside of your heart.
You can see him in that problem you have.
Jesus is here; if you want, you can follow him.

Psalm 42

As the deer pants for the waters
so my soul longs for you, O Lord.
Day and night I am thirsty for you.
Only for you will I seek.
Fill me, fill me, Lord.
Give me more, more of your love,
I am thirsty only for you.
Fill me, Lord.

BIBLIOGRAPHY

Alvarez, Carmelo E. *El Protestantismo Latinoamericano: Entre la Crisis y el Desafío*. Mexico City: CUPSA, 1981.
Arciniegas, Germán. *America, Tierra Firme*. Buenos Aires: Sudamericana, 1943.
Bamat, Tomas, and Jean-Paul Wiest, eds. *Popular Catholicism in a World Church: Seven Case Studies in Inculturation*. Maryknoll, NY: Orbis, 1999.
Bartley, James W. *La Adoración que Agrada al Altísimo*. El Paso, TX: CBP, 1999.
Bastián, Jean Pierre. *Historia del Protestantismo en América Latina*. Mexico City: CUPSA, 1990.
Bataillón, Marcel. *Erasmo y España*. Mexico City: FCE, 1966.
Berr, Henry. *El Ascenso del Espíritu: Balance de una Vida y una Obra*. Mexico City: Editorial Hispano Americana, 1962.
Bromiley, Geoffrey W. "Misticismo." In *Diccionario de Teología*, edited by Everett F. Harrison, G. W. Bromiley, and Carl F. H. Henry, 350. Jenison, MI: TELL, 1990.
Camorlinga, José María. *El Choque de Dos Culturas*. Mexico City: Plaza y Valdés, 1992.
Canals, Vidal F. *Filosofía y Pensamiento Medieval*. Barcelona: Herder, 1985.
Canclini, Arnoldo. *Tras el Alma de América Latina: Una Introducción a la Sociología Latinoamericana*. El Paso, TX: CBP, 1992.

Cardona, María, ed. *El Pequeño Larousse Ilustrado*. Mexico City: Larousse, 1998.
Caro Baroja, J. *El Carnaval*. Madrid: Taurus, 1965.
Casas, Bartolomé de las. *Los Indios de México y Nueva España*. Mexico City: Porrúa, 1966.
Castle, Brian C. *Sing a New Song to the Lord. The Power and Potential of Hymns*. London: Darton, Longman and Todd, 1994.
Clavijero, Francisco Xavier. *Historia Antigua de México*. Mexico City: Porrúa, 1964.
Cook, David. *Thinking about Faith: A Beginner's Guide*. Leicester, UK: InterVarsity, 1986.
Corbitt, J. Nathan. *The Sound of the Harvest*. Grand Rapids: Baker, 1998.
Dana, Harvey E. *Manual de Eclesiología*. El Paso, TX: CBP, 1993.
Deiros, Pablo A. *Historia del Cristianismo en América Latina*. Buenos Aires: FTL, 1992.
———. *Protestantismo en América Latina*. Nashville: Caribe, 1997.
Delahoutre, Michel. "Mística." In *Diccionario de las Religiones*, edited by Paul Poupard, 1199. Barcelona: Herder, 1987.
Dussel, Enrique, ed. *Historia General de la Iglesia en América Latina, Tomo I*. Barcelona: Sígueme, 1983.
Eliade, Mircea. *Lo Sagrado y lo Profano*. Madrid: Guadarrama, 1973.
Equipo Seladoc. *Panorama de la Teología Latinoamericana*. Salamanca, Spain: Sígueme, 1975.
———. *Religiosidad Popular*. Salamanca, Spain: Sígueme, 1976.
Escobar, Samuel. "El Reino de Dios, la Escatología y la Ética Social y Política en América Latina." In *El Reino de Dios y América Latina*, edited by René Padilla, 127–56. El Paso, TX: CBP, 1975.
Fink, Peter E. "Liturgy and Spirituality: A Timely Intersection." In *Liturgy and Spirituality in Context*, edited by Eleanor Bernstein, 47–61. Collegeville, MN: Liturgical, 1990.
Gutiérrez-Marín, C. L. *Místicos Españoles del Siglo 16*. Mexico City: CUPSA, 1946.
Hawn, C. Michael. "The *Fiesta* of the Faithful: Praising God in Spanish." *The Chorister* XLIX, no. 7 (January 1998) 11–13.
Iturriaga, José N. "Fiestas Mexicanas: El espíritu de un pueblo." mexico@quikmail.com, November 1, 1998.
———. "Las Fiestas Mexicanas." mexico@quikmail.com, November 1, 1998
Krickeberg, Walter. *Las Antiguas Culturas Mexicanas*. Mexico City: FCE, 1964.
Lebon, Jean. *How to Understand the Liturgy*. London: SCM, 1987.
León-Portilla, Miguel. *Los Antiguos Mexicanos*. Mexico City: FCE, 1970.
Lovelace, Austin C., and William C. Rice. *Music and Worship in the Church*. New York: Abingdon, 1960.
Mackay, Juan A. *El Otro Cristo Español*. Mexico City: CUPSA, 1952.
Maldonaldo, Luis. *Introducción a la Religiosidad Popular*. Santander, SP: Sal Terrae, 1985.
Martínez-Garcia, Carlos. *Secta: Un Concepto Inadecuado para Explicar el Protestantismo Mexicano*. Mexico City: CUPSA, 1991.
McAleer, Miguel. *Los Aspectos Culturales del Carismatismo en América Latina*. Mexico City: Convención Regional Bautista Central, 1995.
Méndez, Dinorah B. "La Esfera Socio-Religiosa de la Cultura Mexicana y su Influencia en la Teología y Práctica de las Iglesias Bautistas de México." BTh thesis, Seminario Teológico Bautista Mexicano, 1989.

———. *Evangelicals in Mexico: Their Hymnody and Its Theology*. Brussels: Peter Lang, 2008.
Mitchell, Robert H. *Ministry and Music*. Philadelphia: Westminster, 1978.
Northcott, C. *Hymns in Christian Worship*. London: Lutherworth, 1964.
Osorio, César. *Misticismo y Locura*. Buenos Aires: Partenón, 1945.
Padilla, Raúl N. "El Sincretismo Religioso en Hispanoamérica." *Revista Certeza* 19, no. 74 (July–September 1979) 46–49.
Paz, Octavio. *El Laberinto de la Soledad*. Mexico City: FCE, 1967.
———. *Sor Juana Inés de la Cruz o las Trampas de la Fe*. Obras Completas 5. Mexico: FCE, 1993.
Pannet, R. *El Catolicismo Popular*. Madrid: Marova, 1976.
Pike, E. Royston. *Diccionario de Religiones*. Mexico City: FCE, 1960.
Pobleto, Renato. "Evangelización de la Cultura, Religiosidad Popular y Religiosidad Pentecostal." In *Cultura y Evangelización en América Latina*, 155–56. Santiago, Chile: Paulinas/ILADES, 1988.
Riding, Alan. *Vecinos Distantes: Un Retrato de los Mexicanos*. Mexico City: Joaquín MortizPlaneta, 1985.
Routley, E. *Christian Hymns Observed*. Princeton: Prestige, 1982.
Ruitenbeek, Hendrik M. *El Individuo y la Muchedumbre*. Buenos Aires: Paidós, 1964
Russell, Anthony. "Sociology and the Study of Spirituality." In *The Study of Spirituality*, edited by Cheslyn Jones, Geoffrey Wainwright, and Edward Yarnold, 33–38. London: SPCK, 1992.
Schreiter, Robert J. *Constructing Local Theologies*. Maryknoll, NY: Orbis, 1985.
Segler, Franklin M., and Randall Bradley. *Christian Worship: Its Theology and Practice*. Nashville: Broadman, 1967.
Sejourné, Laurette. *Pensamiento y Religión en el México Antiguo*. Mexico City: FCE, 1957.
Tolosana, Carmelo Lisón. "Aragón Festivo: La fiesta como estrategia simbólica." In *Antropología Social y Hermenéutica*, 43–83. Madrid: Akal, 1983.
Toro, Alfonso. *Compendio de Historia de México. Tomo II: La dominación española*. Mexico City: Sociedad de Ediciones y Librería Franco-Americana, S.A., 1926.
Van Gennep, Arnold. *Les Rites de Pasaje*. Paris: E. Nourry, 1909.
von Allmen, Jean-Jacques. *Worship: Its Theology and Practice*. Oxford: Oxford University Press, 1965.
Verrill, Hyatt A. *Viejas Civilizaciones del Nuevo Mundo*. Buenos Aires: Argonauta, 1947.
Vila, Samuel. *Diccionario Etimológico de Sinónimos Castellanos Adaptado a la Predicación y la Literatura Evangélica*. Barcelona: Libros CLIE, 1986.
Webber, Robert E. *Worship Is a Verb*. Waco, TX: Word, 1985.
Westermeyer, Paul. "The Functions of Music in Worship." In *The Complete Library of Christian Worship, Vol. 4: Music and the Arts in Christian Worship, Book 1*, edited by Robert E. Webber, 99–103. Nashville: Star Song, 1994.
White, James F. *Introduction to Christian Worship*. Rev. ed. Nashville: Abingdon, 1990.
White, Susan J. *Groundwork of Christian Worship*. London: Epworth, 1997.
Wiersbe, Warren W. *Real Worship*. Nashville: Nelson, 1988.
Wilson-Dickson, Andrew. *The Story of Christian Music*. Oxford: Lion, 1992.
Yañez, Agustín, Coord. *Enciclopedia de México en Diez Tomos*. Vol. II. Mexico City: Instituto de la Enciclopedia de México, 1967.

SECTION III

Forming Worshipers

NARRATED LIVES AND TESTIMONIES AS PART OF RECAPITULATING THE HISTORY OF SALVATION IN LITURGY

Toward an Open, Multicultural Experience

Israel Flores Olmos

The church described in this essay is taking its first steps to becoming an intercultural community, open to newcomers from other parts of Spain as well as from Europe, Africa, and Latin America, and learning from each other through narrated lives. Telling our stories and sharing our experiences enrich the community, keeping it open to others and committed to its mission to promote the kingdom of God. As the worship liturgy recapitulates the story of salvation, people's life narratives promote the meaning, the history, and the purpose of the church community and bring hope to its members. Telling these narratives in an environment so diverse and pluralistic allows us to know each other better and sensitizes people to the various needs of both newcomers and those already in the community. In this essay we suggest that including testimonies—life narratives—in the worship liturgy helps to break down barriers, create bonds of empathy, and challenge one another to greater levels of faith.

AN EXOTIC COMMUNITY IN GRANADA

The community we studied is a Protestant church in Andalusia, a region in the south of Spain, and specifically in the city of Granada. This is a church of the diaspora, a minority church community, which finds itself on the margins of a wider society that is traditional and very conservative.

This church community has faced a number of different challenges over the years. In addition to finding itself in a minority position and socially excluded in the history of Spain, its history has been marked by persecution and harassment by both civil and religious authorities. Now the situation has changed with a more tolerant political and social climate, yet the community continues to face great challenges.

Merely being Protestant in the middle of a traditional and conservative Roman Catholic social environment raises questions about our identity as a community. Yet in the wider context of growing indifference to religion, the church is seen as a community of the past with little relevance in an increasingly secularized society.

In spite of this, the number of young people and couples joining the church has increased. There are people in this intergenerational community who are familiar with the traditional forms and rhythms of worship, but with the influx of people from a younger generation come different expectations about what it means to be a worshiping community. At the same time, families from different geographical backgrounds have been integrating into congregational life, resulting in a community that is both diverse and adaptable. This diversity of people coming from other regions of Spain as well as from abroad has brought different perspectives on the world around us and made us open to other forms of worship. While most come from Protestant backgrounds, there are some who bring their own understanding of what it means to be a Protestant. When they integrate into the community, they can find their traditional understanding challenged at both cultural and religious levels. It may lead to the deterritorialization of their symbolic-religious values. But through shared experiences and understanding, we have discovered new dimensions to our faith.

Thus, while this community is on the margins of its geographical and cultural setting, it is open to new experiences, making possible new opportunities for growth in its faith and life.

AN ADAPTIVE LITURGY FOR A DIVERSE CHURCH COMMUNITY

The arrival of new members from different contexts has enriched the liturgical practices of this community with new songs, new music, and sometimes new musical instruments. The worship structure mostly follows traditional Presbyterian liturgy, but little by little it has been adapted to allow a more participative dynamic.

Worship services bring together people who have different cultural, social, ecclesial, and liturgical backgrounds. This represents a real challenge, but it's also an opportunity for growth. A variety of liturgical forms can reinforce mutual understanding and enrich community life, making the worship service conducive to the integration of newcomers from other contexts without neglecting their spiritual experience.

Some who come to this community have had the traumatic experience of migration and the search for refuge. Some students or families come to Granada to settle for a period of time, and some stay permanently.

We propose that in this kind of context, life narratives (testimonies) within worship can enrich the community in the experience of life and faith. These stories of life can accompany the liturgy in each stage and can be reinforced with liturgical gestures, biblical passages, or hymns.

Testimonies can focus on good or bad situations in which people saw the hand of God, even when the situation has not yet changed. Or the testimony can be a declaration of faith or a personal story in which God was the protagonist as Creator or Provider. Here we describe the first way.

LIFE DESERVES TO BE NARRATED, SUNG, AND CELEBRATED

Worship as a Life History

Christian worship is the "recapitulating of the history of salvation," Jean-Jacques von Allmen reminds us.[1] In its structure, worship contains a meaning, narrating the history of salvation both chronologically and theologically. In the chronological sense, it speaks of the creation of the world, perhaps in psalm readings. Then, in confession, it refers to the evil in the world. Next, through the preaching of the word, we

---

1. von Allmen, *Culto cristiano*, 31–40.

talk about the promise of redemption and its fulfillment in Jesus Christ. Finally, it tells about Christ's death, his resurrection, and his return when celebrating the Eucharist. Thus, the worship in itself narrates the history of salvation, in which God is constantly seeking relationship with humans, and its culmination in the ministry of Jesus Christ. In this way the worship is an anamnesis, a memorial of the work of salvation in Christ in the form of a re-enactment of history that commits to itself all those who participate in the liturgical assembly. Worship is thus a testimony to the saving action of God in history.

Worship also tells us the history of salvation in the theological sense because it expresses the salvific will of God. That is, worship expresses the divine desire to save human beings seen from Genesis to the prophets. Second, there is the reconciliation that makes possible the saving will of God through Jesus Christ; and finally, God himself protects and defends the efficacy of that salvation through the action of his Spirit. All this manifests or expresses itself in worship as a whole as a narrated story of salvation—"recapitulating the history of salvation."

Worship as a recapitulation of the history of salvation speaks of God's action in the world and bears witness to the life of Jesus. This testimony of the life of Jesus, present in worship through the liturgy of the word and the liturgy of the upper room, is finally the testimony of a life that is being narrated in the worship. Thus, the ministry of Jesus in Galilee as one who appears preaching the gospel of the kingdom of God is present in the liturgy of the word. And the ministry of Jesus in Jerusalem, with his passion, death, and resurrection, is reflected in the liturgy of the upper room. The worship, even in its structure, recapitulates the history of salvation on the basis of the ministry of Jesus.[2]

But this recapitulation not only refers to the past—it also points to the present and to the future of the consummation of the kingdom. As it narrates the history of salvation, worship updates and communicates. Thus, it shows its alterity and breaks into chronological time to incorporate us into a different kind of time in which the past, present, and future converge. This happens especially in the celebration of the Eucharist because it is done "in memory" of Jesus. It is an action that, when performed, points to life and to the sayings and deeds of Jesus as a salvific work, and it is updated. In this way, worship is testimony: it is a story that presents the action of God in history and its actualization. The

---

2. von Allmen, *Culto cristiano*, 31–40.

events of the life of Jesus, his words and his actions, manifest the salvific work inasmuch as it was told to others.

In this way, Christian worship is testimony, a narrative that presents the action of God in history and updates it. Jesus' words, his actions, and the events of his life are a salvific work of the arrival of the kingdom of God, because through those words, actions, and events he transformed the lives of others. Jesus' life was defined by his relationships with others, especially the poor, foreigners, women, the sick, and other marginalized people. The Gospels testify to the way Jesus lived, the irruption of the kingdom of God, transforming the lives of those around him who became protagonists in the history of salvation because of their relationships with Jesus.

The irruption of the kingdom of God continues today. It is a historical project that is growing, breaking into lives and adding new protagonists. Their testimony to God's saving action in their lives through Jesus and the Holy Spirit fits into worship as part of that history of salvation that continues to be carried out. Their stories are especially relevant when they are the testimony of the victims of this world, the marginalized and the excluded, like many of the stories in the Gospels that have been incorporated into the history of salvation. We could even say that these life stories *should* be told: "We tell stories because, after all, human lives need and deserve to be narrated. This observation acquires its full force when we evoke the need to save the history of the vanquished and losers."[3] Adding to this, we would say that life stories of suffering can finally find meaning in and deserve to be told as part of the history of salvation. All human suffering is a reminder of the suffering of Jesus, and the memory of Jesus is "dangerous," in the words of theologian J. B. Metz, because before his suffering we can hardly remain indifferent.[4]

Life as a Narrative History

Human existence is experienced in temporality, which links time and narrativity. The art of telling a story is itself a fundamental anthropological and ontological category. As Ricoeur has shown, our identity is

---

3. Ricoeur, *Temps et récit I*, 115.

4. Metz, *Fe*, 120–26. Thanks to my colleague Julio Cézar Adam for indicating this relationship with the political theology of Metz.

narrative, because we understand ourselves by telling our own story.⁵ The self can thus be said to be refigured by the reflective application of narrative configurations.⁶ Therefore, the narrative identity allows the subject to appear constituted both as a reader and a writer of his own life. It is not a lonely story, but the refiguration of one's own life makes it a fabric of narrated stories. Testimonies in worship serve precisely to show how relationships with others, in this case with the person and message of Jesus Christ and of believers, is woven into personal history, community, and the history of salvation. It is about the lives not only of individuals, but also of groups or communities that can give testimony of their struggles, their challenges, and their pains, but also of their dreams, their faith, and their hopes.⁷

Telling a story is not just transmitting information but building a world. Storytelling unites actions among themselves within a causal relationship.⁸ In the case of the testimonies to which we refer, telling a story means narrating the way in which lives and communities are linked to a world, in this case to the world of the kingdom of God with its values and challenges.

In addition, Ricoeur notes, to narrate is to "open a text"—the text of life, an open work directed to an indefinite succession of possible readers. The text by which we understand the self is, among other things, human action.⁹ This action is endowed with intelligibility when, from a succession of events, a configuration is extracted, thanks to the structuring process of the plot and the mediation that it exercises between a multiplicity of incidents and a unique history: "Life is a story in search of a narrator." Therefore, our lives, both personal and collective, are the field for the constructive activity of the narrative intelligence and imagination through which we find, in the stories that we forge, the identity that constitutes us.¹⁰ By giving testimony of the salvific action in one's personal or collective history, the narrator identifies in worship with those who have also lived

---

5. Ricoeur, *Temps et récit III*), 349; Ricoeur, "Epilogo," 479. The narrative identity is Ricoeur's response to the demand for a hermeneutic that seeks, through phenomenology, a non-substantial identity.

6. Ricoeur, *Temps et récit III*, 355.

7. Even narrative testimonies that are difficult or tragic need to be shared to give full expression to human lives. César López writes about the necessity of liturgical lament in his essay in this book.

8. Todorov, *Grammaire*, 10.

9. Ricoeur, *Du texte à l'action*, 190–91.

10. Mauleon, *Imaginario*, 198.

that salvific action in another moment. Or it is an invitation to hearers or to oneself to be open to that saving action given through the preaching of the gospel or through the testimony itself. Thus the testimony holds a moment of solidarity, sending, and commitment.

How does it happen? Ricoeur acknowledges, together with H. Paul Grice, that any narrative through which an interlocutor intends to signify something implies that the speaker wants a reciprocal exchange of ideas. On the one hand, it is necessary to recognize that the speaker does not speak only for himself; there must be another who acts as the interlocutor. On the other hand, it is necessary that the listener intends to understand what is being said. In this sense, the interlocution raises a circularity of intentions that implies a disposition toward the other.[11]

Therefore testimony, Emmanuel Levinas suggests, becomes a provocation to be and act *otherwise*.[12] The testimony is intended to discover and approach the other. In this sense, there is an ethical component to the testimony, and it involves a decisive moment that makes us say: Here I am! Therefore, the narrated life is not ethically neutral. The narrator and the listener are led to an ethical option: openness to the other. For all these reasons, we consider the importance of testimony in worship for communities that seek mutual recognition of groups or people within the community, despite cultural distance. Such testimony can promote empathy by way of encountering and understanding of the other through his narrated history. In this way the congregation enters into communion by sharing the worship space as a space of faith and commitment. The task of the listener is to take a stand before the various propositions of ethical loyalty that the testimony offers him and that the history of salvation, when recapitulated in the worship, demands.

Testimony Is More than a Story

In a globalized context where there seems to be no place for great narratives and where every story is suspect because it is presented as inconsequential, it is necessary to take up the stories of victims. Enrique Dussel affirms that the testimonies of victims could seem insignificant, exceptional stories in relation to the immensity of globalized, urbanized, modernized society, but this is not so, because what victims experience every day is a testimony

---

11. Ricoeur, *Soi-même comme un autre*, 60.
12. Lévinas, *De otro modo*, 97–115.

of what happens in the environment of the excluded. Though sometimes unnoticed, these stories are an expression of the great tragedies, struggles, and hopes of the victims.[13] We ask ourselves how the story of life is transformed when it is presented in worship as an act of faith, especially in the church of which we are speaking, in which there is a confluence of lives, cultures, and experiences of faith so diverse that sometimes it is not easy to recognize the great diversity of all it.

Testimony has two parts: the one who gives the testimony and those who listen to it. Listening to someone's testimony, one can believe or not the reality of the narrative. For the listener, it is an act of faith to assume the truth of the testimony—that is, listening to someone's narrative testimony demands openness to the one who narrates. Therefore, narrative testimonies should focus on the truth of lives that have been transformed by the action of the gospel, becoming in worship part of the recapitulation of the salvation story and appealing to the faith of the listeners.[14]

Articulating one's life narrative as a testimony enriches the worshiping community, helping it to remain open to others and to become aware of its mission as a promoter of the kingdom of God. Such an encounter with the sacred reinforces the experience of faith as a human experience that can be narrated—indeed, it even *asks* to be narrated. The church community survives in part because it is supported by its own life stories.

Testimony is a form of revelation of victims, especially of those who suffer from the injustices of the current world order. Denied subjects appear with all their strength, narrating their experiences of exclusion. Their testimonies highlight the persistent evil and suffering caused by the structure of the world, revealed in the cry of the subjects themselves.[15]

Life narratives from the margins promote the meaning, the history, and the purpose of the Christian community and project hope for its members. They also strengthen and reaffirm the abilities and hopes of those who share their life story. Exposing the story of life in such a diverse environment allows congregants not only to know each other better, but to strengthen ties and become sensitive to the realities and needs of those who come to the community as well as those already in it. It helps to break down barriers and create bonds of empathy and challenge toward one another. In this sense, testimony is a prophetic

---

13. Dussel, "Retorno de lo excluido," 163–69.
14. Lévinas, *De otro modo*, 100–101.
15. Dussel, *Ética de la liberación*, 523.

expression because the witness speaks of the tensions of the world, the kingdom, and the anti-kingdom.

Testimony also has a confessional meaning, an integration of fact and meaning, narration and confession. This is not done without internal tensions like those present in the testimony of the Gospels. The writing of the Gospels came from directly recording the prophetic words attributed to the living Christ and from eyewitness memories of the actions of Jesus of Nazareth. There is a deep unity of the witness of facts and events and the witness of meaning and truth.[16] Consequently, testimony is both an act of self-consciousness and an act of historical understanding about the signs the absolute gives of itself. The signs that the absolute gives of itself are at the same time the signs in which the conscience recognizes itself. In this, according to Ricoeur, lies the hermeneutic of the testimony, because finally the testimony gives listeners something to interpret.[17] We suggest that in worship, the testimonies of the lives transformed by faith and the events that have marked these lives in the context of the kingdom of God bring new perspectives to the history of salvation. "The man who saw it has given testimony, and his testimony is true. He knows that he tells the truth, and he testifies so that you also may believe" (John 19:35).

NARRATED LIVES: A DANGEROUS MEMORY OF CHRIST

Narrative testimonies are people's stories of the real world that sometimes include painful descriptions of war, persecution, and harrowing migration experiences. On other occasions they are the testimony of those who have been marginalized or segregated because of their religious, political, and/or sexual beliefs. Sometimes people describe a deep emptiness, a sense of life having no meaning until they find new meaning in the light of the gospel. There are testimonies of women who historically have been marginalized and relegated to the background in a patriarchal society. And there are testimonies from people that live in the consequences of ecological destruction, relating the pain of seeing the dry fields, the suffering of the fauna, and the resulting poverty. These testimonies reveal

---

16. Ricoeur, *Fe y filosofía*, 121–22.

17. Ricoeur, *Fe y filosofía*, 127–28. Ricoeur details in this text the elements of a hermeneutic of testimony, but this goes beyond the intentions of this essay.

the world's many challenges and the church's mission in response. Do worship and testimony help this process of awareness?[18]

Von Allmen explains that worship is an "epiphany" of the church.[19] When the church worships, it becomes a liturgical assembly. By means of the worship it makes itself, confesses itself, and above all becomes what in the Old Testament was called the *qâhâl Yahweh*: the people's assembly freed from Egypt and confirmed as the people of God at Sinai (Deut 4:10).

First, von Allmen explains, the church reveals itself in worship as a baptismal community—that is, a community that has died for this world and is raised in Christ. In other words, worship distinguishes the church from the world. The church is not a mundane way of being; it does not belong to the world. Christian worship shows that the church is not a natural society; those who worship have been baptized into it. Thus, worship is celebrated with forgiveness and reconciliation.

Second, the church also manifests itself in worship as a nuptial community, declaring itself to be the faithful wife of Christ. In worship the church declares "yes" to the word and call of its Lord. The church offers itself in fidelity and does not honor other gods. So in worship the church is a community of faith and love.

Von Allmen says the church appears as a catholic community in worship. In the act of worship, all social and anthropological walls are broken, and the church becomes a place of welcome for all. Worship unites what the world divides. In addition, the church is a catholic community in the sense that it transcends time and space. Worship unites people across the centuries. It reminds us of what happened in the history of salvation and keeps a memory of what God has promised from the creation to the end of the world. Worship manifests the church as a catholic community in the sense that it spans sociological, anthropological, spatial, temporal, and cultural differences.

Fourth, the church is a diaconal community called to serve. It does not work for itself, but to serve God and human beings. Worship invites

---

18. My thoughts about liturgical theory are very close to those Júlio Cézar Adam describes in his essay in this book. I, too, consider worship to be a space where the congregation's participation can contribute to the process of the decolonialization and enculturization of the gospel. The gospel relates to and interacts with the culture when the life and history of community are reflected in worship.

19. von Allmen, *Culto cristiano*, 41–56.

church members to help each other in solidarity. Its vocation is for the edification of the whole body.

Finally, von Allmen says, in worship the church becomes a missionary community. It is an alternative to the world, not a society within it. But worship also forces the church to go out into the world. Worship, then, is a call to adoration, but it is also a sending, a commission, and a mission.

These five ways in which the church is revealed can be affirmed and enriched through testimony, by people narrating their real-life stories, including their suffering. Testimony can also help to make the church aware of the ways in which it must reaffirm its baptismal and catholic meanings, its nuptial and diaconal aspects, and its missionary task.

We speak of the church's catholicism because, by offering their testimonies, people from different countries and regions provide living examples of the universality of the church that goes beyond physical, linguistic, and cultural borders. Such testimony shows that in the end, in worship the overarching language is the language of faith. The walls that mark borders have fallen. There are no foreigners or upstarts; all are members of the family of God. In the diaconal and missionary senses, through testimonies the church can become aware of the needs that exist in the world and can then work in ways that affirm the kingdom of God or challenge the powers that be.[20]

Testimony also highlights the need for reconciliation and forgiveness in the world and exposes the suffering that happens without reconciliation. Facing the need for hope in a world where there is so much pain, discomfort, restlessness, and despair, the church must live into its baptismal character and be an evangelical community, bringing the gospel of reconciliation into the world, giving meaning and hope. Testimony can sensitize the church to people's basic needs and the suffering that people live with: poverty, hunger, ignorance, injustice, and death. A victim's testimony will give witness to the struggle for survival, to the search for food, clothing, health care, and shelter. Worship, then, must transform the community into a diaconal church, a "Samaritan community." The church must sympathize, support, share with, and

---

20. Muñoz, "Experiencia popular de Dios," 161–79. Muñoz presents some of the ways in which the church can organize its mission based on the needs that exist in the world. We follow this scheme in describing what the testimonies show about the needs of the world.

heal those who suffer, providing a welcoming place for all those who are tired, sick, and needy.

When people talk about their loneliness and isolation and their need for affection, understanding, companionship, and fraternity, worship can be a home where those who arrive feel like family, joining a celebration where there is freedom to express joy, where bonds of friendship and affection are created or strengthened. When people describe their marginalization, and sometimes their abuse and persecution, the church must be an open and fraternal community willing to host an inclusive table of joy and glee.

When people testify to the denial of rights and injustice for so many people, worship must encourage the church to resume its prophetic character, denouncing the injustices, the impunity of evildoers, and the sin that oppresses the world, and promoting the righteous ways of God according to the justice of his kingdom.

When people narrate their need for God, for a spirituality that puts things in their place and gives meaning to life, worship must be for participants a place where the presence of God is palpable, where people can encounter God, pray, and sing to a living God who loves life.

Narrative testimonies can be told throughout the worship service, paired with liturgical elements that highlight the meaning of the testimony. What follows is an example of a liturgy that we used in our community. Mr. Oli is a man who came to Spain from Cameroon. He crossed the desert, was assaulted, arrested, and finally liberated, but without papers. His story is not unusual for a migrant. But he is a Christian, a person who knows God. In a special celebration in our church, we integrated Mr. Oli's testimony into the worship service as a narrative of the history of salvation, as a dangerous memory of Christ.[21]

> *Prelude*
>
> *Welcome*
>
> *Testimony from Mr. Oli*
> I come from Cameroon. In my country there are twenty-six national parks, six wildlife sanctuaries, and five wildlife reserves. I

---

21. This is the order of worship from a service in our church following the liturgical structure proposed by Eleventh International Migrants Day (December 18, 2010) by Cláudio Carvalhaes. See also the World Council of Churches' work on migration: http://www.oikoumene.org/en/programmes/justice-diakonia-and-responsibility-for-creation/migration-and-social-justice.html.

come from one of the lowlands, the Benue Valley, with its great river. Water is our life, and the animals and plants that live there. The rain is always welcome. The plain is glad and the river rejoices. Today I am here with you to adore the God who has created the world, who has given us the river and gives us the rain.

Call to Worship

Leader: Who are we?

Congregation: We are all immigrants in this world.

L: Where did we come from?

C: We came from everywhere. We came from our ancestors' wombs, those who prepared the way for us all.

L: Where do we find our worth?

C: Our worth is not in documents or passports, but in God's holy name.

L: Where is our home?

C: Our home is in God's unfenced, undocumented, and gracious kingdom. Our home is next to each other, in each other's arms.

L: What are we doing here today?

C: We are here to praise God for God's unbounded grace, mercy, and love.

L: Let us worship God.

C: Let us worship God.

Opening Prayer from an Immigrant

Hymn

Testimony from Mr. Oli

I left Cameroon. The poverty in my land and the divisions and violence that exist force us to go and look for a better future for our people. Many others leave because they are persecuted or because there is no work. I left because they tell us that in Europe there is work and you can make progress.

There are no means to go out with dignity. You leave with the idea of crossing the desert quickly, but there they assault you, or they deceive you. Halfway through the desert they charge you more money than they told you at the beginning.

The road is very tiring. You eat little and you fall asleep. That happened to me. I fell asleep, and I fell out of the car and they left me there. I was walking for three days. I did not separate from the path, but I experienced the most intense loneliness of my entire life. You leave your family, your land, your friends, and suddenly you find yourself alone. I had never been so alone.

Prayers of the People

Between each prayer, say: "Let it begin with us."

Testimony from Mr. Oli

I remembered the stories of the Bible with which I grew up about the people of God in the desert. I had never experienced the presence of God until that day, when I could have died and I was afraid. Just thinking that God is also in the desert helped me to walk.

After three days a car passed by and picked me up. I think that my grandmother and my mother prayed a lot for me. I felt born again when I got back into a car and crossed the desert.

We did not have a good time on the road from Cameroon to Morocco. Moving to Melilla was also very difficult. You go hungry and very thirsty. I arrived "dry" in Spain because I did not have to take a boat. The Red Cross helped me to enter Spain, but even so it was not easy. It is a lot of pain and loneliness.

I have also suffered here. It has not been easy. They intern migrants in centers. It was not as bad as others, but it's not easy. You regret having left, but on many occasions you have no other choice—you go, or you die like some of my companions. Some people who work with migrants have helped me. . . . The Lord freed me.

Now I live in the house of the Red Cross. I am already a volunteer. I have learned Spanish quickly and I also speak English, French, and two other languages of my land. That is why I have been invited to work with them. I always talk about my experience of solitude, danger, and scams, but God has not left me.

Prayer for Illumination

Scripture Reading
Use various Scriptures related to immigration.

Sermon
"God in the Desert" (1 Cor 10)

Testimony from Mr. Oli
The road to Spain was not easy, and even now it is not easy. I remember from the songs of my church how big the desert is, and I remember a few months ago I read a text in the Bible that I did not understand. I asked what it means that the people were baptized in the cloud in the desert (1 Cor 10). When it was explained to me, I identified with the Israelites who were in the desert and walked a lot. God baptizes in the desert.

The Immigrants' Creed[22]
I believe in Almighty God, who guided his people in exile and in exodus, the God of Joseph in Egypt and of Daniel in Babylon, the God of foreigners and immigrants.

I believe in Jesus Christ a displaced Galilean, who was born away from his people and his home, who had to flee the country with his parents when his life was in danger, and who upon returning to his own country had to suffer the oppression of the tyrant Pontius Pilate, the servant of a foreign power. He was persecuted, beaten, tortured, and finally accused and condemned to death unjustly. But on the third day, this scorned Jesus rose from the dead, not as a foreigner but to offer us citizenship in heaven.

I believe in the Holy Spirit, the eternal immigrant from God's kingdom among us, who speaks all languages, lives in all countries, and reunites all races.

I believe that the church is the secure home for all foreigners and believers who constitute it, who speak the same language and have the same purpose.

I believe that the communion of saints begins when we accept the diversity of the saints.

I believe in forgiveness, which makes us all equal, and in the reconciliation, which identifies us more than race, language, or nationality.

---

22. José Luis Casal, "The Immigrants' Creed," https://www.discipleshomemissions.org/wp-content/uploads/2017/05/Immigrants-Creed-Jose-Luis-Casal.pdf.

I believe that, in the Resurrection God will unite us as one people in which all are distinct and all are alike at the same time.

I believe in the eternal life beyond this world, where no one will be an immigrant but all will be citizens of God's kingdom that has no end. Amen.

—Rev. José Luis Casal

Testimony from Mr. Oli

Sometimes there was nothing to eat, but what little there was you shared with the ones you were with. You look for others because it is not good to eat alone. Bread tastes better with others. I learned that on the way to Morocco, through the desert, and in Melilla. Now I give glory to God that I can eat the Lord's Supper with all of you.

Eucharist

The Lord's Prayer

Sending

Now, brothers and sisters, don't forget that there are 200 million people waking around the globe. We as churches of Jesus Christ need to help defuse public hostility toward them. More than that, we must provide hospitality to people in Jesus' name. Go and figure out together how to welcome people in our midst!

Benediction

BIBLIOGRAPHY

The Book of Common Worship: 2018 Edition. Louisville: Westminster John Knox, 2018.
Dussel, Enrique. *Ética de la liberación en la edad de la globalización y la exclusion.* 2nd ed. Madrid: Trotta, 1998.
———. "El retorno de lo excluido: La vida humana cotidiana como el lugar privilegiado de la experiencia religiosa." In *Resistencia y solidaridad: Globalización, capitalismo y liberación,* edited by Raúl Fornet-Betancourt, 163–70. Madrid: Trotta, 2003.
Lévinas, Emmanuel. *De otro modo que ser o más allá de la esencia.* 3rd ed. Translated by Antonio Pintor Ramos. Salamanca: Sígueme, 1999.
Lópes, César Márques. "Learning Empathy: Removing Lament from the Null Curriculum." In *Worship through Latin American Eyes,* edited by María Eugenia Cornou and Noel Snyder, 150–74. Eugene, OR: Cascade, 2026.

Mauleon, Xabier Etxeberria. *Imaginario y derechos humanos desde Paul Ricoeur*. Bilbao: Desclée de Brouwer, 1995.

Metz, Johann Baptist. *La fe, en la historia y la sociedad: Esbozo de una teología política fundamental para nuestro tiempo*. Madrid: Cristiandad, 1979.

Muñoz, Ronaldo."Experiencia popular de Dios y de la iglesia." In *Cambio social y pensamiento cristiano en América Latina*, edited by José Comblin et al., 161–80. Madrid: Trotta, 1993.

Ricoeur, Paul. *Du texte à l'action: Essais d'herméneutique II*. Paris: Seuil, 1986.

———. "Epilogo, Narratividad, Fenomenología y Hermenéutica." In *Horizontes del relato: Lecturas y conversaciones con Paul Ricoeur*, edited by Gabriel Aranzueque, 197–215. Madrid: Cuaderno Gris, 1997.

———. *Fe y filosofía: Problemas del lenguaje religioso*. 3rd ed. Buenos Aires: Prometeo, 2008.

———. *Soi-même comme un autre*. Paris: Seuil, 1990.

———. *Temps et récit I: L'histoire et le récit*. Paris: Seuil, 1983.

———. *Temps et récit III: Le temps raconté*. Paris: Seuil, 1985.

Todorov, Tzvetan. *Grammaire du Décaméron*. Approaches to Semiotics 3. Mouton: La Haye et Paris, 1969.

von Allmen, Jean-Jacques. *El culto cristiano: Su esencia y su celebración*. Salamanca: Sígueme, 1968.

LEARNING EMPATHY

Removing Lament from the Null Curriculum in Public Worship

César Márques López

In the early hours of Tuesday, May 1, 2018, the Wilson Paes de Almeida Building, a high-rise in the old downtown area of Sao Paulo, Brazil, was engulfed by a fire that ended up compromising its structure to the point of spectacular collapse. Dozens of graphic images—of the fire itself, of the firefighters' failed attempt to rescue one of the building's residents, and of 500 residents camping out at a square nearby—appeared constantly on TV and in social media. The subject dominated local and national conversation throughout the week.

But the momentous event seemed to have had little to no effect on how Sunday services were conducted in Sao Paulo's evangelical churches a few days later. This essay will consider this apparent apathy in relation to public events unfolding in the broader Brazilian context and suggest ways to develop public worship that is more empathetic. I will use curriculum theory constructs, such as explicit and null curriculum, to suggest that the incorporation of lament may enhance both the worship experience of the community and the missional perspective of the local church.

In the first section I will describe the regular public worship practices of a local church in relation to the general characteristics observed in the Presbyterian tradition in Brazil and in the broader national evangelical field. In the second section I will discuss and define lament as a biblical category integral to the worship experience of the people of God in the Old Testament. In the third section I will suggest that the apparent apathy toward the events surrounding us in the broader society is a general characteristic of public worship in Brazilian evangelical churches, and at this local church more specifically. I will also discuss how the current ethos of public worship in Brazilian evangelical churches tends to place lament in what the literature in curriculum theory defines as "null curriculum," and I will explore the effects of that placement from an educational perspective.

The guiding principle of this essay is that local churches may benefit from considering empathy as a viable learning outcome of bringing lament to the explicit curriculum of their Christian education, whether this curriculum is intentionally developed or not.

THE WORSHIP PRACTICE AT VILA NOVA CHURCH AS A SAMPLE OF BRAZILIAN EVANGELICAL WORSHIP PRACTICES

At 1:30 AM on May 1, 2018, the national holiday of Labor Day in Brazil, a short circuit ignited a fire at the Wilson Paes de Almeida Building. The fire spread quickly, but almost all of the estimated 500 residents were evacuated safely. At 5:30 AM, in a scene somewhat reminiscent of what the world saw in New York City on 9/11, the fire compromised the twenty-six-floor structure of the building enough that it collapsed in flames and ashes.

More than an isolated tragic incident, the fire synthesizes a number of issues Brazilian society faces. The Wilson Paes de Almeida Building had a unique history. Built in the 1960s as an advanced architectural project, it was never intended to be a residential building. It housed a number of businesses but was eventually transferred to the federal government for payment of a tax debt. It housed the Sao Paulo branch of the Federal Police for nearly a decade. After some ill-explained legal problems, the building was simply abandoned and remained empty from 2001 to 2003, when it was occupied by an organized homeless movement through a sort of squatting process. Homelessness is a serious social problem in Brazil in general and in Sao Paulo especially. In 2015, there were an estimated 15,000 people living in the streets of the city.¹ Evangelical churches do have some outreach in terms of feeding, clothing, and evangelizing the street population. However, the problem is largely ignored in our circles.

While the squatting situation at the Wilson Paes de Almeida Building remained in the gray area of litigation, people kept living there, obtaining their electricity illegally and distributing it through flimsy connections. They divided the wide offices on the first ten floors with plywood and cardboard. They got into the habit of dumping their trash in the unused elevator pits. Such conditions were blamed for the spectacular collapse of the building.

The fire's location in an iconic central area of Sao Paulo, the personal stories told on television news, and the impressive scenes of hundreds of former residents just camping out at a nearby square occupied the national conversation in the following days. People talked about it on social media, at lunch breaks, and with their families.

Unusual Days, Usual Services

Against this heavy backdrop, five days after the fire, the folks at Vila Nova Independent Presbyterian Church gathered for their Sunday service.² The church is located in a smaller town nestled in Sao Paulo's larger metropolitan area, which is home to about 20 million people. Smaller towns like the one Vila Nova is in can be described as lower-middle class suburbs, although these words mean different things in Brazil. "Suburb" commonly refers to a medium- to lower-income commuter neighborhood. Its residents ride public transportation for up to two hours to get from their homes to their blue-collar jobs.

Vila Nova's service happened as usual. An officiant welcomed the congregation, invited people to stand and read a Bible verse, and then to sing a hymn. Another passage was read; a solo was sung. The congregation was invited to make their offerings, and then came an extended moment of praise: five songs connected by some comments from the worship

---

1. Gomes, "Divulgação do censo," lines 6–7. Note that this is pre-pandemic number. The post-pandemic number shows a skyrocketing of this population, with newer estimates coming in around 54,000. See https://agenciabrasil.ebc.com.br/direitos-humanos/noticia/2023-09/populacao-de-rua-em-sao-paulo-cresce-em-junho-aponta-levantamento.

2. The name of the church has been changed to protect the privacy of the local community.

leader. The pastor took the pulpit to preach, and after some individual prayer, a final song, and the apostolic blessing, the congregation was sent to their mission in the world. The tragedy at Wilson Paes de Almeida building was mentioned briefly during the moment of prayer at the beginning of the service, when a congregant prayed about the aftereffects of the fire from several angles, including for the families that were in such a stressful situation. However, the entire tone of the celebration remained basically unchanged relative to other services. The song selection for the extended moment of praise also seemed to be absolutely unchanged.

General Context in Praise and Worship

The service at Vila Nova Church described above is in many ways typical for evangelical churches in Brazil, though it is impossible to give broadly accurate descriptions. However, it is fair to say that Brazilian evangelical churches follow a low-structure liturgy with large chunks of time dedicated to corporate singing and to the sermon.[3]

As with many churches in emerging or developing countries,[4] corporate singing has grown in importance in the last fifty years for churches across the evangelical spectrum in Brazil, and in the 1980s many transitioned from traditional hymns to more contemporary songs and rhythms.

Two musical tendencies emerged. First was a liberationist approach that dialogued with Latin American theologies and was marked by the use of typically Brazilian rhythms. Songs representing this tendency used a language of liberation versus oppression, of resistance and hope, of struggle and conflict with powers of death.

In the early 1990s, Simei Monteiro performed an extensive analysis of songs used by Brazilian Evangelical churches. She devoted some attention to songs written from a liberationist perspective, and her conclusion about them was that "whether in hymnology or theology, the liberationist perspective was always threatened by a utopic attitude."[5]

Latin American theologies did not dedicate much attention to liturgy and worship. One exception in the broader evangelical universe

3. For another description of the Brazilian liturgical context, please refer to Adam's essay in this book, "Liturgy, Daily Life, and Performance." Adam also provides a more extensive description of worship in Brazil in *Worship with a Brazilian Face*.

4. Miller and Yamamori, *Global Pentecostalism*, 148.

5. Monteiro, *Cântico da vida*, 176. Translations throughout this chapter by César Lopes.

was the Anglican Jaci Maraschin, who used a language fairly close to that "utopic attitude":

> Liturgical celebration affirms how life wins over death and engages us in the ecological movement of all the human beings at the planet. [. . .] Liturgical celebration becomes the hope for the revelation of the full life in God, in the world and in human communities. When holding this kind of expectation, we begin to experience happiness. Happiness is always the opening to affirm life in front of the powers of death.[6]

The liberationist perspective did not firmly establish itself in the long run. However, a second tendency stemming from 1980s corporate worship did succeed and is stronger now than ever. Usually referred to as "gospel" (we do use the English word) music, it has grown to a point where corporate singing in most local churches across the evangelical spectrum in Brazil is greatly influenced by a handful of groups with a strong media presence.

For Magali Cunha, some of the most distinguishing characteristics of corporate singing in Brazil under the influence of the "gospel" movement include:

- an emphasis on the "modern" and "mediatic," which connect communities to the present time but at the same time generate some distaste for traditional Christian music or for anything "not gospel," meaning congregations sing only what is promoted in popular media;
- music and musicians becoming indoctrinators of local communities with this emphasis on the predominant gospel culture; and
- a new conception of what a worship service means. The time for praise is interpreted as a "special moment" highlighted and independent from other parts of the service, and at times it becomes a "service within the service," including every element of the other parts of the service (prayer, biblical readings, and even some preaching of the Scripture).[7]

In Brazil, some of the most well-known gospel groups are Diante do Trono, Renascer Praise, and Trazendo a Arca, while some of the individual artists are Aline Barros, Ludmila Ferber, David Quinlan, and Ana Paula

---

6. Maraschin, *Beleza da santidade*, 70–71.
7. Cunha, "Demandas pedagógicas, 87.

Valadão. Current literature and studies in the Brazilian context point to a certain prevalence of individualistic songs emphasizing success and prosperity.[8] Once more, it is important to stress that such emphases are not uncommon in the evangelical churches in developing countries.[9]

Later in this essay I will define the biblical category of lament, but it is important to point out now that, even though apparently occupying opposite sides of the spectrum of contextuality in terms of theology and style, both Brazilian worship music tendencies—liberationist and contemporary "gospel"—tend not to include lament in their creations.[10]

Evangélicos and Presbiterianos in Brazil

At this point it is also important to briefly describe some key components of the evangelical field in Brazil in order to clarify the language used throughout this essay. First, in Latin America *evangélicos* (the same word in Portuguese and Spanish) usually refers to non-Catholic Christians in general. From Presbyterians to Assemblies of God, from Methodists to Baptists, from Reformed to Pentecostals, we are all evangelicals (*evangélicos*).

This simple description includes a very strong identity feature of *evangélicos* in Latin America and especially in Brazil: we are non-Catholics. For many years the evangelical identity in Brazil has been defined as an opposition to Catholicism being the country's *de facto* official religion. To be an evangelical Christian would mean to *not* venerate the saints, to *not* light candles in honor of the dead, to *not* avoid meat on Fridays, etc. The relationship was tense on both sides: even in the mid-twentieth century, evangelicals were persecuted in Brazil.[11]

---

8. See, for example, Baggio, *Música cristã contemporânea* and Dolghie, "Igreja Renascer em Cristo."

9. Steuernagel also touches on this issue in his essay in this book ("Songs from Other Heartlands"), in which he describes worship practices at local communities in Brazil, India, and Mozambique.

10. A case can be made that Protestant worship since the Reformation has emphasized celebration and joy at the expense of lament or a general "sadness." Sánchez M. highlights in his essay in this book ("Theologian by Day") how Luther himself thought of music as something that "alone produces what otherwise only theology can do, namely, a calm and joyful disposition," and that "it is the function of music to arouse the sad, sluggish, and dull spirit."

11. For more on the issue of the evangelical presence in an overwhelmingly Catholic context, see Israel Flores Olmos's description in this book of an evangelical community in the context of Andalusia, Spain ("Narrated Lives and Testimonies").

On this issue of tensions between Catholicism and the evangelical presence, Dinorah Méndez's essay in this book points out that in Mexico,

> The clash among the Spanish and Indigenous cultures was violent, marked by "the sword and the cross." This produced a forced process of evangelization which, instead of bringing about authentic conversions to the Christian faith, engendered a syncretism between existing Indigenous religious beliefs and practices and the newly introduced Roman Catholic ones. We still see this combination or religious mixture in the salient features discussed above. *Mestizo* people since the Conquest were able to adopt the new ideas externally while internally keeping their own existing ideas.[12]

There are profound similarities and differences between the colonial experience of these two Latin American countries. Apart from the obvious fact that the Portuguese, not the Spanish, colonized Brazil, colonization was in both countries a process motivated and promoted by the sword and the cross. On the other hand, the extermination of the Indigenous population in Brazil was more violent and more fully accomplished, similar to what happened in the United States, making Indigenous cultural influences less visible than in Mexico. However, the strong presence of African slaves meant their culture replaced the Indigenous cultures in the equation Méndez describes above. The Brazilian religious ethos is indeed influenced by this mixture of Catholicism and African religions. As a result, the evangelical identity in Brazil is also defined in opposition to African-Brazilian forms of religiosity.[13]

Magali Cunha highlights one specific feature of this evangelical identity construction through differentiation from a Catholic religious matrix that concerns the matter of lament. Cunha proposes that the Catholic relationship with death is marked by fear, while Protestant converts

> began to remake their relationship with their conception of life and death. Death would not be the end, but a passage to eternal life. There is no need to fear it anymore. Before conversion, death is terror; after conversion, it is blessing; this is why, in the evangelical culture, death is commonly referred to as

---

12. Méndez, "Contextualizing Evangelical Worship."

13. This is a rich topic that has been deeply studied. A more recent trend, especially among new Pentecostal churches, is to use elements of African Brazilian religions in a sort of reverse syncretism. A good analysis of the paradoxical relationship, available in English, is Silva's "Neo-Pentecostalism and Afro-Brazilian Religions."

"being promoted to glory," "living with the Lord," "sleeping in the Lord," or "being taken to the eternal tabernacles."[14]

As we see, there may already have been an element of avoiding grief and lament inherent in the very construction of evangelical identity in Brazil.

A second key component of the evangelical field in Brazil is described in the most accepted academic typology of evangelicals in Brazil, produced by Antônio Mendonça in the 1980s. It divides Brazilian evangelical churches and denominations into three categories: immigration Protestantism (mostly Lutherans and Anglicans); missionary Protestantism (ranging from Baptists to Presbyterians, Congregationalists to Methodists); and Pentecostals (which Mendonça further divides into "first wave," such as Assemblies of God and *Congregação Cristã no Brasil*, and "second wave," such as Foursquare Church and *Deus é amor*).[15]

Contemporary scholars, though, highlight the emergence of the *neopentecostais*, the new Pentecostals.[16] With a very strong media presence, the *neopentecostais* in Brazil grew to a point in which one of the largest evangelical denominations in the country is the *Igreja Universal do Reino de Deus* (Universal Church of the Kingdom of God), a *neopentecostais* denomination with about 2.5 million members. It is not a coincidence that the second-largest television network in Brazil is owned by this same denomination.

Such new Pentecostalism is marked by a prosperity gospel theology.[17] Furthermore, many of the groups and songwriters of the "gospel music" worship tendency are influenced by this theology, which is reflected in their lyrics.[18] Their popularity guarantees that other denominations and local churches are also influenced by this theology through worship. This is certainly the case at Vila Nova Presbyterian Church.

Presbyterians, who are part of the missionary Protestantism mentioned above, have been in Brazil since the 1870s and are known for their emphasis on doctrine and on teaching and preaching centered in a more traditional, historical-grammatical interpretation of the Scriptures as opposed to a more Pentecostal or experiential reading. Presbyterian liturgy

14. Cunha, *Explosão gospel*, 181–82.
15. Mendonça, *Celeste Porvir*, 179.
16. Pierucci and Prandi, *Realidade social*; Mariano, *Neopentecostais*.
17. Campos, *Teatro, tempo e mercado*; Mariano, *Neopentecostais*.
18. Cunha, *Explosão gospel*; Cunha, "Demandas pedagógicas"; Mariano, *Neopentecostais*.

falls into the low-structure description offered above, although there is generally an attempt to observe a call for worship, a moment of confession, and affirmations of faith. However, the corporate singing and the preaching are the larger, more carefully prepared parts of worship.

Corporate singing in Presbyterian denominations in general and specifically in the Independent Presbyterian Church denomination in Brazil (I will use the acronym for its Portuguese name, IPIB) generally follows the broader tendencies of Brazilian evangelical churches, though perhaps with less emphasis on prosperity songs. IPIB is a denomination with about 100,000 members. It held some affinity in the second half of the twentieth century with the Presbyterian Church (USA), but in 2016, the dialogue and partnerships were interrupted by a decision of its General Assembly about sexual morality. The IPIB is, however, a significantly more progressive denomination than its counterpart, the Presbyterian Church in Brazil, from which IPIB divided in 1903.

The song selection at Vila Nova Church, which belongs to the IPIB, fits the description of Presbyterian worship given above. The church tends to emphasize christological songs, with lyrics focusing on the Lordship of Jesus, and it intentionally uses traditional hymns. IPIB encourages its churches to use the denominational hymnal, *Cantai todos os povos* (*Sing Out, Every Nation*), as a way to affirm its historic identity and heritage. At Vila Nova Church, such hymns are usually used in the early stages of the service, or else after the preaching. It is interesting to observe that in the "service within the service," as Cunha referred to the extended time of singing praise, hymns are not often used.

However, as mentioned above, it is possible to perceive the influence of the "gospel movement" both in the song selection and in the performance of the musical group. From time to time the worship leader may offer a short homily, usually emphasizing personal struggles and the small or larger victories a believer will have both in the present life and eternally. Furthermore, the music leaders' body language reflects the ethos seen in the YouTube videos of some larger, more mediatic churches: eyes closed, hands up in the air, and a smile on the face indicating the worshiper's confidence in the provision of God.

It is very important to stress that these characteristics are not inherently problematic. They can be viewed as fair and sincere expressions of praise and worship. However, the intention here is to point to the fact that even in a time of mourning and suffering in the community context, these practices continue to be the standard mode of public worship.

Lament and Grief in Contemporary Brazilian Culture

In light of this overall description, it is clear that it is not possible to equate the absence of liturgical lament with an attitude of apathy by evangelical churches. In other words, there are many historic factors contributing to such an attitude. There are even other contextual factors not discussed so far. For example, there is a stereotypical impression of Brazilians having a joyful disposition that makes us not prone to grief. We also see ourselves as a people that never gives up, so there may be an attitude of "grieve quickly to fight quickly." It is interesting to note that in the Brazilian culture, when someone dies the body is usually buried on the same day or the next.

The tendency to grieve quickly is even stronger among evangelicals. According to Leonildo Campos, the focus of evangelical memorial services is helping survivors to not let themselves lose faith in face of pain caused by the loss of a loved one. It is not uncommon to use a burial ceremony as an evangelistic opportunity.[19]

On the other hand, the proliferation of news about local and international tragedies might be causing a sort of a "lament burnout." People may feel that they are just quickly moving from a natural disaster to a terror attack to a human-caused accident within a short period of time. There are even anthropological studies on how mourning in the contemporary Brazilian urban context has been both shortened and moved to the digital sphere and the social networks while in concrete social interactions people are expected to grieve privately.[20]

On the same note, for Methodist professor Blanches de Paula, in the Brazilian contemporary culture "there seems to be a disbelief in the need of grieving as a search for justice and ethics in social relations. Such an attitude cloaks pain and loss, as well as pushes away possibilities of reconciliation with life. Getting astonished by violence is a rare experience."[21] Apathy thus is not a characteristic exclusive to worship practices.

Nevertheless, the main thrust of this essay is that empathy may be intentionally learned by a community that allows itself to lament. But how can we define lament biblically and theologically? What are the theological and personal implications of standing before God and questioning God about the suffering God has allowed?

19. Campos, "Protestantes brasileiros," 153.
20. Koury, "O luto no Brasil."
21. de Paula, "Olhar pastoral sobre o luto," 105.

A BIBLICAL-THEOLOGICAL UNDERSTANDING OF LAMENT

Lament in the Old and New Testaments

Although lament is somewhat an exception in how God's people relate to and publicly worship their Lord nowadays, the same cannot be said of lament in Scripture. The most evident instances of lament are in the Old Testament, especially in the Psalter and the whole of Lamentations.

Old Testament scholar Claus Westermann, however, highlights the presence of lament throughout all of Old Testament literature: "From the beginning to the end, 'the call of distress,' the 'cry out of the depths,' that is, the lament, is an inevitable part of what happens between God and man." Furthermore, the author continues, "all the psalms of lament in the Psalter (and in Lamentations) constitute only a portion of the laments contained in the Old Testament."[22]

Westermann's two definitions of lament are the essence of what we understand as lament in this work: a "call of distress," a desperate plea to the Lord for help, and a "cry out of the depths" emphasizing an agonizing existential situation.

More than a simple expression of grief and suffering, lament can be a way of resignifying these experiences, since "the lament is the language of suffering; in it suffering is given the dignity of language: It will not stay silent!"[23] It is important to perceive the double movement developed by the author: on the one hand, there is a notion of a person or a community sinking in pain and suffering; at the same time, it seems lament is the very turning point for this situation, as the refusal to stay silent and the initiative to voice suffering is the starting point for a liberation that the petitioner trusts will come from God.

In the same tone, Brazilian biblicist Luiz Carlos Susin expresses the idea that lament is a natural and healthy reaction against suffering, either experienced or witnessed, especially in the case of "innocent suffering":

> Lament is, at the same time, confession of misery and protest for justice. It is a feeling that leads to truth. In face of evil, human feelings lead to a place that cannot be reached by reason. Lamentation, grief, and expressions of pain are a higher language than philosophy and theodicy. No doctrine is fair

22. Westermann, "Role of the Lament," 23.
23. Westermann, "Role of the Lament," 31.

enough to the suffering that is voiced by lament. To the obscure excess of innocent suffering, only the transcendent excess, paradoxically bright of a larger mystery, may be worthy of trust and surrender.[24]

In evaluating such expressions of pain, theologian Paulo Roberto Gomes inventories common Christian reactions to suffering.[25] He points to suffering seen as the defeat of human pride, in which God acts pedagogically to teach human beings of their limitations; to suffering happening by God's ordination or permission because of God's "mysterious ways" or omniscience; to suffering as a punishment, as retribution for the evil done by people; to suffering as destiny, as an accident, a way of thinking that invites people to apathy and inaction; and to suffering as something positive, as a way God uses to draw us closer to God or to promote growth. Theologian Walter Brueggemann, however, invites us to refuse such passive explanations by adding an interesting active theological dimension to lament, describing it as the essence of the relationship between the people of God and their testimony:

> First and perhaps most crucially, Israel asks and wonders about Yahweh's reliability and fidelity. Israel had a sense of being abandoned.... The question lingers in Israel. It lingers because Israel is so honest in its testimony and because lived reality does not easily conform to the core testimony of Israel. Old Testament theology must recognize that this question lives at the center of Israel's most convinced testimony.[26]

John Witvliet describes lament in the Psalter as highlighting the psalmist's anger but often at the same time anticipating liberation. This expression may be individual or collective:

> Lament psalms . . . are texts that begin with laments to God about the brokenness and pain of life. Most laments move from expressions of anger to expressions of trust and praise (with Ps 88 as a notable exception). Scholars often divide these texts into "community laments" (such as 80, 85, or 137) and "individual lament" (such as 3, 22, or 42).[27]

---

24. Susin, *Criação de Deus*, 144–45.
25. Gomes, *Deus Im-potente*, 36–41.
26. Brueggemann, *Theology of the Old Testament*, 322–23.
27. Witvliet, *Biblical Psalms*, 70.

For Westermann, there is also a somewhat rigid structure for the psalms of lament: address, the lament itself, a confession of trust, petition, and a vow of praise.[28] Brueggemann develops a slightly different structure:

> The lament psalms, then, are a complaint which makes the shrill insistence: 1. Things are not right in the present arrangement; 2. They need not stay this way but can be changed; 3. The speaker will not accept them in this way, for it is intolerable; 4. It is God's obligation to change things.[29]

Notice that while Westermann understands the last two stances of lament as petition and vow of praise, Brueggemann interprets the petitioner's attitude as being a bit more aggressive. For him the petitioner places in God not only a passive hope, but a more proactive boldness, making God accountable for changing the situation of suffering.

It is important to acknowledge that lament is not as common in the New Testament as it is in the Old. New Testament scholar Klaus Berger notes that the most common laments in the Gospels are the "woe" texts, in which there is an "announcement of disgrace" and the "'woe' is essentially an expression of sadness in general."[30] This is the case in texts such as Matthew 23:13–39 or Luke 6:20–26. A more similar usage to Old Testament lament, Berger says, happens in Revelation with the genre of laments of decay, whose starting point is a contrast between the greatness of the past and ruin in the present, followed by an exhortation for hope.[31] But Westermann contends that lament is still a valid action for Christians:

> I also know no text in the New Testament which would prevent the Christian from lamenting or which would express the idea that faith in Christ excluded lamentation from man's relationship with God.... Only in the paraenetic sections of the New Testament letters does the admonition to bear suffering with patience and humble self-resignation start to gain the upper hand.[32]

In fact, Westermann returns to his concern with actualizing lament in the New by pointing out connections between psalms of lament (especially Ps 22) and Jesus' words on the cross, concluding that the language of

28. Westermann, *Praise and Lament*, 52.
29. Brueggemann, "Costly Loss of Lament," 62.
30. Berger, *Formas literárias do Novo Testamento*, 185.
31. Berger, *Formas literárias do Novo Testamento*, 189.
32. Westermann, "Role of the Lament," 25.

suffering "would receive a legitimate place in Christian worship, as it had in the worship of the Old Testament."[33]

Lament and Suffering in Latin American Theology

In a very broad generalization, I suggest that in Latin American theology and biblical interpretation lament is seen with three emphases. First, there is a very little regard for the dimension of pain conveyed by a lament; second, there is a strong emphasis on the element of resistance against situations of oppression; and third, there is an emphasis on the solitary dimension of lament. The first two may even be considered distortions, but the third seems to be conducive to a liturgical use of lament.

In the first section of this essay, I pointed to the tendency of the liberationist perspective in worship to adopt a "utopic attitude." The first two Latin American emphases mentioned above are simply another aspect of such an attitude. Consider, for example, how Marcelo Souza perceives the issue: "Lamentation, which sets the tone for half of the 150 psalms, adopts the character of supplication and of such loving hope to the point that lament becomes resistance and a pathway to victory."[34]

Such a tendency seems to stem from a perspective more concerned with Latin American contextual issues. For example, in his classic work *A Theology of Human Hope*, Rubem Alves seems to suggest a sort of militant suffering:

> Suffering is . . . the mother of hope. When it engenders the negation of what it is, it prepares the way for a new day. It is historical suffering that keeps hope radically historical . . . The community of faith, consequently, came to see that in order to participate in the politics for a new tomorrow it is necessary to participate in the sufferings of today.[35]

For Alves, suffering is a sort of anchor that makes hope a historical reality, and it seems almost necessary because for him it actually gives birth to hope. Jon Sobrino, a Spanish Jesuit theologian in El Salvador, fully expresses this idea by emphasizing happiness even in the face of suffering:

---

33. Westermann, "Role of the Lament," 34.
34. Souza, "Oração forte de lament," 53.
35. Alves, *Theology of Human Hope*, 120.

> Happiness beats sadness. In situations of great suffering it seems foolishness to speak about happiness, but this is possible, and even necessary. Happiness may be found in poor communities. They gather to sing and celebrate, to express their happiness for being together (in plenitude). And they can make it, since, as Gustavo Gutiérrez heard from a poor people community, "the opposite of happiness is not suffering, but sadness. We suffer, but we are not sad."[36]

Brazilian biblicist Luís Solano Rossi points in a direction similar to Brueggemann above. Rossi stresses the dimension of suffering in lament more than other Latin American counterparts, emphasizing that lament is an initiative from the petitioner, an active refusal to accept the situation as God has left it.

> Lamentations is a book that speaks about pain, of praying in tragedy, and about nurturing hope. Its objective is to find meaning in current events and the face of God amid pain. Lamentations might hold the most catastrophe and pain in the entire Bible. It feels as if it is existing in an atmosphere of death and decay. It is pain that causes groaning—not just any groaning, but excruciating cries of pain. Cries and clamors are everywhere. However, they are cries of liberation. After all, the one who hurts also cries. In a certain sense, we may say Lamentations holds a cry that liberates. For this reason, it is also an educational text; i.e., it teaches that those who do not know how to cry their pain also lose their ability to fight with God and exercise their own faith.[37]

One interesting contribution to this discussion comes from Jon Sobrino. In the wake of a 2001 earthquake in El Salvador, he wrote a small book called *Where Is God?* One extended quote highlights the dimension of solidarity I mentioned as present in the Latin American view of lament:

> There is a lot to do when an earthquake strikes, but the first thing—without which nothing else we do is enough—is to let ourselves be affected by the tragedy, not to turn away or soften it. This is not a way of promoting masochism, or demanding what is psychologically impossible. It simply requires an initial moment of honesty toward the reality. To turn away from tragedy, subtly or blatantly, is a way of escaping the reality of our world. But we must be aware of the consequences: unless we become fully present in the reality we cannot help the people in need

36. Sobrino, *Fora dos pobres não há salvação*, 156.
37. Rossi, *Como ler o livro das Lamentações*, 7.

around us, nor can we meet our internal needs. To let ourselves be affected, to feel pain over lives cut short or endangered, to feel indignation over the way we have ruined this planet, that we have not undone the damage and are not planning to do so, all this is important. It motivates compassion and immediate emergency assistance, but more importantly it sheds light on the most effective way to help in the tragedy.

There is also a salvific aspect to truly letting ourselves be affected by tragedy. It roots us firmly in the truth and forces us to overcome the unreality in which we live.[38]

In fact, Sobrino's theology and Latin American theologies in general propose a radical solidarity with those who suffer:

> How can we overcome the scandal of death, which seems to put an end to all hope, whether we are poor or non-poor? The answer is undeniably personal. However, we may suggest a way: to stand before the wider scandal of injustice which *already* causes victims to die, and try to overcome it praxically.[39]

Gomes agrees with this perspective of a sort of active lament of solidarity, qualifying it as a specific kind of love at the origin of the process that remains always active, directing and configuring diverse elements. For Gomes lament is in reality an action, or else a reaction to the suffering of others, taking on the demands of justice and the prophetic denunciation of those who provoke unjust suffering.[40]

PUBLIC WORSHIP, LEARNING, AND CURRICULUM

Vila Nova Church's answer to Sobrino's question above about how to overcome the scandal of death seems to be "by not talking about it." Such an answer even in the wake of an intense local tragedy like the Wilson Paes de Almeida building fire seemed to also be that of other Independent Presbyterian Churches in the Sao Paulo metropolitan area. Friends, colleagues, and students of mine from five different local churches observed in their services the week of the fire, one of their congregations prayed for the victims, but in the other four churches

---

38. Sobrino, *Where Is God?*, 7.
39. Sobrino, *Fora dos pobres não há salvação*, 154.
40. Gomes, *Deus Im-potente*, 157.

the incident wasn't even mentioned. It seems our services in the face of suffering and death are marked by *apathy*.

More than an isolated incident or a coincidence, there appears to be a consensus in the Brazilian evangelical world that our churches and our services are mostly impermeable to the happenings that surround us. We do pray for specific topics, especially when there is some sort of call to prayer by national or denominational leaders, and we do pray for special circumstances such as elections. Occasionally there are sermons dealing with hot political topics—seemingly a growing tendency with debatable results, as the country lives in a time of intense polarization with evangelicals on both sides of the spectrum questioning the testimony of their political opposites. But there is little intentional dedication to change the tone of the service in response to current events, least of all the "mood" of the extended moment of praise.

In this section, I will explore the idea of public worship as a learning experience, emphasizing how apathy mentioned above, although certainly unintentional, is a concrete outcome of the worship experience in its current iteration. I propose we may be able to learn how to develop sensitivity and empathy by thinking about the general design of public worship services and song selection as "curriculum development."

Worship and Learning

Some people may object to the idea of learning as an objective of worship, and it is a reasonable objection. Old Testament scholar Daniel Block, for instance, even resists using the word "objective" to discuss the idea of the triune God being the exclusive *object* of our worship.[41] Certainly the central objective of public worship is to glorify the Lord, but learning can still be a byproduct. By focusing on the learning aspect of worship in this essay, I am not making it the main objective, but rather looking at it always within the framework of being intentional about the educational consequences of the act of worshiping.

A second objection may be the idea that by focusing on learning or learning outcomes we are emphasizing a rationalistic dimension of worship. However, our focus here is that there are attitudinal and affective objectives that may be accomplished with curriculum development. Although we usually think about curriculum development as focusing

---

41. Block, *For the Glory of God*.

on a list of objective, factual, or propositional truths to be learned or memorized, we will explore the idea that curriculum design also involves attitudinal, moral, and affective dimensions.

It is important to mention that, in a sense, the other side of this possible tension between worship and learning is somewhat reinforced by the typical view of learning in the context of the church: that Christian education happens almost exclusively in the realms of Sunday school, preaching, and study groups. But Christian educators should also focus on the learning dimension of worship.

In fact, Reginaldo Braga highlights the holistic effect of learning through worship and liturgy:

> When thinking of education and liturgy, I cannot think about education exclusively in terms of conveying contents, simply acquiring abilities, learning creeds, and reciting faith propositions. I think of [liturgy] and education as a process of humanization of the text, a context in which while living, I am *becoming*.[42]

Finally, Debra Murphy also highlights this learning dimension by emphasizing "that it is in public worship that the lives of Christians are most acutely formed and shaped."[43] She also affirms that "what we do and how we act in the liturgical assembly shape us in particular and powerful ways and are formative of identity and catechetical in the most basic sense."[44]

A Brief Discussion of Curriculum Constructs

If we accept learning as a viable outcome of public worship, we open space for a discussion on imagining possible learning outcomes and how to plan, offer, and evaluate learning experiences. Such a discussion is, in other words, about curriculum. In fact, a central feature of this essay is the exploration of definitions of curriculum that include explicit, implicit or hidden, and null curriculum, especially by highlighting this third branch. This section will briefly discuss these expressions.

For curriculum in general we may use a somewhat informal statement from theological educator LeRoy Ford. He asserts that "an effective curriculum involves somebody (the learner), in learning something (the scope), in some way (the methodology and the instructional and

42. Braga, "Liturgia e educação," 197.
43. Murphy, *Teaching That Transforms*, 10.
44. Murphy, *Teaching That Transforms*, 20.

administrative models), somewhere (the multiple contexts), for some purpose (the educational goals and objectives)."[45]

Some of the dimensions listed by Ford contribute to our reflection. First, there is a proper focus on the learner. Different educational models and practices may place their focus on the content to be taught or on the role of the teacher, but it is not within the scope of this essay to debate this. But I do affirm the importance of focusing on the learner when we are talking about an affective objective such as empathy.

Ford also talks about establishing learning goals and objectives. This is especially important in our discussion, since I suggest that apathy is an unintended learning outcome of public worship impermeable to situations happening around us. Purposefully establishing another learning outcome, such as empathy, and designing learning experiences that may achieve it is the necessary movement of removing something from the hidden or null curriculum and placing it in the explicit curriculum.

Such a tripartite approach to classify curriculum was proposed by curriculum theorist Elliot Eisner.[46] The explicit curriculum is the set of ideas, knowledge, and practices that the teacher overtly sets out to teach. It is the official body of knowledge a regulatory agency wants its students to learn. The hidden curriculum is implicitly taught by means such as the structure of the school or learning place, by the peers, and by social interactions. Students learn how to decode the implicit curriculum and build a set of values around it that usually do not coincide with the values of the explicit curriculum. For Michael Apple, a hidden curriculum encompasses the tacit teaching of norms, values, and dispositions simply by students living in and coping with institutional expectations and routines.

Null curriculum is what a place of learning, intentionally or not, does not teach. It refers to a whole set of knowledge that is either intentionally or unconsciously excluded from a curriculum. Every curricular decision will have a dimension of exclusion and inclusion, but by refusing to incorporate some relevant alternatives to standard or hegemonic approaches, educational agencies may disqualify such alternatives as invalid or of less importance.

> Everything consists in un-hiding the hidden curriculum. Part of its efficacy resides precisely in its hidden nature. Implicit in the hidden curriculum notion is the idea that, if we are able to

---

45. Ford, *Curriculum Design Manual*, 50.
46. Eisner, *Educational Imagination*.

un-hide it, it will become less efficient, it will lose the effects it has for the only reason that it is hidden. Supposedly, this is the awareness that will allow any possibility of change. To develop awareness of the hidden curriculum means, in some sense, to disarm it.[47]

Placing something in the null curriculum may have the power to suppress a certain idea, knowledge, or practice. Eisner says:

> It is my thesis that what schools do not teach may be as important as what they do teach. I argue this position because ignorance is not simply a neutral void; it has important effects on the kinds of options one is able to consider, the alternatives that one can examine, and the perspectives from which one can view a situation or problem.[48]

Eisner points out three areas of the null curriculum: intellectual/cognitive processes (schools emphasize logical, linear thinking); subject matter (entire areas of study or subjects that are just not studied); and affect (morals, emotions, values, attitudes, empathy).

Classic examples of ideas placed in the null curriculum area at school systems may be issues such as racism, sexism, or the perspective of Indigenous people about the conquest of the Americas. Although these issues are certainly a feature of many of our societies, by not discussing such issues or by not even naming them, school systems delegitimize the plight of those who suffer. Placing something in the null curriculum therefore has sociopolitical implications, as does removing something from it.

A concrete example of null curriculum from the Brazilian context is the matter of our African heritage. Even though more than 50 percent of our population is of African descent, school curricula in Brazil did not include African history and culture until the early 2000s. Moving this theme from the null curriculum into the explicit curriculum was not (and has not been) easy. There is, for example, a strong reaction by evangelicals against it because they believe African traditional religions are being promoted when teachers speak about African culture.

---

47. Silva, *Documentos de identidade*, 80.
48. Eisner, *Educational Imagination*, 97.

Lament and Null Curriculum

To close this section, we may reflect on the accuracy of the proposition that lament is placed in the null curriculum of a holistic Christian education that has a preoccupation with public service. In a North American context, there are two strong supports for this idea. The first comes from evangelism professor Soong-Chan Rah. Although clearly addressing his own context, his words strike a chord in our own Brazilian situation:

> The triumph-and-success orientation of our typical church member needed the corrective brought by stories of struggle and suffering. These stories should not merely provide a sprinkling of flavor for the existing triumphalistic narrative that furthers the privilege of those in the dominant culture. The tendency to view the holistic work of the church as the action of the privileged toward the marginalized often derails the work of true community healing.[49]

The emphasis for our reflection on null curriculum is how the absence of an important learning element derails a more holistic development. In fact, Rah follows a reasoning very similar to the one critical curriculum theorists have developed. Placing something in the null curriculum is an exercise of power and has the concrete effect of silencing a dissenting voice. In terms of lament,

> The balance in Scripture between praise and lament is lost in the ethos and worldview of American evangelical Christianity with its dominant language of praise. Any theological reflection that emerges from the suffering "have-nots" can be minimized in the onslaught of the triumphalism of the "haves."[50]

I must reiterate that although Rah is speaking from a North American point of view and toward that same context, we find many similarities in our own setting that make this reflection worth of consideration.

Support for this perspective comes from Walter Brueggemann, who, although not speaking exclusively about worship, candidly asks in a similar fashion to his Latin American counterparts:

> What happens when appreciation of the lament as a form of speech and faith is lost, as I think it is largely lost in contemporary usage? What happens when the speech forms that redress

---

49. Rah, *Prophetic Lament*, 20.
50. Rah, *Prophetic Lament*, 23.

power distribution have been silenced and eliminated? The answer, I believe, is that a theological monopoly is reinforced, docility and submissiveness are engendered, and the outcome in terms of social practice is to reinforce and consolidate the political-economic monopoly of the status quo. In other words, the removal of lament from life and liturgy is not disinterested and, I suggest, only partly unintentional.[51]

In fact, "docility" and "submissiveness" are the exact opposite of the kind of militant solidarity we saw Latin American theologians proposing as a form of lament. Our observation on the practice of Brazilian evangelical churches in general supports this view.

A REFLECTION ON LEARNING EMPATHY THROUGH LAMENT IN THE LOCAL CHURCH

This essay has focused on the issue of lament, and one of its recurring themes may now be better fleshed out. I have been insisting on the inclusion of lament in what we have been calling the explicit curriculum of the holistic Christian education project of a community. Quite honestly, it is very uncommon in the Brazilian evangelical context for local churches to formally or consciously develop such a curriculum. In communities such as Vila Nova Church, as well as in so many others across the country, it is much more common to think of "curriculum" as the materials provided to Sunday school teachers, with the caveat that Sunday school is also a declining institution in our context.

However, it is definitively reasonable to assume that a committed local pastor may establish a sort of informal curriculum for their community, a set of knowledge, attitudes, and values they hope to help their community develop over time. The point is thus to include empathy as a learning outcome and lament in public worship as an instructional method.

The exercise of lamenting in public worship will certainly cause resistance. In a book about the struggle between apathy and what he calls sympathy in Christianity, theology professor Edson Almeida claims that lament is not only unwelcome in the context of a church that emphasizes victory or happiness, but also in our past and current societies:

> An instinctive repulsion characterizes human trajectory when it stands before death in all the ages. It is true that this

---

51. Brueggemann, "Costly Loss of Lament," 59–60.

repulsion is intensified by the modern secularization process, which broadcasted a utopic trust in the virtual sanitizations and in the absolutization of earthy life. However, its roots are older and more complex.[52]

In terms of liturgical practice, even John Witvliet, in his extensive work about using the Psalter in public worship, acknowledges that it is challenging to lament in worship. He suggests interspersing the lament of this kind of psalm with silence before proclaiming or singing of its hopeful thanksgiving:

> More challenging are psalms of lament, in which a salvation oracle, whether explicit or implicit, functions as a hinge that transforms a lament into an anticipation of thanksgiving. Thunderous silence cries out from between the lines of Psalm 6:7–8. Quite possibly, in the ancient temple liturgy, words of assurance or an oracle of salvation was spoken at this point. In our use of the Psalter, the very least we might do is to interpose a brief time of silence if speaking the Psalm or a brief musical interlude when singing the Psalm.[53]

One final difficulty with lament in worship is that songs with a tone of lament are not abundantly available in Portuguese. But lament is just one of many instructional strategies for adding empathy to the list of desired learning outcomes for public worship.

In summary, what could have been different at the Vila Nova Church service just a few days after the Wilson Paes de Almeida fire? What could we all, as Christians in the metropolitan area, have done differently?

As a congregation, we could have taken action as a result of being sent out in mission. At least two different local churches in São Paulo did go to the area around the fire where the residents were camping (and where, as I write more than two months later, some residents are still camping) to pray and to talk with them. Other institutions, whether Christian or not, promoted food and clothes drives. People did contribute individually, but we could have done better as a community.

In worship, the usual celebratory tone could have been replaced by a more sober one, with biblical readings and song selections emphasizing pain and suffering but also solidarity, hope, and deliverance. We could have included moments of silent reflection on the reality of people

---

52. Almeida, *Do viver apático ao viver simpatico*, 106.
53. Witvliet, *Biblical Psalms*, 80–81.

being left homeless overnight. A sermon could easily be developed on some passage describing Israel in exile—a homelessness of sorts. The expected learning outcome of such public worship practices would reasonably be a more empathetic attitude of solidarity.

BIBLIOGRAPHY

Adam, Júlio Cézar. "Worship with a Brazilian Face." In *Worship and Culture*, edited by Gláucia Vasconcelos Wilkey, 239–61. Grand Rapids: Eerdmans, 2014.
Almeida, Edson Fernando. *Do viver apático ao viver simpatico*. São Paulo: Loyola, 2006.
Alves, Rubem. *A Theology of Human Hope*. New York: Corpus, 1969.
Baggio, Sandro. *Música cristã contemporânea*. São Paulo: Editora Vida, 2005.
Berger, Klaus. *Formas literárias do Novo Testamento*. São Paulo: Loyola, 1998.
Block, Daniel. *For the Glory of God: Recovering a Biblical Theology of Worship*. Grand Rapids: Baker, 2014.
Braga, Reginaldo. "Liturgia e educação." In *Teologia do culto: entre o altar e o mundo*, edited by Cláudio Carvalhães, 191–212. São Paulo: Fonte, 2012.
Brueggemann, Walter. "The Costly Loss of Lament." *Journal for the Study of the Old Testament* 36 (1986) 57–71.
———. *Theology of the Old Testament*. Minneapolis: Fortress, 1997.
Campos, Leonildo. *Teatro, tempo e mercado: organização e marketing de um empreendimento Pentecostal*. Petrópolis/São Bernardo do Campo: Vozes/UMESP, 1997.
———. "Protestantes brasileiros diante da morte e do luto: observações sobre rituais mortuários." *Rever* 16, no. 3 (September–December 2016) 144–73.
Cunha, Magali. "Demandas pedagógicas no contexto das igrejas evangélicas no Brasil em tempos de cultura gospel." *Revista de Educação do Cogeime* 16, no. 16 (December 2007) 83–94.
———. *A explosão gospel*. Rio de Janeiro: Mauad, 2007.
de Paula, Blanches. "Um olhar pastoral sobre o luto e a violência." *Revista Pistis Práxis, Teologia Pastoral* 10, no. 1 (April 2018) 101–16.
Dolghie, Jacqueline Ziroldo. "A Igreja Renascer em Cristo e a consolidação do mercado de música gospel no Brasil: uma análise das estratégias de marketing." *Ciências Sociais e Religião* 6, no. 6, 201–20.
Eisner, Elliot W. *The Educational Imagination: On the Design and Evaluation of School Programs*. New York: Macmillan, 1994.
Ford, LeRoy. *A Curriculum Design Manual for Theological Education*. Nashville: Broadman, 1991.
Gomes, Paulo Roberto. *O Deus Im-potente*. São Paulo: Loyola, 2007.
Gomes, Rodrigo. "Divulgação do censo da população de rua em São Paulo é marcada por dúvidas." *Rede Brasil Atual*, May 13, 2015. https://www.redebrasilatual.com.br/cidadania/2015/05/censo-da-populacao-de-rua-de-sao-paulo-e-marcado-por-questionamentos-e-acusacoes-3031/.
Koury, Mauro Guilherme Pinheiro. "O luto no Brasil no final do século XX." *Caderno CRH* 27, no. 72 (September-December 2014) 593–612.
Maraschin, Jaci. *A beleza da santidade*. São Paulo: ASTE, 1996.

Mariano, Ricardo. *Neopentecostais: Sociologia do novo pentecostalismo no Brasil*. 2nd ed. São Paulo: Loyola, 2005.

Méndez, Dinorah B. "Contextualizing Evangelical Worship within Mexican Religiosity." In *Worship through Latin American Eyes*, edited by María Eugenia Cornou and Noel Snyder, 106–30. Eugene, OR: Cascade, 2026.

Mendonça, Antonio Gouvêa. *O Celeste Porvir: a inserção do protestantismo no Brasil*. São Paulo: EDUSP, 2008.

———. *Introdução ao Protestantismo no Brasil*. São Paulo: Loyola, 2002.

Miller, Donald, and Tetsunao Yamamori. *Global Pentecostalism: The New Face of Christian Social Engagement*. Berkeley: University of California Press, 2007.

Monteiro, Simei. *O cântico da vida*. São Paulo: ASTE, 1991.

Murphy, Debra Dean. *Teaching That Transforms: Worship as the Heart of Christian Education*. Eugene, OR: Wipf and Stock, 2004.

Pierucci, Antonio Flavio, and Reginaldo Prandi. *A realidade social das religiões no Brasil: religião, sociedade e política*. São Paulo: Hucitec, 1996.

Rah, Soong-Chan. *Prophetic Lament*. Downers Grove, IL: InterVarsity, 2015.

Schneider-Harpprecht, Christian. "Aconselhamento pastoral." In *Teologia Prática no contexto da América Latina*, 291–317. São Leopoldo, BR: Sinodal, 1998.

Silva, Tomaz. *Documentos de identidade: uma introdução às teorias do currículo*. Belo Horizonte, BR: Autêntica, 1999.

Silva, Vagner Gonçalves. "Neo-Pentecostalism and Afro-Brazilian Religions: Explaining the Attacks on Symbols of the African Religious Heritage in Contemporary Brazil. *Mana* 3, no. 1 (April 2007) 207–36.

Sobrino, Jon. 2008. *Fora dos pobres não há salvação*. São Paulo: Paulinas, 2008.

———. *Where Is God? Earthquake, Terrorism, Barbarity, and Hope*. Maryknoll, NY: Orbis, 2004.

Souza, Marcelo de Barros. "A oração forte de lamento e da resistência do povo de Deus." *Revista de Interpretação Bíblica Latino-Americana—RIBLA* 13 (1993) 50–60.

Susin, Luiz Carlos. *A criação de Deus*. São Paulo: Paulinas, 2003.

Vicente da Silva, Andreia. "'A partida da promessa': o rito de luto evangélico e os objetos dos mortos." *Interseções* 15, no. 1 (June 2013) 149–71.

Westermann, Claus. "The Role of the Lament in the Theology of the Old Testament." *Interpretation* 28, no. 1 (January 1974) 20–38.

———. *Praise and Lament in the Psalms*. Atlanta: John Knox, 1981.

Witvliet, John. *The Biblical Psalms in Christian Worship*. Grand Rapids: Eerdmans, 2007.

ENRICHING AND DEEPENING CONGREGATIONAL WORSHIP LIFE BY DEVELOPING YOUTH

Lessons from a Latino Congregation in Texas
—The Roots and Wings Framework

Elizabeth Tamez Méndez

"Do you hear what these children are saying?" they asked him. "Yes," replied Jesus, "have you never read, 'From the lips of children and infants you, Lord, have called forth your praise'?"

—Matthew 21:16

Perhaps your congregation can identify with this, as other Latino[1] communities do: Many children and youth are present week after week, filling the congregation with their energy. We see them running down the church halls and filling the back pews. Yet when it comes to issues of public worship, there is not much designed for them to actively participate in, much less lead. The adults in the congregation plan and lead every

---

1. Although the terms Hispanic and Latino have different meanings, they are used interchangeably in this piece to reflect all preferences. The US Census Bureau uses the term "Hispanic" in its reports; others, such as the Pew Research Center, use the term "Latino." The terms "Latino" and "Latina" are used for ease of readability, and I acknowledge this terminology is limited in its connotation of inclusivity and could be best expressed through variations of the term such as Latino/a, Latino@, Latinx, Latine, and Hispanic-Latino.

aspect of the worship service, reflecting their own ideas and preferences for expressing honor, reverence, and gratitude to God.

Our congregation in East Texas found itself in this situation. We were replicating the public worship practices common in other churches in our denomination. These practices served us well for a season. Still, demographic changes made children and youth the majority in our Latino community, and in our congregation came the need to find worship practices that connected with all participants in our intergenerational worship services. This is the story of how our congregation adapted our public worship practices by integrating aspects of applied theology and concepts of human development that help young people thrive.

OUR WORSHIP PRACTICES

The worship services held three times a week in our congregation resembled those traditionally held in Baptist churches. We met Sunday mornings for a worship service after Sunday school, then again later in the evening, and again on Wednesday nights. In every worship service there is a topic or theme that runs throughout the liturgy and is reflected in the Scripture readings, the music, the songs chosen for congregational singing, and the sermon. The services include private and communal prayer times, and the congregation is invited to come to the podium or altar area and kneel during prayers as a sign of a special request or gratitude. There are also times dedicated to the giving of tithes and offerings and the sharing of testimonies attesting to how God was present during the week in our everyday lives. Other worship practices in our congregation include observing the Lord's Supper once a month, fasting when the congregation needs to make a major decision, prayer vigils that last six to eight hours, celebrating baptisms when an adult decides to make public their decision to follow Christ, and a special time of consecration when a new baby is born. The worship services are intergenerational, with all family members, from grandparents to schoolchildren, coming together in public worship—or so we hoped.

At the time of this story, our congregation was implementing a plan to intentionally reach out to the middle school and high school youth in our congregation and to their friends at school. For about four years, our church had offered several programs and service projects where youth could find constructive experiences designed to nurture their spiritual and personal growth. We were seeing positive results. Youth were engaging with the congregation and enjoyed coming to church every week. Sunday school classes were relevant and interactive, and youth enjoyed fulfilling leadership and responsibility roles within that time of Bible study. They also looked forward to the shared congregational meal after the Sunday morning worship service, especially when it was their turn to help serve the food. Each month there was a community service project or a fundraising activity planned largely by the youth.

Yet amid our intentional efforts to engage youth in our congregation, there was a blind spot when it came to our congregational worship practices. Thankfully, when youth trust you, they tend to honestly and visibly express themselves when they don't like something or aren't interested, but somehow, in the midst of all the activities, we church leaders were missing their cues. When teenagers sit in the back of the sanctuary and spend much of the worship service time looking down at their phones and tuned out, it is clear that there is a disconnect between our worship practices and how the young members of our congregation perceive and engage with these.

UNDERSTANDING THE TIMES: THE LATINO POPULATION IS DEFINED BY ITS YOUTH

It would have been tempting to perceive this disconnect between the youth in our congregation and the public worship practices of our church as an issue that would resolve on its own, or to simply say, "This is the way things are, and young people must learn to adjust." But as with most challenges, there is more to it than meets the eye. As Latinos in the United States, we are facing historical moments that are creating exciting challenges and opportunities for our congregations and communities, with youth at the center of it all. Our public worship practices play a substantial and strategic role in the efforts to foster intergenerational connections in which youth are nurtured. Thus, not proactively working to resolve the disconnect is not really an option.

Reports and demographic forecasts from the US Census Bureau indicate that by the year 2045, racial and ethnic "minorities" will together be the majority of the US population.[2] The Anglo/Euro-American population will no longer be the majority. According to the US

---

2. Frey, "U.S. Will Become 'Minority White' in 2045."

Census Bureau, as of 2019 the Hispanic population in the United States was more than 60 million people,[3] up from 56.5 million in 2015.[4] From 2018 to 2019 the Hispanic population increased by 930,000 people, and since 2010 Hispanic people represented more than half of US population growth.[5] By 2060, the total Latino population is estimated to be around 111.2 million, at which point it will be nearly 27 percent of the total projected US population.[6]

Even more important than its rapid growth, the Hispanic population in the US is younger on average than the rest of the US population, making it the largest and youngest "minority" group in the United States.[7] In 2018 Latinos accounted for 25 percent of the US population under the age of 18.[8] Overall, the Hispanic population in 2019 was much younger that the rest of the population in the US: the median age of Hispanics was thirty years, compared to non-Hispanic whites with a median age of forty-four years.[9] The Latino population is defined by its youth. No other ethnic or racial group in the United States has as high a percentage of children, teens, and millennials (young adults born between 1981 and 1996) in its demographic composition.[10]

This boom of young Hispanic people not only has changed the face of the US, but will continue to play a substantial role in reshaping and redefining the nation's future—and the future of the church. First, it is estimated that by the year 2030, half of Latinos will be Protestant.[11] Despite the decline of people in the cultural majority who identify as Christians or as having a religious affiliation, the number of Latinos who identify as Protestant is steadily growing.[12] The Public Religion Research Institute reports that more than half of the young Christian population (ages eighteen

---

3. The US Census Bureau does not include in the count institutionalized population or those in the armed forces living off post or with their families on post.

4. US Census Bureau, "QuickFacts United States"; Flores, "2015, Hispanic Population."

5. Noe-Bustamante et al., "U.S. Hispanic Population Surpassed 60 Million."

6. US Census Bureau, "Hispanic Population to Reach 111 Million"; US Census Bureau, "Projections on the Size and Composition of the U.S. Population."

7. Patten, "Nation's Latino Population."

8. "Child Population by Race and Ethnicity."

9. Noe-Bustamante et al., "U.S. Hispanic Population Surpassed 60 Million."

10. Patten, "Nation's Latino Population."

11. Pew Research Center, "Latinos Who Are Evangelical Protestant"; Franco, "Mapped."

12. Mulder et al., *Latino Protestants in America*, ix.

to twenty-nine) in the US are ethnic minorities.[13] The Decade of Change report also points out that racial/ethnic minority congregations have a higher rate of retention of their younger congregants.[14] Furthermore, various studies have highlighted that religion plays a more important role in the lives of Latino youth than for their white peers.[15]

By virtue of sheer numbers, if we want to see substantial impact and long-term ministerial results, youth are the demographic group in which to invest and focus our efforts on *today*. It is vital for churches to align their ministry approaches to these trends with a commitment to Latino youth and their needs. If your congregation notices a disconnect between young congregants and the public worship practices of your church, as ours did, it is time to take an intentional look at what is and isn't connecting, and, most importantly, why. Understanding the times (1 Chr 12:32) means giving ourselves the space and discipline to search, learn, discern, and interpret what is taking place in our midst so that we may know what to do. Intergenerational connections must be intentionally nurtured within our congregations in order to reach all involved.

A TREASURE TO GROW AND PROTECT

If young people are not connecting with the public worship practices our congregation follows, is it not up to young people to learn to embrace them? Our congregation had to grapple with this question and came to understand that the answer is both yes and no.

Our church's youth outreach team at the time consisted of six adults, and we were working with approximately fifty youth ranging in age from middle school to junior college. As leaders, we were learning together new concepts and frameworks that were informing and guiding our work. Our explorations included designing and modeling congregational practices in ways that connected with the particular needs of young people in our community and congregation. This was the first step in the process toward reimagining our public worship practices.

Our theological understanding of Genesis 1:27–28 gave us a model for the "why" and "how" of reaching the next generation. We are called

---

13. Cox and Jones, "America's Changing Religious Identity"; PRRI, "2020 Census of American Religion."

14. Roozen, "American Congregations 2010."

15. Hernández, "Religious Experience of Latino/a Protestant Youth."

to multiply "images of God," and God bestowed upon Adam and Eve the divine blessing to fulfill the mission of multiplication, which continues from generation to generation. Jacob blessed his twelve sons (the tribes of Israel), and consequently the generations since (Gen 49). This theological perspective, grounded in Scripture, outlines for us the divine design where a pattern of blessing is established—within both our familial and congregational relationships—and the next generation flourishes as a result of the spiritual legacy that the preceding generation passes on to them.[16] If we want youth in our community to reflect God's image, our task is to implement strategies that intentionally bestow spiritual blessings upon them by serving and guiding them in their journey (Deut 6:6–7; Prov 22:6) rather than always expecting them to adjust to us.

THE ROOTS AND WINGS FRAMEWORK[17]

At this point in our congregational exploration process, we came across Positive Youth Development Theory (PYD),[18] which provided us with the theoretical and philosophical stance for establishing the next phase of our work with youth, especially as we took a deeper look at the challenges we were facing and had to rethink our approach to public worship. PYD is a theory of contemporary applied human developmental science that is concerned with the lens through which youth and youth development are viewed.[19] PYD proposes two key concepts for our work: 1) youth development is holistic, and 2) youth should be seen as assets to develop, and not problems to manage (potential vs. deficit perspective).[20]

To understand what is meant by "holistic," it serves us to know that developmental science points out six core needs of youth: a sense of security (psychological and emotional support), a sense of connection (physical and social), identity development (self, ethnic, sexual, etc.), desire to learn (cognitive), meaning in life (depth, direction, contribution, and empowerment), and spiritual growth (transcendence, convictions, and values). These key areas are manifested in both the internal (individual and psychological characteristics) and external (contextual and relational

---

16. The idea of "pattern of blessing" is inspired by Kim and Lee, "Intergenerational Ministry."
    17. Méndez, "Rethinking Latino Youth Ministry."
    18. Benson et al., "Positive Youth Development."
    19. Lerner et al., "Positive Youth Development."
    20. Lerner et al., "Positive Youth Development."

features of the social environment) dimensions of a person.[21] The needs of young people in each of these six areas and in both dimensions must be tended in order for them to grow up healthy and to thrive.[22]

The holistic perspective promotes the importance of tending to all six core needs of young people when designing and implementing the tactical and strategic goals of youth-serving models and programs.[23] It recognizes that the human development process simultaneously entails body, mind, and spirit. To this end, Scripture intentionally points out that "Jesus grew in wisdom and stature, and in favor with God and man" (Luke 2:52). Youth are in a formative stage that will guide the rest of their lives. It is like an interconnected web: for one area of their lives to grow and develop, the other areas also must be tended to simultaneously. If we want to see young people flourish and have a deep encounter with Christ, the other aspects of their lives must be nurtured through our ministries too. This approach ultimately allows us to make deep, meaningful, and lasting connections with young people that in turn support not only their spiritual development, but also their engagement with and contributions to the congregation.

This holistic approach is in line with the second key concept of PYD, which sees youth as assets to be developed, not problems to be managed. This is an important concept to understand because research studies have historically focused on a "deficit" perspective toward young people, highlighting their involvement in high-risk behaviors and situations such as drug and alcohol use, teen pregnancy, suicide, or juvenile incarceration, and looking for ways to prevent those behaviors.[24] This approach affected the models and programs of youth-serving organizations, including youth ministry. In their pedagogy and curriculum, youth were to be passive recipients sitting in a pew listening to a sermon or Sunday school lesson with a message focused on telling them what to do and how to behave, emphasizing the need to stay out of trouble. In shifting perspectives, as PYD proposes, youth are rather seen and valued for their "assets"—their potential and the positive characteristics they already possess (interests, skills, abilities, talents, and knowledge) that can be further developed

---

21. Lerner et al., "Positive Youth Development."
22. Nakkula and Toshalis, *Understanding Youth*, 1–39.
23. For more on connecting the core needs of youth with congregational practices, see Méndez, "Reaching the Next Generation."
24. Lee and Zhou, *Asian American Youth*, 2–9.

when caring adults invest in finding ways to nurture them and provide youth with hands-on opportunities to put them to use.[25]

In PYD, the family and social contexts (home, school, church, etc.) with which youth interact are denominated ecological contexts. Some characteristics that must be present in the contributing ecological contexts to support youth's positive development include: (1) healthy and sustained adult-youth relationships, (2) opportunities for youth to be actively engaged with activities that strengthen their skills and competencies (leadership, teamwork, planning, public speaking, etc.), and (3) mutually beneficial relationship between the context and the young person where youth are making meaningful contributions.[26] In a sense, the contributing factors in PYD could be summed up with an equation-like expression of:

> Positive Relationships + Positive Experiences + Positive Environments = Positive Youth Development[27]

The more these ideal dynamics are fostered in our congregations, the more our congregations become supportive environments for young people to thrive—and our public worship life is a space in which to do so.[28] To apply these PYD concepts within our congregational settings, I propose the use of two key words that illustrate and summarize the concepts in a framework of action: *roots* and *wings* (Eph 3:17–18; Isa 40:28–31).

Roots provide a tree with stability, a place to grow, and a conduit by which life-giving nutrients are drawn from the soil and distributed throughout the tree so that all of its parts—trunk, branches, and leaves—can flourish. If the roots are severed from the tree, the tree dies, no matter how magnificent and strong the tree's other components are. Ephesians 3:17–18 points out that a person can comprehend the length, width, height, and depth of God's love when there are roots that draw from the love and relationships of a faith community.

Wings can lift an entire eagle swiftly and with strength, allowing the eagle to soar magnificently above even the harsh winds and storms. Isaiah

---

25. Lerner et al., "Positive Youth Development."

26. Damon et al., "Development of Purpose during Adolescence"; Larson and Hansen, "Development of Strategic Thinking"; Overton, "New Paradigm."

27. Youth.gov, "Safe Youth, Safe Schools."

28. For further insight into aspects of PYD in congregational life, see Méndez, "Leadership Development Among Youth."

40:28–31 speaks of the Lord being the source of strength and power to the weak and the weary, the young and the old, so that with wings like eagles they may soar, not grow faint, and reach their full potential.[29]

Every young person needs to have roots in key relationships: a family and a social group to belong to, to protect and provide for them, to be anchored to, and from whom to learn about life, love, and faith. An environment of healthy relationships is the foundation for creating a sense of security and connection, all of which contributes to a young person's identity development. Likewise, every young person needs to be given wings: key relationships, spaces, and experiences in which to grow in knowledge and skills while being empowered and given the opportunity to be actively contributing to the dynamics of the group. This allows young people to have their needs met in their desire to learn, seek meaning in life, and experience spiritual growth. Young people must find our congregations to be an ecological context where their roots can go deep through the support they receive, which will in turn help their wings grow and strengthen so they can personally thrive and make meaningful contributions to society, their family, and their congregation.

This is where our congregation found itself at a crossroads. When the programs and activities were mostly age-specific or outside of the worship service structure, the congregation had an easier time embracing the "roots and wings" framework in our work with youth. It was not so easy when the concepts affected the dynamics of the entire congregation within the worship service. There was an unspoken mindset of "This is *our* time, *our* space as adults. We are open to the changes happening outside the worship service, but in the worship service things will be as we have always done them." But with this posture we were excluding young people from connecting with the public worship practices of our congregation, which meant that in worship our congregation was missing out on an opportunity to provide roots and wings. This initial reaction was understandable; at the time our congregation had not been exposed much to other models of public worship, and some members were new in their faith walk. It was not resistance for the sake of resistance; it reflected a need for a process that would provide the space and guidance to navigate this issue together. Still, it took a major incident for the congregation to be open to considering this issue from a different vantage point.

---

29. Méndez, "Leadership Development Among Youth," 35–37.

THE TIPPING POINT

Our congregation found itself in a rough situation, a season of many transitions. The pastor had relocated to a new city due to work commitments, and our congregation was interviewing potential candidates for his replacement. Unfortunately, one of the church leaders at the time who had served in our congregation for a couple of years decided that he should be the next pastor of our church and that due process should not be followed for interviewing candidates. This triggered many tense moments, misunderstandings among the congregation, and the need for multiple business meetings over the span of several weeks. During one of those business meetings, things got heated. After a while of getting nowhere, many of the church leaders opted to pray while some of the members of the congregation exchanged strong opinions. Thankfully, the situation came to a halt when a church member had had enough and decided to leave the meeting with others following behind. It was a moment that will forever be etched in the memory of our congregation. The group leaving the sanctuary had to stop because the hall was blocked by teenagers on their knees praying, interceding for peace and resolution amid the turmoil in the business meeting. The sight of teenagers on their knees in prayer was what finally jolted the group to stop arguing. Amid one of the worst moments we have ever experienced in our congregation, the Holy Spirit used the youths' expression of faith and worship in that moment to speak to the adults.

Although it was a bitter season to endure, one filled with much pain, from the ashes a new season in our congregation emerged. This unfortunate situation in fact became a blessing for our congregation as it brought about turning points in several areas, primarily public worship. Adults in the congregation now saw the youth in a different light: youth too, they realized, can teach us about faith and set an example to follow in our worship. There was now an openness to consider what needed to shift in our public worship practices so that young people could also connect and feel the desire to participate.

What were some of the underlying issues that stood in the way of considering what aspects of our public worship needed to be redesigned? The idea that youth are people who bring valuable contributions to the congregation was quite a foreign concept to most adults in our congregation. Most had grown up in rural areas of Mexico and Central America and understood parent-child and adult-child relationships to be authoritative, distant, and transactional: children are part of the labor for working the land, tending to the animals, and running the household. It is a loving and caring family dynamic, but the interactions do not lean toward considering the thoughts, ideas, and preferences of the children in the household. In our first-generation, rural Latino context, there was a tendency towards adultcentrism.[30] There was a sense that children are to be seen and not heard, that children play a secondary role within the home, and that adults receive preferential treatment—almost as if a person does not count until reaching adulthood.[31] There was also a tendency to measure children by adult standards and to ignore their perspectives because adults, we assumed, were automatically more knowledgeable. Cultural values of honor and respect also played a role in these dynamics: younger congregants wanted to be respectful of their elders and had a general sense that expressing their opinions, feelings, and ideas to adults was not proper. To this we add the reality that most congregational public worship practices and models are geared towards adults, so there is little to refer to when designing an intergenerational worship dynamic.

Because our congregation was in a season without a pastor and worship minister, our church council leaders agreed that this was a perfect opportunity to evaluate what was working and what needed to be redesigned within our congregational practices and programs to ensure they addressed our current intergenerational needs. One member felt called to serve as interim worship leader, and together with the youth outreach team and the church council we began to talk about our observations surrounding public worship needs.

We addressed the fact that lately our young people were very active and engaged with other aspects of our congregational life, but that there was a disconnect when it came to public worship. Was this disconnect merely a matter of young people learning to embrace our worship practices and adjust? Our congregation had to grapple with this question and came to understand that the answer was both yes and no. Yes, youth should be open to embracing the worship practices that connect with the adults in the congregation, but similarly, adults should be open to embracing the worship practices that connect with the youth in the congregation. After all, isn't worship not about me and my preferences, but rather about a sole focus on expressing honor and adoration to God?

30. Petr, "Adultcentrism."
31. Pinedo and Segura, "*Dejen que los niños vengan a mí*," 6–7.

This crossroads we were at gave us the opportunity for a breakthrough toward a new model of public worship practices that could show that we are all one body in Christ by reflecting the worship characteristics and preferences of *all* involved, not only some.

One Body in Christ

Our congregation was committed to be a place where youth and children matter, where their voices, questions, opinions, needs, and dreams are heard, where there is space for open dialogue and for shared leadership that strengthens the congregation and community and helps youth learn how to lead by doing, thereby allowing them to grow deep roots and strengthen their wings. We understood that the number of young people and children in our Latino community is large, so our youth outreach must not be an afterthought or just a program among many others in our congregation. It must be central to all we do as a congregation. We must ask ourselves how each thing we do will affect the lives of our youth. As leaders, we were committed to understanding the times and acting as strategic leaders, anticipating what is needed for the future as well as planning for the present.

Our commitment led us to host a series of casual yet intentional conversations with the youth in our congregation about their questions, opinions, needs, preferences, ideas, and dreams about making our congregational public worship time more inclusive of and engaging for youth in the congregation. In our theological explorations we dealt with the overarching unspoken understanding that engaging in worship comes with adulthood. But Jesus reminds us that it's really the other way around: "From the lips of children and infants you, Lord, have called forth your praise" (Matt 21:16; cf. Matt 18:2–4). This realization gave the congregation more insight into understanding and expressing acts of worship from an intergenerational perspective.

On Wednesday nights after worship service, over coffee and *pan dulce*, we also hosted conversation sessions with the adults to explore questions such as: What do young people need from our congregation? How can leaders best serve them? What are some ways in which each person in the congregation can reach out to our young people? We wanted to be a congregation that loves and is passionate about youth, that takes time to know the youth in their context, that innovates to find relevant ways of reaching their hearts. This means leading not just differently, but inversely—contrarywise, in reverse, inside out. This is what Latino youth need to thrive: trailblazers who lead from the inside out, who know and understand youth, their heart, their pain, their culture and values, their concrete needs, and their aspirations, and who with that understanding begin to build ways of connecting that make sense to our young people and their families. Such is the kingdom of God: an inverse structure where children always come first (Matt 18:1–6, 10; 19:13–15).

For about three months, our congregation held events where adults and youth spent time together working on projects around the church, helping elderly members of the congregation with lawn care, and attending the sporting events the youth were involved in at school. During those activities, we encouraged the youth and adults to have casual conversations about the church, how they felt about it, and what could be different. It was not an easy process. Having these types of conversations was a foreign practice for both the youth and the adults, but as they spent more time together, trust and openness to one another developed organically. After this time of congregational exploration, we put practical steps into action, and the new model for public worship in our congregation was put into motion.

Our Congregational Worship Tenets

During our explorations regarding intergenerational public worship, tenets of worship emerged that integrated the aforementioned theological and youth developmental theories with our theory of action.

We understood that our public worship model needed to shift from exclusive to inclusive, from youth as spectators to youth as engaged contributors, from adult-centered worship to worship that reflected and included the expressions of all involved. To achieve this, we knew we could not simply do more of the same or replicate what we saw other congregations do, because the needs and interests of youth are different and unique to each congregation. Reaching the heart of our Latino youth requires us to rethink systems, strategies, and frameworks. The process begins with constructing relevant models, *nuestros modelos*, for giving young people the space and holistic support they need for them to engage with all areas of congregational life.

Meaningfully engaging youth meant that we also had to learn as a congregation to see youth as equal partners with adults in the decision-making process. The plans for public worship needed to be developed *with* the youth, not *for* the youth. Our process needed to embrace an equal partnership, with both adults and young people being fully engaged, open to change in how things are done, and accepting that some things will not change, all leading to a unified vision for the project.[32] We have seen public worship models in Latino congregations that lean toward one end of the age spectrum or the other. Either adults are overseeing and making all the decisions regarding public worship, much like our congregation was, or young people are entirely responsible for designing worship with very little mentoring and scaffolding, which also presents a set of challenges and dangers. Achieving a collaborative model takes time and requires learning to be reflective and aware of the responsibility to serve the needs of all in the congregation as much as possible.

When youth have an opportunity to be directly involved in aspects of designing, planning, and coordinating the logistics of public worship, we support their spiritual development, their full engagement with the congregation, and their growth as leaders. We want to provide opportunities for youth to "experience a depth of transformation in church that results in a life of discipleship outside of church."[33] When young people are involved in the decision-making process, it makes it easier for them to accept, adopt, and integrate into their lives the decisions made and the direction taken by the group. This process also sets them on a course to potentially continue this important work in the future within the congregation.

Putting It All into Practice

The youth outreach team, along with the interim worship leader, some of the members of the church council, and youth who expressed interest in getting involved in the public worship redesign all began to think and work together toward how to put these concepts and desires into practice.

It took time, but with each meeting we came closer to forging a new path. We invited youth to think of some first steps they could take to integrate themselves into public worship practices before we considered

---

32. Youth.gov, "Safe Youth, Safe Schools."
33. Baker, *Greenhouses of Hope*, 35.

redesigning anything. The youth began by volunteering to collect the offering, distribute bulletins, greet people as they came into the sanctuary, and give *testimonios* through which they shared with the congregation how they had seen God act in their lives throughout the week.

Through these initial experiential acts, youth gained confidence and felt more at ease with taking an active role in public worship, which ultimately led to greater agency. It also gave the congregation the opportunity to experience the learning process through gradual integration of youth into a more active role via small projects that provided space for everyone to understand and embrace the idea of collaboration across generations.

We then looked at how youth could contribute to music and singing in worship. Again, youth were invited to think of ways in which they could use their skills, interests, and resources in ways that were meaningful to them and that contributed to congregational efforts. In time, the collective public worship project grew to where youth were co-leading music and playing instruments, helping with audio and video technology, and preparing biblical reflections to share with the congregation during the worship service. Our worship music expanded from the traditional piano and acoustic guitar to include electric guitar, trumpet, violin, flute, and drums, and an elementary-school girl began playing the tambourine. The choice of songs also expanded to include music that spoke to a wider range of experiences and styles. The congregation was happy to see that the musical education their children received in school could also be used in the context of the church.

The music was not always played perfectly, but that was not the primary focus. We knew that would improve with practice. Our focus was designing worship practices that were for all, in which everyone could partake—indeed *needed* to partake—so it could truly be a collective expression. Our public worship began to better reflect the intergenerational characteristics of our congregation and the existing worship dynamic of entire families being together during the service.

Involving young people in the leadership of public worship provided a new way for youth to explore and express their faith journey, and it added a new space for discipleship. The music practice meetings included a time for biblical and theological reflection. It was important for youth to understand that being a worship leader entails a special calling and responsibility. It is not simply an operational activity of playing an instrument, singing, or speaking. Those are simply tools for the central ministry of leading the congregation into a time of joint worship. During our times of theological reflection, for example, we discussed what message the song lyrics conveyed and whether the message connected with and felt authentic to their expressions of worship.

Young people in our congregation reported that these shifts in our public worship model gave them a creative outlet, a feeling of deeper connection with the congregation, a sense of belonging and of being active contributors, and ownership. It became in new ways *their* congregation, not just their parents'. Through each step, adults were able to let go of their apprehension about letting younger members actively contribute and lead. They began to let go of the idea that young people are not experienced or knowledgeable enough to exercise these roles. As a congregation we began to understand that our expressions of worship and the way we can spiritually affect one another is not determined by age. This model of intergenerational collaboration in public worship later extended to other areas of congregational work. A young congregant interested in acting proposed creating a clown team. Children, youth, and adults worked together to learn how to produce a clown show and make it part of a worship service. A few times a year our congregation hosted a worship service in a nearby park where families from the community gather. The clown team delivered the sermon along with the puppet team that was later formed. Vacation Bible school and service/mission trips every summer became other ways for the entire congregation to work together, to have opportunities for mutual mentoring and space to discern new worship practices to integrate into our congregational life and to share with the communities we serve.

The Roots That Support Their Wings

It's been seventeen years since our congregation began its work to intentionally encourage intergenerational worship and relationships. New generations of children and youth are coming to our congregation, and with this, changes have continued to take place: more technology, the integration of movement into acts of worship, and an emphasis on worship using both Spanish and English. But the "roots and wings" framework is not about programs or a curriculum to follow; it's about a deliberate choice to shift the mindset within our congregation to create space for practices, views, and relationships that nurture the roots and wings of our young people. This all became part of our congregational identity, and today we continue to see congregational dynamics that support interconnectedness between all age groups.

Our congregation now has space for practical experiences that nurture new leaders, develop intergenerational connections, and create a congregation that truly regards all members as *familia*. Those teenagers and young adults who were the catalyst for change in our congregational practices of public worship are now married and have children of their own, and they continue to be engaged in the congregation, with some in leadership positions such as treasurer, youth pastor, associate pastor, and Sunday school director.

Now their children are growing up, and they too are sharing with their parents what practices connect with them in public worship. During the Sunday evening worship service, the music caters to our youngest members, the toddlers and preschoolers, in both Spanish and English. We project short videos with animations along with the songs, colored lights complement the environment, and children are invited to come to the front of the worship space to sing and move together while worshiping. This is not the worship style preference of some of the great-grandparents and grandparents in the congregation, but they have learned to focus with joy and gratitude on the fact that their great-grandchildren and grandchildren are engaging in public worship and building their sense of connection with God and with their *familia* in Christ.

We are called to multiply images of God, and if we want youth in our community to reflect God's image, our task is to implement strategies that intentionally bestow blessings upon them, guide them in their journey, and provide them with spaces to flourish (Deut 6:6–7; Prov 22:6). Our congregation learned to embrace a paradigm that understands that we live in a constantly changing society and that we are best served by having more questions than prescribed answers or fixed models. Youth and children have modeled that for the community and our congregation. After all, if we desire to minister to younger generations, who better to render an "expert opinion" on how to do that than youth themselves? The youth in our congregation bring insight from multiple perspectives; they can "code switch," be cultural translators, and negotiate multiple identities of faith, ethnicity, and culture. These are valuable skills and insights that help our congregation be more effective in connecting with them and the community around us as demographics change.

Youth are the barometer of the health and future of our ministries and indeed of the church at large. Youth define our Latino population. If young people are not finding pathways of active engagement and empowerment in our congregation, they will find other outlets, and we will be overlooking the most precious assets we possess as Latinos and as a faith community. Young people have the capacity to contribute in great ways to our congregations while developing their skills and their power to lead. They are looking for adults who will walk alongside them and fully empower them to do so. May our congregations always be spaces where youth can be rooted and spread their wings.

BIBLIOGRAPHY

Baker, Dorie Grinenko, ed. *Greenhouses of Hope: Congregations Growing Young Leaders Who Will Change the World.* Herndon, VA: Alban, 2010.

Benson, Peter L., et al. "Positive Youth Development: Theory, Research, and Applications." In *Handbook of Child Psychology: Theoretical Models of Human Development,* edited by R. M. Lerner and W. Damon, 894–941. Hoboken, NJ: Wiley, 2006.

"Child Population by Race and Ethnicity in United States." The Annie E. Casey Foundation Kids Count Data Center. https://datacenter.aecf.org/data/tables/103-child-population-by-race-and-ethnicity#detailed.

Cox, Daniel, and Robert P. Jones. "America's Changing Religious Identity." PRRI, September 6, 2017. https://www.prri.org/research/american-religious-landscape-christian-religiously-unaffiliated/.

Damon, William, et al. "The Development of Purpose during Adolescence." *Applied Developmental Science* 7, no. 3 (2003) 119–28.

Flores, Antonio. "2015, Hispanic Population in the United States Statistical Portrait." Pew Research Center, September 18, 2017. https://www.pewresearch.org/hispanic/2017/09/18/2015-statistical-information-on-hispanics-in-united-states/.

Franco, Marina E. "Mapped: Power of Latino Protestants." Axios (website), August 6, 2022. https://www.axios.com/2022/08/06/latinos-protestants-catholics-republicans.

Frey, William H. "The U.S. Will Become 'Minority White' in 2045, Census Projects." *The Avenue,* Brookings, March 14, 2018, https://www.brookings.edu/blog/the-avenue/2018/03/14/the-us-will-become-minority-white-in-2045-census-projects/.

Hernández, Edwin I. "The Religious Experience of Latino/a Protestant Youth." In *Pathways of Hope and Faith among Hispanic Teens: Pastoral Reflections and Strategies Inspired by the National Study of Youth and Religion,* edited by Ken Johnson-Mondragón, 291–319. Stockton, CA: Instituto Fe y Vida, 2007.

Kim, Mitchell, and David Lee. "Intergenerational Ministry: Why Bother?" In *Honoring the Generations: Learning with Asian North American Congregations,* edited by M. Sydney Park et al., 21–38. Valley Forge, PA: Judson, 2012.

Larson, Reed, and David Hansen. "The Development of Strategic Thinking: Learning to Impact Human Systems in a Youth Activism Program." *Human Development* 48, vol. 6 (2005) 327–49.

Lee, Jennifer, and Min Zhou, eds. *Asian American Youth: Culture, Identity, and Ethnicity*. New York: Routledge, 2004.

Lerner, Jacqueline V., et al. "Positive Youth Development." In *Handbook of Adolescent Psychology*, Vol. 1, 3rd ed., edited by R. M. Lerner and L. Steinberg, 524–58. Hoboken, NJ: Wiley, 2009.

Lerner, Jacqueline V., et al. "Positive Youth Development: Processes, Philosophies, and Programs." In *Developmental Psychology*, 2nd ed., edited by Richard M. Lerner, et al., 365–92. Hoboken, NJ: Wiley, 2013.

Méndez, Elizabeth Tamez. "Leadership Development Among Youth in Latino Congregations: The Relationship of Religious Participation to Social Service Involvement and Engagement in Leadership Tasks." PhD diss., Andrews University, 2018. https://digitalcommons.andrews.edu/dissertations/1667.

———. "Reaching the Next Generation: Ministry to Culturally and Ethnically Diverse Youth and Young Adults." *Communitas: Journal of Education Beyond the Walls* 12, no. 12 (2015) 12–18.

———. "Rethinking Latino Youth Ministry: Frameworks that Provide Roots and Wings for Our Youth." *Apuntes: Theological Reflections from the Hispanic-Latino Context* 37, no. 2 (2017) 42–91.

Mulder, Mark T., et al. *Latino Protestants in America: Growing and Diverse*. Lanham, MD: Rowman & Littlefield, 2017.

Nakkula, Michael J., and Eric Toshalis. *Understanding Youth: Adolescent Development for Educators*. Cambridge: Harvard Education, 2006.

Noe-Bustamante, Luis, et al. "U.S. Hispanic Population Surpassed 60 Million in 2019, but Growth Has Slowed." Pew Research Center, July 7, 2020. https://www.pewresearch.org/short-reads/2020/07/07/u-s-hispanic-population-surpassed-60-million-in-2019-but-growth-has-slowed/.

Overton, Willis F. "A New Paradigm for Developmental Science: Relationism and Relational-Developmental Systems." *Applied Developmental Science* 17, vol. 2 (April 2013) 94–107.

Patten, Eileen. "The Nation's Latino Population Is Defined by Its Youth." Pew Research Center (website), April 20, 2016. https://www.pewresearch.org/hispanic/2016/04/20/the-nations-latino-population-is-defined-by-its-youth/.

Petr, Christopher G. "Adultcentrism in Practice with Children." *Families in Society: The Journal of Contemporary Human Services* 73, no. 7 (1992) 408–16.

Pew Research Center. "Latinos Who Are Evangelical Protestant." *Religious Landscape Study*, 2014. http://www.pewforum.org/religious-landscape-study/religious-tradition/evangelical-protestant/racial-and-ethnic-composition/latino/#demographic-information.

Pinedo, Enrique, and Harold Segura. *Dejen que los niños vengan a mí: Pistas Bíblico-teológicas para el ministerio con la niñez y la juventud*. San José, CR: Movimiento Juntos con la Niñez y la Juventud, 2015.

PRRI. "The 2020 Census of American Religion." July 8, 2021. https://www.prri.org/research/2020-census-of-american-religion/.

US Census Bureau. "Hispanic Population to Reach 111 Million by 2060," October 9, 2018. https://www.census.gov/library/visualizations/2018/comm/hispanic-projected-pop.html.

US Census Bureau. "Projections on the Size and Composition of the U.S. Population: 2014 to 2060." March 2015. https://www.census.gov/content/dam/Census/library/publications/2015/demo/p25-1143.pdf.

US Census Bureau. "QuickFacts United States." https://www.census.gov/quickfacts/fact/table/US/PST045219, accessed July 23, 2020.

Roozen, David A. "American Congregations 2010: A Decade of Change in American Congregations 2000–2010." Faith Communities Today. https://faithcommunitiestoday.org/wp-content/uploads/2019/01/Decade-of-Change-in-American-Congregations.pdf.

Youth.gov. "Safe Youth, Safe Schools." https://youth.gov/feature-article/safe-youth-safe-schools.

www.ingramcontent.com/pod-product-compliance
Lightning Source LLC
Chambersburg PA
CBHW031427150426
43191CB00006B/428